Networking
with
Personal NetWare®

Networking with Personal NetWare®

Cheryl Currid & Company

Tony Croes

Josh Penrod

Paul Penrod

JOHN WILEY & SONS, INC.

New York • Chichester • Brisbane • Toronto • Singapore

Associate Publisher: Katherine Schowalter
Editor: Tim Ryan
Managing Editor: Angela Murphy
Editorial Production & Design: SunCliff Graphic Productions

Designations used by companies to distinguish their products are often claimed as trademarks. In all instances where John Wiley & Sons, Inc. is aware of a claim, the product names appear in Initial Capital or all CAPITAL letters. Readers, however, should contact the appropriate companies for more complete information regarding trademarks and registration.

This text is printed on acid-free paper.

This publication is designed to provide accurate and authoritative information in regard to the subject matter covered. It is sold with the understanding that the publisher is not engaged in rendering legal, accounting, or other professional service. If legal advice or other expert assistance is required, the services of a competent professional person should be sought.

Library of Congress Cataloging-in-Publication Data

Currid, Cheryl
    Networking with Personal NetWare / Cheryl Currid
        p.   cm
    Includes index.
    ISBN 0-471-30759-9 (alk. paper)
        1. Personal NetWare.   2. Local area networks (Computer networks).
I. Title.
TK5105.9.C87   1994   94-10693
004.6 ' 8—dc20

Printed in the United States of America

10 9 8 7 6 5 4 3 2 1

In memory of my father, Charles M. Clarke,
   who taught me how to learn.

C.C.

To Beckie,
   for patience and understanding beyond the call of human endurance.

T.C.

To Delia,
   who makes it all worthwhile.

J.P.

To my loving wife Lori,
   for her patience and continuous support.

P.P.

Contents

Chapter 6   Increasing Productivity with Personal NetWare DOS Utilities   **105**

Chapter 8   Network Security   153

Chapter 9   Administrative Chores for the Network   179

Chapter 10   Working with Other Versions of NetWare   213

Chapter 11   Advanced Topics: Troubleshooting   225

Appendix A   Upgrading NetWare Lite Resources   251

Acknowledgments

Tony Croes would like to thank:

Tim Ryan and the rest of the crew at John Wiley & Sons, for pulling off a miracle in the eleventh hour.

Tom Mattingly, for unbelievable response time and real answers to difficult questions.

Diane Bolin, who edits, coordinates, scolds, and otherwise keeps the rest of us in line. Without her, any book project would be completely unmanageable.

Mike Ellerbe, for his willingness to share his technical knowledge of NetWare at all hours of the day, night, weekend, etc.

Josh Penrod would like to thank:

Paul Penrod, for agreeing in a moment of ignorance to be abused night and day throughout the manuscript production. Thanks Paul, you made the difference.

Tim Ryan, for persevering through endless delays. Thanks Tim, you are a real pleasure to work with.

The cheerful voice on the other end of the telephone, who usually said "Mike's tech support. Do you have your credit card ready?" Thanks, Mike.

Tom Mattingly, for the patience to put up with all of our questions.

Paul Penrod would like to thank:

Tom Mattingly, for cutting through the volumes of red tape and providing timely answers and updates.

The Lost Boys for leading me by the nose through the book berthing process.

Introduction

Networking with Personal NetWare was written to provide you with a complete and readable explanation of the challenging task of creating and managing a Personal NetWare network. We have provided you with more than just commands and procedures—you'll find information and examples that show you *why* you should do something as opposed to simply *how* to do it. The first law of networking is contant change. We hope our focus will help you handle those nasty unforseen circumstances that always seem to crop up when technology is involved. To this end, we have tried to cover a wide range of topics from the basics on general network theory to advanced management subjects such as dealing with other versions of NetWare. Overall, this book will provide you with an understanding of how to implement a Personal NetWare network, as well as give you the knowledge to use it effectively to increase your productivity.

This book contains a wide variety of information that is intended for the beginner through the intermediate user. If you fall into the beginner category, you should read the first three chapters closely to gain some background information about networking and Personal NetWare. If you are an intermediate user, you may wish to skim these chapters in order to get to the "meat" of the book, beginning with the installation procedures.

This book is organized into four parts: Chapters 1 to 4 explain many networking basics including: what a network is, types of networks, networking theories and concepts, and the different components and technologies that allow network communication. This section also covers considerations for the planning and implementation of your Personal NetWare network and what it can do for you.

Chapters 5 to 7 provide you with a brief look at what the DOS and Windows utilities offer, and a detailed explanation of how to use them. These chapters were written with the user of a Personal NetWare network in mind. Examples are tailored to help the user become more productive with the network.

Chapters 8 to 11 deal mainly with the administrative issues that affect everyone on the network. Topics include discussions on Personal NetWare security, application management, and backup. Later chapters discuss network issues and concerns with other versions of NetWare and troubleshooting methods for maintaining and tuning the network.

Finally, Appendixes A and B deliver discussions on migrating NetWare Lite resources to the Personal NetWare network and the NetWars interactive, three-dimensional "video" game.

Chapter 1

Introducing Network Computing

Whether we realize it or not, hundreds of computers participate in our lives daily. From a self-tuning car engine to a simple phone call to a friend, computers help make nearly everything in our technically advanced society work better. While we are still learning how to more closely integrate computers into the way we entertain, shop, study, and live computers have already had drastic effects on the way we conduct ourselves in business. Yet, digital computers are relatively young when considered in terms of the most important discoveries. Inexpensive personal computers linked into networks provide a means with which corporations, both large and small, fundamentally change the way they do business.

In the Beginning, There Were Mainframes...

Computer technology exploded onto the scene in the last part of this century. Within the span of forty years, we saw an incredible move from the vacuum tube driven ENIAC to a vast array of desktop, notebook, and palmtop computers that can be used virtually anywhere. But, it took a lot more than a wave of the magic wand to get us from there to here. Like most new technologies, early computers were unreliable and not particularly suited to business needs. These computers used tremendous amounts of power, generated enough heat to keep

1

entire buildings at a cool 120° F, and literally required teams of people to manage their care and feeding. The capabilities of these early computers is greatly exceeded today by common pocket calculators we sometimes call "four-bangers" because they can only add, subtract, multiply, and divide.

In the early sixties, the government and military spent a considerable amount of money and tremendous effort to bring us into the nuclear age. Advances in technology refined early computers sufficiently enough to become useful to a wider range of organizations, and to large businesses in particular. These early computers, commonly called mainframes (interchangeable with the word dinosaur), were still large, difficult to use, and expensive.

Mainframes required special climate controlled environments (lovingly called "glass houses") to prevent the excessive heat from damaging them and a full-time staff of computer gurus who performed the magical process of programming them. Although information processing on these computers was unwieldy, it was still faster and more efficient than having hordes of workers generate data by hand as had been done in the past.

The centralized computing theory also fit very well with the hierarchical corporate structure that was prevalent at the time. Despite the early awkwardness and high price tag associated with mainframe computing, MIS departments managed to carve out a place for themselves in the business setting of the sixties.

Enter the PC

The computing world remained the undisputed domain of the mainframe and minicomputer (smaller versions of the mainframe) until the revolutionary IBM Personal Computer fundamentally changed the marketplace in the late seventies and early eighties. The phenomenal success of the IBM PC is largely due to the fact that the software that made the system run (called the Operating System) was developed by a small, relatively unknown (at the time) company called Microsoft. This operating system opened the door to other third parties capable of developing software packages. A PC buyer didn't have to rely on IBM to develop the software they used—anyone with a useful idea for a program could develop and market it.

In the Darwinian struggle for market share that followed, software packages had to be written with the consumer in mind in order to succeed. Packages that not only helped a person with a particular task, but also paid attention to people needs (user friendly software) met with greater and greater success. The IBM Personal Computer became popular for business and personal use so quickly that it lent its name (desktop computers are most often referred to as PCs) to an entire industry that sprang up virtually overnight to copy or clone the PC. Most of these early PC clones used the same Intel microprocessor and IBM design, which eventually became known as the Industry Standard Architecture (ISA).

The business community was not slow to cast its vote. Suddenly a tool was available that could be used to increase productivity by allowing *real people* (not just specially trained computer gurus) to create documents, analyze numbers, or query databases. PCs were also relatively cheap: For typically less than ten thousand dollars, a worker could be outfitted with a PC or PC clone and software. The power of computers, which was once the exclusive tool of the military, the scientific community, and large corporations, blossomed into an invaluable part of many businesses.

Business Changes Affect Our Use of Computers

Inexpensive personal computers linked into networks running Personal Net-Ware provide a means with which companies, both large and small, fundamentally change the way they do business. As the needs of business change, computing products also change. Downsizing, rightsizing, streamlining, empowering. Sound familiar? These buzzwords are spoken everywhere in the corporate world. Open the paper, turn on the television. You'll read or hear about tougher economic times punctuated by layoffs, hiring freezes, and unpleasant economic indicators. Economic waters are (seemingly) rougher than they used to be, margins are slim, and it's increasingly difficult for individuals and businesses to make a buck.

There is only so much you can do to improve sales in a tight economy, so businesses have to look elsewhere for a means to increase profitability. Trimming the waste and "fat" is fast becoming the avenue of choice, and corporations are learning hard lessons about efficiency. Increased productivity for everyone is the goal—make do with less and still provide a superior product. The days of endless budgets have been replaced with a new emphasis on looking at where and how companies spend their cash.

This emphasis on a leaner corporate environment and improved ways of doing business changes the way we conduct ourselves professionally. In today's fast-paced business environment, organizations can no longer wait for decisions and ideas to pass through the cumbersome and frustrating channels of the bureaucratic past. The well-entrenched hierarchy of the past is quickly giving way to the much more flexible and responsive matrix management theory, or virtual corporations. When you need specialized information, you just go to the source without worrying about or waiting for the information you need to pass through official routes of communication. More and more often, important information is obtained and decisions are made in the informal atmosphere of a phone call, a quick e-mail message, a walk down the hall, or a casual conversation over a cup of coffee in the break room.

Larger companies are now learning what small operations have known for years: Work is done more efficiently and problems are solved faster, with fewer mistakes and less expense and hassle by bringing people with the various necessary talents together into workgroups and giving them free reign with their imaginations.

Why Network Computing?

By now you must be wondering what the preceding "soap box" speech has to do with computers. Well, let's put the pieces together. Middle management ranks are being hit the hardest as corporate America struggles to regain profitability. This is naturally thrusting more responsibility on everyone else, forcing them to be more productive. (By the way, productivity is not just an issue for large corporations. Small organizations need increased efficiency more desperately than their larger brethren because small companies most likely do not have the financial staying power to afford "dead wood" in the organization.)

One of the most effective ways of increasing productivity is to give workers access to information they need in order to make educated decisions, when they need it. People make decisions more rapidly when they have adequate information. Conversely, people will delay decision making (sometimes inevitably) when they have insufficient information. Network computing is a tool that arms workers with fast access to information gathering and manipulating tools.

Information is the most important asset a company can possess in today's economy. Reports and statistics on market trends, production amounts and timetables, and customer feedback from sales personnel are just some of the ways information can prove invaluable to an organization in making major directional moves. Processing and reacting to important information quickly is normally the mark of a successful company, and often is the difference in obtaining and maintaining valuable business relationships.

Business Tools That Make Sense

Personal computer networks provide us with valuable tools for communicating. Everyone in your company can be within easy reach of a quick electronic mail message. E-mail does not play "phone tag," it doesn't forget to give you the message, and the message is in writing. Generally, people put more thought into written requests than verbal ones. A simple go or no-go business decision can transpire in a matter of seconds—less than the time it would take to walk down the hall.

A group schedule program can be invaluable for coordinating meetings with co-workers who are usually moving in fifty different directions at once. Network-based faxes can be sent directly from a word processor or spreadsheet at your desk—no more waiting to get to a fax machine. When companies get really sophisticated, they can avoid wasting paper by filing documents electronically.

Recent trends are proving that most of you are also becoming *mobile workers*. You might work in the office, on the road, or at home. It is fairly easy to equip your networks with software and modems that allow you to access the network from remote locations. *Mobile connectivity* also allows you to work when it's most convenient for you. When a creative idea hits a mobile worker, it's relatively simple for them to log into the network from a remote location and jot a few notes or blast off a few e-mail messages. Although the idea of working at home or on the road initially might shake your company to the core, more and more companies are embracing the idea.

The second major benefit of network computing is that it provides you and your co-workers with the tools necessary to get the job done. Word processors make document creation a snap with spelling and grammar checkers providing a useful backstop against embarrassing mistakes. Mix a good word processor with spreadsheets, graphics packages, a scanner, and a good quality printer, and you have the recipe for outstanding reports, sales tools, and proposals that look like they were produced by a professional.

Network computing also allows you to maintain and share databases of useful information. Inventories, customer databases, and phone lists are just a few examples of the types of information that can be kept and accessed easily by anyone who needs it. Searching high and low for phone numbers could become a thing of the past.

Yet computers and networks are not magic. They don't do things for you; rather, they help you get things done. It sometimes requires creativity and a little patience to derive the most benefit from computers; but, with a little imagination, tremendous possibilities for improving your company's productivity and efficiency are at your disposal.

Chapter 2

What Is Personal NetWare?

Personal computer networks are built on a few relatively simple concepts. Nevertheless, there is still tremendous confusion—fueled to a great extent by claims and promises we see in advertising—about what networks can and cannot do. It may help to always keep in mind that personal computer networks are not a panacea for solving business problems; rather, they are a tool used by *people* who solve business problems.

In this chapter, we intend to set (or possibly reset) your basic expectations of what networked computers can and cannot do. We'll try to stay away from the nasty details of how networking technologies work at the bit level and stick to basic concepts that apply to almost all networking software. We'll introduce you to basic computing concepts, describe the two primary types of PC networks, and, finally, we'll tell you a little about Personal NetWare and how it fits into the overall scheme of things.

Basic Computing Concepts

When you fire up a stand-alone computer, it's really not a very smart machine. It has a few instructions stored in read-only memory (ROM) that tell it how to use devices like floppy drives, hard disk drives, input/output ports, and keyboards. Using these instructions, called a Basic Input/Output System or BIOS, the computer will search for and attempt to load an operating system. The operating system is software that sets up the computer's "personality," it tells the computer how to interact with you, the user, and with other devices and data in the system.

Applications are the programs the user generally works with. They run "on top of" the operating system. When you start an application like a word processor or spreadsheet, your computer's operating system loads the application into memory from a local disk drive. At this point, you have several layers of software running on your computer: a BIOS, an operating system, and an application. Each of these layers plays a part in translating your instructions into tasks performed by the computer, like loading, saving, or copying a file on one of the computer's disks. In the same fashion, when you're ready to print, your application and operating system sends printing instructions directly to a printer attached to your computer.

In both cases, software is controlling devices that are either part of or attached to your computer. What you can do with your computer is largely determined by your software and devices that we call *resources*. Hard disk space and memory are good examples of computer resources, as are other computer peripherals such as CD-ROM, tape, and diskette drives, as well as modems, printers, and scanners.

Stand-Alone Computing Environments

Let's back up a minute and take a look at how we use computing resources in a stand-alone environment. Each stand-alone computer has a certain set of resources that give additional capabilities to the computer. When you need additional resources (or better ones, like a laser printer instead of a dot-matrix printer, or a color printer instead of a laser printer) you either have to purchase and install them on your system or go to another computer equipped with the resources you need. In many cases, only one computer in an office might be equipped with resources you need, like a printer, plotter, modem, or CD-ROM drive.

We sometimes call office environments like this *sneaker networks*, because you'll often see a person copy a document onto a diskette, saunter over to another computer, interrupt the current user, and borrow the workstation. This kind of work environment is not only disruptive, but also potentially hazardous. Without intending to cause harm, a user might exit an application on someone else's workstation without saving that person's work.

When several users need access to a data-intensive application, like a customer database or accounting package, each user might keep a separate copy of the data on his or her workstation. There is no inherent security and no control over these data-intensive applications. Even worse, if more than one user has a copy of an application's data, it eventually becomes impossible to tell who has the most up-to-date version. The system completely breaks down when more than one user edits his/her copy.

No matter how cautious and careful users are in an environment like this, tremendous effort and work are often lost. Someone will simply forget to follow procedure or get in too much of a hurry, and the system will fail. Fortunately, personal computer networks can eliminate nearly all of these problems.

Basic Networking Concepts

Simply put, personal computer networks allow computers to be connected together in such a way that they can share their resources. Networks add another layer of software (or in some cases, completely replace a layer) at the workstation that permits it to see other computers on the network. These computers are connected together by network controllers and a common wiring scheme called a *medium*, both of which we explain in Chapter 3.

Some computing resources can be shared, while others either cannot be shared or the methods we would have to employ would make sharing them impractical. Examples of nonsharable computing resources are display cards, memory, and sound boards. Examples of sharable resources are hard disk space, printers, plotters, tape or CD-ROM drives, and modems. Computers that provide resources to the network are called *servers*. As Figure 2.1 shows, conceptually you can think of a network server as a hard disk, printer, or other resource stretched away from your computer by a longer-than-normal cable. The main difference is the fact that networking software makes these resources sharable with other users. As Figure 2.2 shows, these resources can be attached to other personal computers acting as servers, or they might be completely self-contained servers (like a network modem or network printer).

Networking from the User's Point of View

When your workstation is attached to a network, there are some subtle changes that occur within applications that are "network aware." From within most applications, additional resources like new disk drives or printers simply appear to be attached to your computer. Most modern Windows and DOS-based

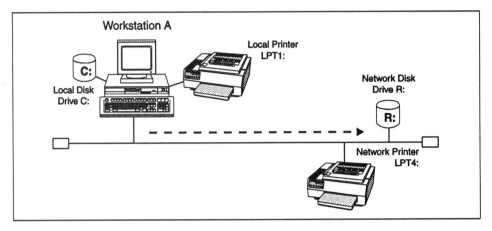

Figure 2.1 **A simple way to think about networks.**

applications are capable of dealing with networks. In general, network drives will appear as new drive letters beyond your local drives, and network printers will appear in your printer listings.

Loading applications across a network also occurs differently than at a stand-alone workstation. The network client software running on your workstation

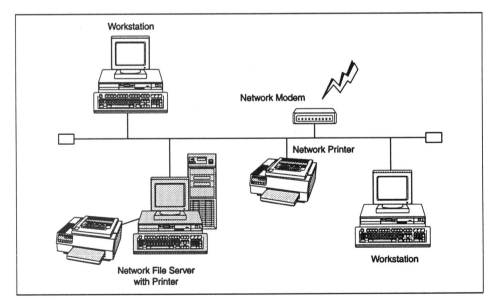

Figure 2.2 **Diagram of a network.**

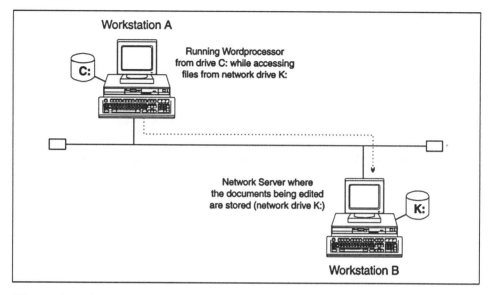

Figure 2.3 Accessing applications and data across a network.

determines if the drives you are accessing are local resources or network resources, and directs your instructions appropriately. As Figure 2.3 shows, the
applications and data you access might be on a local drive or on a network drive,
and you can access both local and network drives simultaneously.

Network Software Types

There are two basic models of how today's network software operates: cli-
ent/server and peer-to-peer. You have chosen peer-to-peer software because
Personal NetWare falls under that category, but we will explain both as there is
good possibility you will have to deal with both if you are a part of a larger
network.

Client/Server

The client/server model is a network that has at least one computer dedicated
as a file server. This server and/or other servers act as network traffic cops,
controlling access to data and resources across the network. They also provide
a central location for file storage and can provide services such as printing,
database access, communications, and e-mail to the network. Workstations

(called clients) establish network *sessions* with one or more of these servers in order to use network resources.

The term client/server is often a source of confusion for computer users because it not only describes networks, but also specially developed software applications as well. To clarify, we'll divide client/server into two distinct definitions, one for client/server networks and one for client/server applications. Client/server networks are networks in which client workstations access data and resources from servers. Application processing (using word processors and spreadsheets for example) occurs on the client workstation using its processor and RAM. The server merely provides access to file and print services.

With a client/server application, the application's processing tasks are divided between the client computer and a server. The server is dedicated to performing part of the work, instead of just providing access to information. Both computers dedicate resources (like CPU power and RAM) to running the application.

Client/Server Confusion

The term client/server is often a source of confusion for computer users. Client/server also describes specially developed software applications in which the application processing tasks have been divided between a client computer and a server.

On a client/server network, like NetWare 2.x, 3.x, and 4.x, entire computers are dedicated to providing services to the network. These might be file and print services (as with NetWare) or application services (as with dedicated fax, database, and e-mail servers). Each server runs a special application (and in some cases, a special operating system) designed to provide network services.

Peer-to-Peer (Desktop)

A peer-to-peer method of networking is somewhat different from the client/server network model in that there is no need for a dedicated server on the network. Instead, some workstations on the network *publish* their own hard drives, printers, and other resources to other nodes on the network. These workstations are, in effect, both servers and clients. If your computer is configured as a server, the resources on your network workstation become available to your peers, and the resources of other servers become available to you.

A peer-to-peer network is in some ways more flexible than a client/server network. For starters, they are cheaper and easier to install because the need for a dedicated file server running a special operating system or application has been eliminated. A peer-to-peer network can be set up by adding network software, a network interface controller (NIC), and wiring to each workstation. Though there may be minor configuration changes, the operating system and applications on the workstation stay the same. In environments with highly savvy PC users, administrative tasks can also be distributed around the network—each user can control and take care of the information and applications on his or her own hard disk.

The main drawback to peer-to-peer networking is that it can't realistically handle many users. Personal NetWare can theoretically handle up to 50 users in a workgroup setting, but its effective user level is probably more along the lines of 20 to 30 depending on the applications and services being provided. Each node configured as a server forces its processor to perform dual duties; not only is the processor responding to the user on the workstation, but it is also providing processing power for the user's application and for service requests from users at other workstations. It doesn't take many users trying to access a large database before a performance decline is noticed. Fortunately, Personal Netware allows you to control how much processing power the network can use from a server. By default, the network can use up to 5 percent of the CPU, while the workstation user keeps 95 percent.

What Is Personal NetWare?

As we mentioned in Chapter 1, the whole idea behind building and using networks is to provide workers with a set of tools that make their jobs easier and make them more efficient at doing them. In general, there is a certain set of tasks we must do in order to perform our jobs. The group of people we normally interact with in order to accomplish these tasks is called a *workgroup*. Personal NetWare is networking software designed to help us collaborate with other people in our workgroup so that we can accomplish our tasks more efficiently. We call this collaboration and use of networks *workgroup computing*. Therefore, Personal NetWare is software that facilitates workgroup computing.

Sometimes, Personal NetWare is also known as desktop computing or *peer-to-peer* software. All of these terms have basically the same meaning. Personal NetWare allows you to connect your computer (your desktop) to the other computers in your workgroup. In this way, the set of resources available to the network is made up of the computing resources attached to all of the workstations in the workgroup.

What Does Personal NetWare Do?

Personal NetWare is designed to work the way we work. It combines the resources of many workstations (and people) on the network into logical entities called workgroups. Workgroups are a way of gathering the people you work with daily into efficient (and secure) groups. Every workgroup has a set of network resources associated with it, including all of the servers, network disk volumes, users, and printers provided by workstations configured as workgroup members.

We call this method of viewing the network as a single workgroup entity a *network centric* point of view. You can create as many workgroups as you need to support the way your organization operates. In large environments with both peer-to-peer and client/server networks, there might be hundreds of workgroups constructed along the organization's functional boundaries or other divisions that make sense.

From an individual user's perspective, each workgroup is accessible with a single user name and password, and each workgroup provides a certain set of privileges and resources to the user. As the user needs to work with different groups of people or with different resources, he/she simply logs into another workgroup. The end result is a very flexible, organic network infrastructure that changes as rapidly as the organization does.

Conclusion

We've covered quite a bit of material in this chapter. We talked about how stand-alone computers differ from networked ones, and we discussed some of the problems inherent with stand-alone computing environments. We presented information about the two primary types of networking software: peer-to-peer and client/server. And we indicated where Personal NetWare falls in the spectrum. In the next chapter, we'll take a look at what makes networks tick and help you define an efficient architecture for your network.

Chapter 3

Designing Your Personal NetWare Network

Introduction

Creating a network is not a simple process. There are many variables that need to be understood and taken into account. The most important preparation is to design a plan that will make your Personal NetWare network easy to implement, use, and maintain. To begin to understand the variables you need to plan for, this chapter will discuss network theory and the concepts behind the parts of a network, highlighting the different topologies, protocols for accessing the network, and the equipment necessary to network computers.

With that foundation, we can begin to use some common sense to create a blueprint for our network. We'll include some tips on network documentation, recommend the equipment and software to buy, and direct the placement of your equipment and cable runs. Finally, we will point out some areas of concern that you should consider before jumping into a network setup. This is a lot of material, so tune out everything else for a little while, and read on.

Network Building Blocks

The first order of business is to choose the topology and network access protocol. Based on these two items, you should be able to choose the equipment you will need. Because Personal NetWare is ideal for the small office or the workgroup setting, the suggestions and recommendations here slant toward this audience. Small offices and workgroups are often under financial constraints, and money must be spent on the variables that matter. We also will consider the need to leave room for growth.

Network Topology

One of the more important pieces of the network puzzle is topology. A network's topology describes how the workstations of that network are connected with cabling. Topology can have an effect on both the cost and performance of a network, as well as the ease with which that network may be administered. Topology itself can be influenced by the method with which your network nodes communicate and also by the length and type of network cabling that you plan to use to connect the various nodes. There are presently three different types of topology: *ring, bus* or *linear*, and *star*.

Ring

Ring topology is what it sounds like. The cabling connects all the nodes to form a large ring; so there is no real beginning or end to the network cabling (see Figure 3.1). Each node, however, is only connected to the two neighboring nodes located on either side of it in the cabling structure.

Ring topology, as described above, is not currently in use in PC networking today. It is mentioned, nevertheless, to help you understand the concept of *token passing* communication protocols to be discussed later.

Bus/Linear

The second type of topology is called *bus* or sometimes *linear*. The cabling begins with a node on one end of the network and connects the next node and the next after that until all the nodes have been connected. Unlike a ring, however, a bus or linear topology has two distinct ends to the cabling as shown in Figure 3.2. Both of these ends usually need to be *terminated* or grounded so that network nodes will have a point of reference from which to interpret the electronic signals transmitted by the cabling.

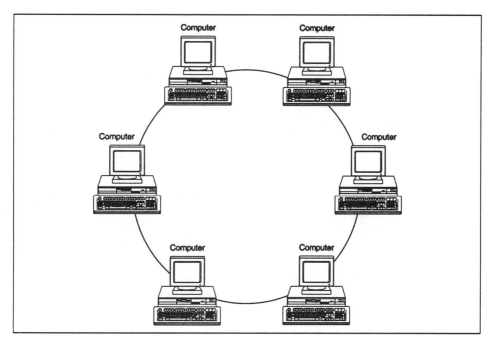

Figure 3.1 Ring topology.

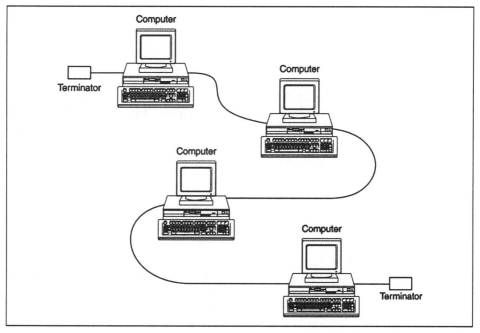

Figure 3.2 Bus topology.

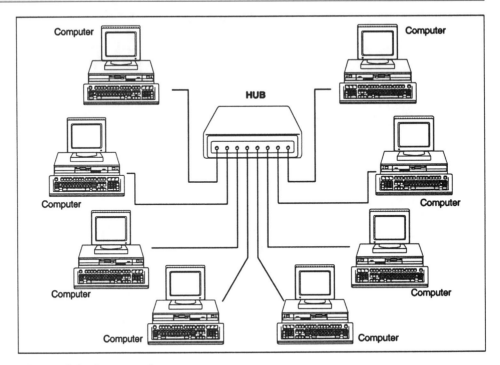

Figure 3.3 Star topology.

Star

The third type of network topology is called *star*. In a star topology, each node has its own length of cable connecting it to a piece of equipment called a network *hub* located in a central location (see Figure 3.3). When the hub receives a signal from one node connected to it, the hub will repeat the signal simultaneously to all the other nodes that are connected to it.

Which Topology to Use: Bus or Star?

Star topology is probably best suited for you. Although the bus topology is cheaper in that you use far less cabling and do not need hubs to connect the nodes of a star topology network, the bus topology limits you to only Ethernet and ARCnet of the relatively more inexpensive protocols. Both are good protocols to use, but if you're going to have to interface with IBM mainframes, now or in the future, you should consider Token Ring as a choice for your network access protocol.

Another good reason to use the star topology is expandability. A structured wiring plant will enable you to add more nodes and at a greater distance. Remember that a bus topology must visit every node on the network with what amounts to a single cable. There are limitations, depending on the length and type of cable used as well as which protocol is employed as to how far a network signal can be effectively transmitted. If you have a lot of nodes to visit, you could be asking for communication problems with a bus topology. You can extend the distance a signal can travel with *repeaters* (another name for a hub), but if you're going to spend the money for repeaters, you would be better off considering the extra cost up front, and have the flexibility of a structured wiring plant from the beginning.

Probably the best reason from your point of view for a star topology is that it makes line errors easier to recover from. With a star network configuration, you can isolate a malfunctioning node or wiring segment so that the other nodes can still operate. With a bus topology, you always run the risk of a jabbering node or a cut or fatigued line bringing your network to its knees. Also, finding a bad cable or station is much easier with a star network when all you have to do is isolate one segment at a time. This is accomplished by disabling it from the hub or using the hub management facilities to check out port activity. Finally, the potential administration hassles you can avoid will make the extra cost of a star topology worthwhile.

In general, bus topology works well for small networks where the number of nodes is few, and they are close together. If there is a break in the cable or a bad connection, the problem can be traced and fixed relatively easily with a small bus network. The larger the network, though, the more trouble you are going to have administering a bus network. Then, the benefits of having a star network will start to outweigh the cost savings of a bus. If you plan for network growth, it is advisable to consider using a star topology from the outset rather than trying to convert later.

Network Access Protocols

Another factor that will have a major effect on the topology you choose is the network access protocol you decide to use. A network access protocol is a standardized way for nodes to access the network to send packets of information to each other, how those packets of information are structured, and how fast they can get to the node for which they were intended.

Contention vs. Token Passing

There are two main schools of thought on how to access the network: the *contention-based* scheme and the *token-passing* scheme. The contention-based form of accessing the network allows a node to transmit whenever it has a packet of information ready to go. The node will then listen for confirmation from the node for which the packet was intended, verifying that the packet was received in good order. If a confirmation message is not received, the node that sent the original packet will resend it. If two nodes transmit at the same time, their packets will corrupt each other. This occurrence is known as a *collision*. The nodes that transmitted at the same time will both resend their respective packets after a random amount of time. The nodes, in a sense, are contending for use of the network medium. The contention-based scheme can use both star and bus topologies.

In contrast, the token-passing scheme is quite different from the randomness of the contention-based access method. A token-passing method of communication is most often used on a star topology network. It might help at this point to remember the ring topology and think of the star topology as a *collapsed ring* where the ring is actually inside the hub, as illustrated in Figure 3.4. A special

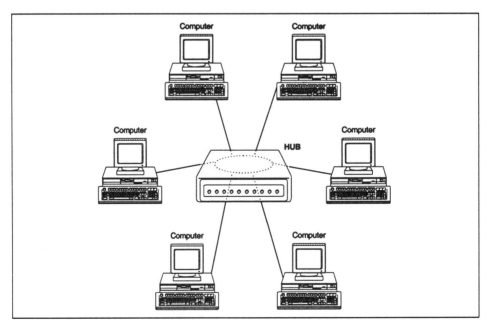

Figure 3.4 A collapsed ring.

information packet or *token* is passed around the star (collapsed ring) from node to node. A node is not allowed to transmit unless it is in possession of the token, so ideally there are no collisions with this scheme. A good analogy would be a circle of musicians passing around a single trumpet. Only the person with the trumpet can play music.

When node A needs to transmit a packet to node B, it will wait until the token is transmitted to it, and then node A will transmit its packet instead of resending the token. The message is transmitted to the next node, which will do nothing to the message but pass it on since the message was not addressed to it. When the message is finally passed to Node B, it will copy the packet for its own use and then pass the packet on. When the packet returns to node A, node A will then send the token to the next node in the ring. When the token reaches node B, it will hold the token while it transmits a confirmation packet to node A before releasing the token again. If node A does not receive confirmation, it will wait for the token to come around again and then resend its original packet. Figures 3.5A and B illustrate basic token passing theory.

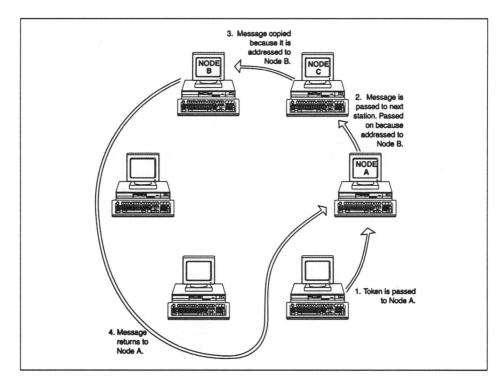

Figure 3.5A Token Passing—Part 1.

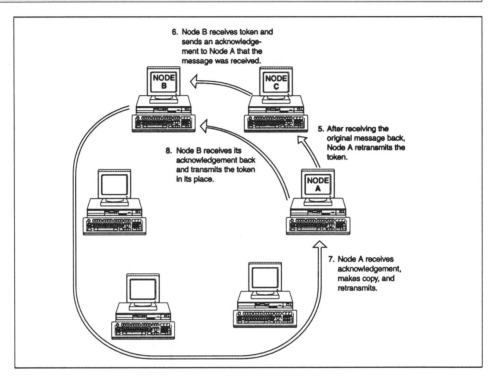

6. Node B receives token and sends an acknowledgement to Node A that the message was received.

NODE B

NODE C

5. After receiving the original message back, Node A retransmits the token.

8. Node B receives its acknowledgement back and transmits the token in its place.

NODE A

7. Node A receives acknowledgement, makes copy, and retransmits.

Figure 3.5B   Token Passing—Part 2.

ARCnet

Attached Resource Computer NETwork or more commonly known as ARCnet is a very popular token passing protocol. Although a little slow in comparison to other protocols, ARCnet is extremely reliable and adaptable. Most ARCnet LANs normally transmit at a speed of 2.5 Mbps (Mbps = Megabits per second) but can be configured to run at a much higher speed of 20 Mbps. Despite this slow speed of 2.5 Mbps, ARCnet still is popular because of its ability to use any type of networking cabling in either the star or bus topologies. This flexibility, coupled with ARCnet's proven reliability, make it a good alternative for a small LAN.

Another factor is that the equipment needed, network interface controllers (NICs) and hubs, are very competitive cost-wise. In addition, a de facto ARCnet standard is closely adhered to by equipment manufacturers, thus making reasonably certain that equipment from different vendors will be compatible with each other. If you are setting up a small LAN where speed is not a factor, ARCnet's flexibility, stability, and cost-effectiveness make it a viable option.

Token Ring

Token Ring uses the token-passing scheme and operates on a star (collapsed ring) topology. IBM was one of the major backers of this protocol when it first gained popularity in the early seventies. Token Ring is presently the only protocol that has the blessing of the Institute of Electrical and Electronic Engineers' 802 Committee, and has been codified into the IEEE 802.5 standard.

Since Token Ring runs on a star cabling layout, it needs a central hub called a Multistation Access Unit (MAU). Token Ring operates at two transmission rates: 4 Mbps and 16 Mbps. These two transmission rates can't be run at the same time across the same LAN segment. They could, however, be run on two different LAN segments, which are connected by a bridge or router.

Token Ring has several advantages. Like other token-passing schemes, Token Ring is very stable. It can be run on a variety of cable types from telephone cabling, such as Unshielded Twisted Pair (UTP) and Shielded Twisted Pair (STP), to Fiber Optic. Additionally, Token Ring networks can be easily integrated with IBM mainframe hosts if you still have these legacy systems lurking about. On the flip side, Token Ring NICs and MAUs are more expensive than with other protocols.

Ethernet

Ethernet, today, is truly the workhorse communication protocol for local area networks. The number of LANs using it far outnumbers any other protocol. Ethernet is a contention-based protocol originally developed by Xerox, which wisely allowed it to become an industry standard (IEEE 802.3). Ethernet uses a contention scheme called Carrier Sense Multiple Access with Collision Detection (CSMA/CD) to access the network. CSMA/CD, an improvement over previous contention-based schemes, allows a node to listen for a collision rather than waiting for an acknowledgment or lack of one to detect a collision. This can be described as "listening while talking," and helps minimize the *propagation delay* or the time it takes for a network message to be sent and acknowledged.

Ethernet's strengths are that Ethernet LANs are easy and inexpensive to set up, they can transmit at speeds of up to 10 Mbps over a wide variety of cable (Table 6.1), and they can run on either bus or star topologies. Another plus is the wide industry support it has from manufacturers. Most vendors provide some form of Ethernet interface with their computers no matter what operating system they are meant to run under.

FDDI and CDDI

Fiber Distributed Data Interface (FDDI) and *Copper Distributed Data Interface (CDDI)* are similar high-speed protocols that use a special bidirectional token-passing scheme to obtain speeds of up to 100 Mbps. In fact, the only real difference between the two is price. FDDI is much more expensive to install because it uses fiber optic cable, while CDDI uses ordinary telephone wire (UTP) of data grade quality. Also, FDDI can have segments of up to 2 Km long compared with only 100 meters for CDDI. Both protocols run only on a star topology and require expensive hubs and NICs.

"Fast Ethernet"

Until August of 1993, "Fast Ethernet" was a controversial struggle between differing standards for the designation as the IEEE 802 committee's standard for 100 Mbps Ethernet. Recall that normal Ethernet transmits at only 10 Mbps. Two different schemes have coalesced. The first is called *100BaseX* and is backed by a consortium of vendors lead by Grand Junction. 100BaseX operates under the basic principle of speeding up the transmissions to reach 100Mbps but keeping the access method of CSMA/CD basically the same.

Hewlett Packard's version is called *100BaseVG* (voice grade) which can be implemented over normal UTP phone line. 100BaseVG is a much more radical departure from the normal Ethernet mold. 100BaseVG abandons the CSMA/CD access method and replaces it with a quartet signaling system in order to reach the 100 Mbps transfer rates. Currently, both 100BaseX and 100BaseVG have their own committees to develop two separate standards independent of the IEEE 802.3 Ethernet standard.

Protocol Recommendations

In recommending a protocol to use, we will continue under the assumption that you are planning for a relatively small network with the potential to grow but with a close eye on the pocketbook. The tight budgets with which small networks must work immediately should preclude the 100 Mbps protocols of FDDI, CDDI, 100BaseX, and 100BaseVG. The equipment necessary to implement these protocols is just too expensive for a small network that will not normally need this kind of transmission speeds.

This leaves you with ARCnet, Ethernet, and Token Ring. Of the three, Token Ring is the more expensive and once again, if you do not need Token Ring for a special reason such as networking with IBM mainframes, it would be wiser to budget your money for more important things, such as better grade wire, the extra cable for a star topology, or a managed hub versus an unmanaged hub.

Ethernet is probably your best choice of the two remaining protocols. Ethernet and ARCnet are both sturdy and dependable protocols, and their equipment is relatively inexpensive and well proven. The item that should tip the scale for you is that Ethernet is faster with transmission speeds of up to 10 Mbps, while ARCnet is generally only 2.5 Mbps.

Network Equipment

There are several physical components that make up a network. Depending on the topology and protocol you have chosen, you will need the following items for your local area network:

- Cabling
- Network Interface Controllers (NICs)
- Hubs

Network Cabling

There are four main types of cabling commonly used in LANs today:

- Unshielded Twisted Pair (UTP)
- Shielded Twisted Pair (STP)
- Coaxial (Coax)
- Fiber Optic

The first type of cabling, *unshielded twisted pair (UTP)*, is probably the cabling you're most familiar with, since UTP is most commonly used when cabling telephone systems. Most worthwhile UTP cabling consists of at least two conductors twisted together to form a cable with at least six twists per inch. This twisting of the conductors provides *impedance* or electrical resistance, which helps to compensate for noise that will be produced by the electromagnetic fields of any nearby fluorescent lights, telephone lines, and/or power cables. UTP has several grades of cable, with *voice grade* being one of the cheaper alternatives. The overall price, though, is so inexpensive that you would be wiser to pay the extra one or two cents per foot and purchase the higher grade called *data grade*. Some major pluses for UTP are its price and that any protocol can use it as a network media (FDDI protocol run over UTP instead of fiber optic cable is called CDDI). The downside to UTP is that it is very susceptible to electromagnetic interference since it is "unshielded." You need to be careful as to the placement and the overall length of UTP cable segments.

Similar to UTP, *shielded twisted pair (STP)* also has one or more pairs of conductors twisted together so that they provide the proper impedance. STP, however, goes a step farther by providing a layer of insulating material around the twisted pairs of conductors, and often has a braided shielding conductor around all of that. This layer of insulation and the outer conductor provide better protection or "shielding" against electromagnetic noise. As with UTP, STP has different types, which provide varying numbers of twists and gages of the wire. In addition to the shielding, STP production is generally monitored more closely so the wire twisting is more accurate, thereby providing better impedance. This allows STP to support longer network segments as well as provide better noise protection. The trade-off is obviously in price.

The third type of cabling available is *coaxial (coax)*. Coax cable consists of a core of either one large solid wire or many smaller wire strands twisted together. The core is surrounded by a layer of insulation, which is itself surrounded by a braided wire mesh to ground out electromagnetic interference before it can affect the signal carrying inner core. Coax cable is called "coaxial" simply because the inner core and the surrounding outer conductor share the same axis. Coax cabling's abilities to better resist outside interference and carry a clearer signal over longer distances than other forms of copper cabling make it an ideal, cost-effective alternative to fiber optic cabling for running longer segments or operating in an electronically noisy environment. Coax cable, however, is sometimes difficult to work with. If the wire is not handled correctly, the core can "fatigue" and break, making it useless. Coax can also be bent sharply or "kinked," which could push the core through the insulating layer and ground out the signals you are trying to send between nodes.

The last type of cabling, *fiber optics*, is also the most expensive type to run by far. Fiber optic cable itself is not particularly expensive, but the specialized installation equipment and personnel needed to install the cabling are. Fiber optic cable uses light signals to transmit messages instead of passing electrons along copper wire. Light photons are not normally affected by electromagnetic background noise like electrons are, so fiber optic cable can carry a perfectly clear signal through the electronically noisiest of environments. These segment lengths can be measured in *kilometers*, which makes them useful for connecting different LANs that are not located in the same area.

Network Interface Controllers (NICs)

A *network interface controller (NIC)* is a piece of hardware that allows a network node (workstation or server) to access the network media. In other words, NICs allow the network nodes to send and receive messages to and from other nodes on the network using the cabling. An NIC accomplishes this by taking a message generated by the node A and dividing the message into a packet size consistent with the network access protocol. The NIC then adds the network address of node B and sends the packet on its way across the LAN. The NIC in node B recognizes the address and grabs the packet. The address portions of the message are then stripped off, leaving only the message that is passed on to the node B.

Most people tend to think of the term NIC as "network interface *card*" since a PC add-in card is one of the more common uses that they are exposed to. This, however, is a misnomer since a PC add-in card is not the only use by far. Many network items do not need a PC add-in card to allow them to talk on the network, but have their NICs built right into them. Some examples of such network items are print servers, printers, fax servers, modem servers, and so forth.

Hubs

In a star topology, you need devices called hubs from which network cables run from the hubs' *ports* to each node. The hub becomes the point at which all the cable segments are joined or "concentrated" (hence one of the names a hub is known by, *concentrator*). Basically, a hub takes any signal it receives from one of its ports and repeats it (which gives rise to another name, *repeaters*) to all the other nodes that are connected to it through its other ports.

Most hubs can be categorized into three groups or generations of hubs based on their capabilities and hub technology advancement. The most likely candidates for use in a small network come from the first two types.

First generation hubs are known as *"dumb," "unmanaged,"* or *"unintelligent,"* because they have no port management capabilities other than the ability to do some simple port regulation such as automatically isolating a line with a node on it that is constantly sending messages (*jabbering*) or producing illegally long information packages. First generation hubs are simply boxes that repeat signals, so they tend to be much more inexpensive than other more advanced hubs.

The *second generation* of hubs have added to the first generation's technology management capabilities, such as allowing each port to be turned on or off, obtaining the status of each port, and maintaining basic statistics about the network traffic through each port. With these management capabilities, it is much easier to make decisions about how best to improve network traffic performance and troubleshoot network signalling problems. In effect, the simple "dumb" hubs of the first generation became the *"smart," "intelligent,"* or *"managed"* hubs of the second generation.

In some instances, several hubs made by the same vendor can be added to the network by linking them through special ports and cabling so they can form a *hub cluster* and operate as if they were one hub instead of many. This, of course, means that you will lose a little of your flexibility because your clustered hubs will all have to be located in the same place, but it will mean more ports are available for additional nodes.

Another interesting example of a second generation hub is the hub card. A hub card is a managed hub that is designed to be a PC add-in card with its own NIC. Because the hub card uses the host machine's power supply, chassis, and processor (for management tasks), a hub card can provide you with managed hub benefits for near dumb hub prices. To expand your number of network ports, you simply add more hub cards to your host (these can be linked to form a cluster).

Another similarity between first and second generation hubs is that both can support only one protocol (you buy an Ethernet hub, Token ring hub, etc.), and both have a limited bandwidth. This means that the more traffic on the network, the more the network bandwidth becomes divided as nodes compete for the media. If the pipe is full, you can't shove any more water through it. The net effect is that, if there is too much traffic, your network may slow down. Since a hub is in essence merely a connection for the various network segments, a hub with a limited bandwidth is not able to alleviate a performance problem such as this.

A third generation of hub, the enterprise hub, can connect networks with different access protocols such as Ethernet and Token Ring. Enterprise hubs are also not limited in bandwidth. They are, however, very expensive and not likely to be cost-effective for a small or even a medium-sized network. Enterprise hubs are addressed in more detail when other more advanced networking equipment is discussed.

Choosing the Right Networking Equipment

The decisions you make regarding network topology and access protocol will impact enormously on your decisions as to the type of networking equipment to choose. In the instance of network cable, choosing FDDI as your network access protocol also necessitates that you install fiber optic cable to your PCs. As mentioned before, unless you have a special need for the unique qualities that fiber optic cable can provide, it is probably too expensive for considering running to the desktop setting.

Shielded twisted pair (STP) and coaxial cable also are not very likely choices for the small network setups in which Personal NetWare is most often run. Both are relatively expensive and difficult to deal with. STP is sold in premeasured lengths in most cases, because the connectors are so difficult to put on. This is not a very efficient way to run cable either in materials, or the time it takes to try to figure out segment lengths. Great care must be taken when laying coaxial cable so that the cable does not bend sharply or "kink."

The final candidate for network cabling, unshielded twisted pair (UTP), is the easiest to work with and least expensive of the four types of cabling. If care is taken to lay the cable away from possible points of interference such as light fixtures, you should have no problem with communications. In addition, any protocol can use UTP. If, in the future, the benefits of moving to speedier access protocol such as CDDI, 100BaseVG, or 100BaseX begin to outweigh the costs, the conversion will be much easier since you will not have to rewire your present stations. Make sure that you use data grade UTP for improved clarity. The price difference is only a few cents per foot, and it will enable you to use the high-speed protocols.

Now that you know the topology, access protocol, and cable you are going to use, it should be easy to decide which equipment you will need. As stated earlier, a small network should work very well with Ethernet on a star topology using UTP cabling. Consequently, your hub ports and NIC connections should have 10BaseT (Ethernet over UTP) interfaces. The NICs should also come with NetWare Open Data-link Interface (ODI) drivers so that Personal NetWare can communicate through the NIC. Your best bet for hubs would be to stay with the simple unmanaged hubs. If your network is large enough that you need management capabilities for your hub ports, then hub cards are an economical solution.

Advanced Networking Equipment

Personal NetWare is geared toward the small office and workgroup setting, which means you should not run into too many situations where you will need advanced networking equipment such as bridges, routers, gateways, and enterprise hubs. These items are more common in large internetworks that contain many different LANs and LAN types, as well as hundreds of PCs and even mini-

and mainframe computers. However, if you plan to use Personal NetWare for workgroup computing and you are going to be a part of a much larger network or internetwork, then it might be beneficial for you to understand what this type of advanced equipment does.

Bridges and Routers

Bridges and routers are devices that allow you to connect groups of nodes or networks into larger networks. You could use first and second generation hubs to do this as well, but remember that they only repeat what one port receives through the other ports. If you connect too many nodes in this fashion, you will saturate the entire network with traffic and slow it down. A bridge or router is more selective about the information it passes on. This helps to segment your network and keep traffic congestion on the subnetworks down.

Suppose you have two sets of nodes connected through a bridge or router. The bridge or router will look at each packet of information that is broadcast by any node on either network. Unlike the hubs we talked about earlier, which would blindly repeat the packets of information from one network to the other, a bridge or router will look at the address of the packet and decide whether the packet should be repeated across to the next network.

For example, a node on network A broadcasts a packet of information to another node on network A. The bridge or router sees the packet just like any other node located on network A. However, the bridge or router looks at the address for which the packet is intended and decides not to allow the package to cross over to network B since it is not intended for a node on network B. If the packet had been intended for a node on network B, the bridge or router would have repeated the packet to network B. In this manner, the traffic that is meant only for network A is kept from cluttering up network B and vice-versa.

Bridges and routers also have another advantage over the first and second generation hubs. They can be used to connect networks that use different access protocols. In this manner, you can have Token Ring nodes talking to Ethernet nodes, for example.

There is a definite difference in how bridges and routers work, but explaining that difference is beyond the scope of this book. For our purposes, they will appear to act the same.

Gateways, like bridges and routers, can be used to add computing resources to your network. Whereas bridges and routers help you connect to other PC networks, gateways are used to give PC networks access to devices that have a different architecture and method of communicating such as mainframes and minicomputers. Fax gateways, e-mail gateways, and connections to CompuServe are some common uses of gateways other than connecting to legacy hardware.

Enterprise Hubs

As mentioned earlier, there is another kind of hub called *third generation* or *enterprise* (or *chassis*). They have all the management capabilities of previous hubs, but they are very different in both level of technology and design from the first and second generation hubs because they are meant to connect networks to form internetworks.

Third generation hubs are often capable of performing as bridges and routers, and are based on a chassis design to which you can add modules to expand the number or type of ports. In other words, if you have Token Ring ports already in your hub, and you want to add an Ethernet segment to your network, you would simply buy a module with Ethernet ports and install it in your chassis hub. The bridging and routing functions free you from being limited to only one type of network access protocol as with previously discussed hubs.

Another big improvement is that third generation hubs do not have a limited bandwidth. A third generation hub has a special bus called a *backplane* to which the modules plug in and across which traffic between the modules is carried. Through a process called *micro-segmentation*, this backplane can be divided into several smaller, separate channels or networks, but each still has the capacity to handle the full bandwidth produced by the access protocol of the ports using these networks. For instance, an enterprise hub with a backplane capable of a bandwidth of 100 Mbps can be divided to support ten different Ethernet modules, each with its own 10 Mbps channel. Instead of 100 Ethernet nodes competing for a 10 Mbps bandwidth, as would happen if these nodes were connected with normal hubs, you can divide the nodes up so that only ten nodes are competing for each of the ten 10 Mbps channels into which the enterprise hub's backplane can be segmented.

Designing Your Network

A network is not simply a conglomeration of machinery strung together with cables. A network needs to be built to provide you with good performance, ease of maintenance, and above all, the functionality that will make it worthwhile to install the network in the first place. All of this requires careful thought and planning. The following questions should be taken into consideration when designing your Personal NetWare network:

- What do you intend to use your network for?
- What equipment and software do you already have and what do you still need?
- Where would be the best placement for your equipment?
- How will you run your cabling in the most efficient way?

Intended Network Uses

The answer to the question, what will the network be used for, is easy. A Personal NetWare network allows a workgroup to access and share the same resources and data so that they can accomplish the tasks and solve the problems that they were brought together to do. But that initial question spawns more questions that need to be answered before you move on.

For starters, who is part of the workgroup? Once you have this answer, you then need to think about how often each workgroup member will need access to the network. For instance, if you are going to have workgroup members who will only need to use the network sparingly, you might try and provide a common workstation for them instead of one workstation for each. This, of course, is limited by practicality. It would not be very convenient for your network users to have to move to distant locations in order to perform their jobs.

Next, you will need to determine which applications and the corresponding data each workgroup member will need to access in order to get his or her work done. This will have an effect not only on the software that you need to purchase, but also on the hardware. Some software packages have special hardware requirements or they cannot run properly.

What sort of printing functions are you going to need? This includes the printers that must be available and where they will be best placed based on the needs of your workgroup. Remember, printing is one of the most important functions of your network and should be carefully thought out. You can create spectacular documents and reports with your network, but they won't amount to much if you can't produce an acceptable hard copy in time for the meetings or presentations for which they are intended.

All these questions need to be addressed before you determine the final configuration of your network.

Creating Your Network "Shopping List"

Okay, you've decided who you need to support, how many workstations it will probably take, and the applications and services that you will need to provide to your workgroup through the network in order for them to be more productive. The next step is to determine what you already own. The simplest way to discover this, especially if you are dealing with legacy equipment (equipment that arrived before you did), is to grab a notepad and pencil and inventory all your equipment. Don't just count workstations either, but use this opportunity to do a thorough scrutiny of the equipment and software you already have, what it does, and where it is located. Find out information such as the type of processor chip, amount of Random Access Memory (RAM), size of hard drives, and monitor types.

It would also be useful to know if any special hardware is installed or attached to each workstation such as optical drives, scanners, modems, sound boards, fax boards, and so forth, and which IRQ settings, memory addresses, and/or communication or printer ports this special hardware is using. This information will come in handy when the NICs for each station are installed later.

Find out how many and what types of printers you have. You also need to know if there are any special features such as PostScript. As with special equipment added to workstations, you will need to discover how the printer is presently attached to the workstation so that the printer and the workstation can communicate with each other.

Check each hard disk to find out which applications and utilities are installed and in which directories. Make sure that you locate the original diskettes so that you can reinstall a central copy on one of your servers if need be to suit your new directory structure and naming schemes. Remember that you are trying to maximize the network disk space that is available by sharing one copy of software among users who need it, instead of each user having a copy on his or her own hard drive. You will have to purchase network versions of software that can be shared by your workgroup users if you do not already own such.

Find all the documentation for both the software and the hardware that you already have. This, along with the notes you are now making, could be invaluable in helping to resolve a hardware or software conflict later on.

You now should have a detailed set of notes on all the workstations and the related hardware as well as the software that you can use in a network environment. Next, compare these notes with the decisions you made earlier regarding equipment and software that you still need to purchase. Also, when you are making out your hardware and software shopping list, don't forget about networking equipment that you might need, such as NICs and hubs.

Equipment Placement

After you have discovered what you already have and what you need to buy, the next step is to decide whether you have a good place to put the equipment. In earlier planning sessions, you should have made some assessments as to where your equipment might be best placed. You may have to make some adjustments to your network plan if the proposed equipment placement will not work out well in light of this closer consideration.

Convenient to Users

The first and foremost factor in determining where equipment should be placed is user convenience. The whole idea behind networking computers is to make the resources a user needs (data, printers, applications, etc.) easily accessible. For example, this means that printers should be in a location central to the most likely users or have special stations for scanners. You also want to have workstations either on or near a workgroup member's desk. If the workstation is to be shared by more than one user, then it needs to be in close proximity to all the intended users.

Power Problems

One detail many people overlook is making sure a good power source is available for sensitive electronic equipment like a computer. Most office buildings are not wired very well or with sensitive and power-hungry equipment in mind. Intermittent power flows or "spikes" can be especially damaging to delicate electronics even if the building is well grounded. Electrical storms can also cause these outages or damaging power surges. Make sure that you have surge protectors on all of your workstations, modems, fax boards, and so forth, to protect against sudden power surges.

In many instances, the electrical codes of buildings allows contractors to put more sockets and light fixtures on a particular circuit than you might expect. The draw of too many electrical items could throw the breaker for that circuit at a most inopportune time. Say, for instance, your break room happens to be on the same circuit as a server/workstation in the office next door, and several users are trying to use applications on that server/workstation for projects that have reached the critical mass stage. Meanwhile, someone turns on the microwave to reheat a cup of coffee and trips the breaker for the circuit that the microwave and the server/workstation are on. You can just imagine the blood curdling screams that will follow as the realization sets in with the users that their work is lost.

For reasons like this, it is wise to see if you can get dedicated lines to at least your Personal NetWare servers, if not all of your stations. Also, it would be worth the money to invest in an Uninterruptable Power Supply (UPS) for your Personal NetWare servers. A UPS is basically a box of batteries that can sustain the server's operation for about 15 to 20 minutes following a power loss. This is certainly long enough to help prevent unexpected power losses to the server/workstation. A UPS also acts as a surge protector to help prevent damage from power spikes.

Other Placement Concerns

Another concern to take into account when planning where to place workstations is the possibility of overheating. Computers are outfitted with a small fan to circulate air through the case to keep the circuitry from becoming too hot. You may not have thought about it, but there is quite a bit of electricity involved in running a computer, and naturally some of that energy is going to be released in the form of heat. Usually, the fan alone will do the trick, but if your workstation is left on in an enclosed area with no real ventilation, the fan might not be enough.

Try and choose areas with good ventilation and out of direct sunlight, especially the western sun in the afternoon. This helps to reduce the possibility of damage to machines that must be running constantly even when the air conditioning is off at night and on weekends. Another good precaution is to turn off the monitor when it is not in use. This not only preserves your monitor, but eliminates the heat radiating from it into the room.

Dust and smoke can also cause damage to your workstations. These elements are not very healthy for the circuitry in your workstation and can easily be sucked into a computer case by the fan trying to keep the computer cool. If enough dust accumulates on the fan bearing, the bearing can freeze and prevent the fan from working. If this happens, your computer can become damaged through overheating.

You can prohibit smoking near the workstations, but dust is a different story. Try to keep the area around the computer clean, and periodically check the fan bearing and inside the computer case for dust buildup. Areas with naturally high amounts of any kind of airborne pollution are definitely unhealthy places for computers.

Cabling Concerns

As with everything else, cabling requires planning because there is more to running cable than just stringing it between computers. In most cases, common sense can be an effective guide to good cabling practices. The following tips and suggestions should help you come up with a good plan for cabling your Personal NetWare Network.

- Test the Cable: Whether you run the cable yourself or contract that task out, make sure that the cable runs are tested for a useable signal that can be sent across them. The cables could have a fault in a particular run or could have been damaged during installation. Many things can prevent a successful connection to the network. It will make your life easier if you can rule out cable problems when you are troubleshooting your network.

- Pull More Than You Need: Nothing can be more frustrating than pulling a cable run and finding out that you do not have enough slack to locate the PC where the user wants it. Leave more slack than you think you need. This will save you from having to rerun a line that is too short.

- Pull Redundant Cable Runs: Pull redundant lines to each station location. If one line should become damaged or unusable for any reason, you will have a second line available to connect the workstation without having to re-pull another line.

- Leave Drawstrings in Place: Getting cable through a difficult-to-reach area, such as a conduit or wire tray, sometimes requires ingenuity and a "fish tape." A fish tape is a long, thin piece of metal that you can tape or tie string to and push to the other end of the conduit. You can then use the string to pull your wire through the difficult area. Pull another drawstring with the wire so that you will not have as much trouble the next time.

- Label the Cable: Label your cable with stick-on numbers at each end and periodically along its length so that you can identify them. This can help you when you are trying to correct a line problem.

- Document the Cable Routes: Use a floor plan to document which cables run to which locations and the routes they take. Once again, this will be helpful in correcting line problems.

- Pull Cable in Easy Access Areas: Try to pull cable through easily reached regions such as hallways and common areas. If you should have to pull more cable to correct a line problem, you will not be as disruptive to people trying to work in your cabling route. You will also run into fewer locked doors or difficult-to-reach places.

- Locate Cable Out of the Way: Many buildings have special conduits and wire trays in the ceilings and walls designed to hold wiring. If you do not have these trays and conduits available, it is still best to still try to lay your cable in the ceilings and inside the walls to keep it out of the way. Both you and the cable are protected this way, since employees will not be stepping on the cable (bad for the cable) or tripping over it (bad for the employee). Use tie-wraps to bundle up excess cable at either end of your cable run (neatness counts) for the same reasons.

- Use the Same Routes: Try and use the same routes for your cable runs as much as possible. It is more convenient for troubleshooting line problems if you only have a few routes to work on instead of many. Additionally, there will be fewer disruptions for your co-workers.

- Avoid Interference/Obstacles: It is definitely a good idea to locate your cabling away from electrical machinery and machinery with moving parts. The electrical machinery, such as florescent lights, can create electrical fields that can interfere with your network signaling. Keeping your cable away from machinery with moving parts will remove any chance of it becoming tangled and/or cut.

Coping with a Network's Hidden Costs

There are several costs that most people do not consider when setting up a network. These hidden costs need to be addressed or you could be in for a rude shock. Ask yourself, are you moving from a mainframe environment, setting up a smaller segment on a larger network, or just networking for the first time? Chances are, you are not moving from a mainframe environment all the way down to a small peer-to-peer system like Personal NetWare. This migration is by far the most expensive in both cost and disruption, and is more likely to be a move to a large client/server network in any case.

Still, a new working environment is going to breed some interesting problems you may or may not have considered. What about new software? Do you have what you want now? How are your people going to handle the new network and software? How are you going to install and maintain this network? If you haven't thought about these questions or the answers to them, then it is time you do.

New Software

One of the more easily quantifiable hidden costs is the need for new software. You already know about the cost for Personal NetWare: that is an obvious and predictable expense. Purchasing and/or designing software can seem every bit as expensive as hardware. If you are creating a smaller network segment for your department out of a larger network, you will probably still be able to use the applications and definitely the data from the larger LAN that you had been using before, unless the scope of your new workgroup has changed enough to consider rethinking and retooling your software and data resources.

If you are networking for the first time, you *are* going to have to buy software applications. Resign yourself to that fact, even if you already own software you used on some of the stand-alone computers you are now networking. You will need network versions of this software so that multiple users can use it. You can't do this with regular software designed for one user on a stand alone computer. These network versions are not cheap either. Many times, instead of buying a single copy with the ability to be shared as you might expect, you end up having to also purchase the right to use that piece of software for a certain amount of users or sessions.

Another surprising circumstance is software maintenance. Some software packages are expensive up front, but the periodic upgrades are surprisingly cheap in comparison. The hook is that you need to purchase these upgrades to remain relatively current in the software company's upgrade path. If you do not, when you actually do need to upgrade, you could find the price of an upgrade that covers several steps in the path has grown to nearly that of re-purchasing the software again.

Purchasing new software and remaining current on upgrades should be two important considerations in your initial and ongoing network budgets.

Retraining

Here you are: You have moved up to a first-time network or sectioned off your own department's computing domain from a larger LAN. Either way, you have a new computing environment. Although the new working environment that a network creates means greater efficiency later on, initially, you are going to have to retrain employees and cope with confusion.

Probably the hardest part of this new situation is teaching the new concepts involved. Using a new network, whether client/server or peer-to-peer, is going to be a very confusing process to most of your staff, especially if they have little or no exposure to computers. And, those with computer experience, more often than not, know just enough to get by. They learned the "how" part, but not always the "why." Even your veterans who have computer experience and/or worked in a client/server setting are going to have trouble with the network-centric view of Personal NetWare as opposed to the server-centric view of the immediate past.

The goal here, is not to disillusion you, but to make you aware of a possible hurdle so that you take a realistic outlook: Don't expect your workers to be interacting smoothly with the LAN from day one. There will be a breaking-in period.

Installation and Maintenance

Now that you have this wonderful Personal NetWare to help your office or department improve its efficiency, and you know how it's going to work, what equipment and software you are going to need, and where you want to place everything, have you thought of who's going to install it for you? Do you feel confident enough to do it yourself? Do you really want that kind of hassle? If you don't feel up to the task or do not have the time, there are many competent companies that can give you estimates on a certified cabling installation.

The hidden part of this expense problem is not the installation of your Personal NetWare network, which can be easily quantified, but how your network is going to be maintained. Will you or someone on your team perform routine maintenance or troubleshooting? Will you need to hire someone with this expertise? How much time must be allocated for maintenance and administration activities? Clearly, you will need to take the obvious question of installation and the not-so obvious question of network maintenance into budgeting considerations.

Conclusion

By now, you should have a good idea of where you stand in regard to equipment and software, placement of hardware, software and the cabling runs, and some of the hidden issues that sometimes are forgotton in the shuffle of planning. Through study of your particular situation and what you hope to accomplish by setting up a network, you can combine some basic networking concepts with common sense to build a networking plan that is the right answer for your needs. The next step is to implement your plan, so you can begin installing Personal NetWare on the individual workstations.

Chapter 4

Installing Personal NetWare

Introduction

Now that we have created a network plan and installed the cabling system, we are ready to actually install the Personal NetWare software on each of the workstations. Although the actual installation is rather simple, there are some important options and questions that need to be addressed before and during the setup procedure.

- What hardware and software upgrades need to be made to the workstation that is to be added to the Personal NetWare network?

- What bearing do these additions have on how Personal NetWare will be installed?

- What options for workstation performance and network management does Personal NetWare have?

- How are these and other options configured during the installation procedure?

In this chapter, we will answer these and other similar questions by taking an in-depth look at the installation procedure and any preparatory work that may be necessary. We will explain all the options and features that you can install and configure, what they are used for, and how to modify them.

Installing Personal NetWare

The installation procedure is really quite simple and easy to understand. There will no doubt be some hardware and software upgrades involved, especially if the workstation has never been networked before. Then, a two-part installation process begins using two different utility programs.

There are also two sets of user utilities files, one set for DOS, which actually handles the networking, and a user interface for Windows. These utilities include procedures for installing from both the DOS and Windows environments. The procedures are exactly the same; the only real difference is that the interfaces look different, but the information that is captured and the options that are set are the same.

If you install from DOS and choose to install both the DOS and the Windows utilities, Personal NetWare will be no different than if you installed the software from the Windows environment. For this reason, we will focus on just the DOS installation procedure and use sample screens from that procedure for our examples.

Software and Hardware Requirements

Nearly all of the hardware and software requirements depend on whether you will be running only DOS or DOS and Windows as the operating systems for each workstation. Running only the DOS utilities requires fewer resources than if you choose to run the Windows utilities, since this requires that your workstation be able to run the Windows environment.

You do not have to run all your machines on the network as either DOS machines or Windows machines for Personal NetWare to work correctly. You can use the Windows interface on the machines that are able to run Windows, and the DOS utilities on those that can't run Windows. The Windows and DOS machines will still be able to work with each other since all machines have the DOS software loaded. Remember, the Windows files we will install are only an interface for the Windows environment; the actual networking is performed in DOS.

Personal NetWare is designed to work equally well with both DOS and Windows workstations, which means you can use just about any IBM compatible around today. Any two (or more) IBM PCs, PC ATs, PS/2s, or machines comparable to these models should work well as workstations for your Personal NetWare network. Comparable here means the computer you choose uses the Industry Standard Architecture (ISA) or Extended Industry Standard Architecture (EISA) for its basic design.

Additional hardware requirements for each workstation include 640 kilobytes (KB) of random access memory (RAM) if you are planning to run DOS as your only operating system, or 2 megabytes (MB) of RAM if you are going to run Windows as well. You will also need about 5 MB of hard disk space for the DOS files or around 8 MB of hard disk space for the DOS and Windows files. Each workstation needs a network interface controller (NIC) to enable it to communicate with the network. Finally, you will need a cabling system to physically link all the computers you plan to network (see Chapter 3).

The software requirements are a bit more simple. As already stated, whether you will be using Windows or not, you will need a version of DOS installed on your computer. The minimum acceptable versions of DOS are Microsoft DOS 3.30, Compaq DOS 3.31, IBM PC-DOS 4.0, DR (Digital Research) DOS 6.0, and Novell DOS 7. If you intend to run Microsoft Windows 3.1 on a machine, you must first have a machine that meets the Windows requirements, both hardware and software. As for Personal NetWare's requirements, it will support Microsoft Windows version 3.1 operating either in the Standard or Enhanced Modes. The final software requirement is, of course, a licensed copy of Personal NetWare for each workstation that you intend to network.

Preparing Your Workstations

Preparing a workstation for installation can be a simple procedure if you have done a complete survey of the equipment as outlined in Chapter 3 that you intend to network. This survey should show you valuable information about the way the workstation is configured, what hardware it has, and what software is currently installed.

Upgrading the Workstation

Let's start with the software. A good method for planning what you will need to do is to start with your version of DOS. The survey should tell you what version of DOS the workstation is currently running. If you do not have an acceptable version of DOS on which to run Personal NetWare, you will need to upgrade. This may also entail some hardware upgrades such as memory and/or disk space.

If you intend to run Windows on the machine in question, you will probably have to take into account further hardware upgrades, because Windows requires far more in the way of resources. Finally, you will need to look at what Personal NetWare requires. This should give you a list of the areas where you workstation may be deficient, and what software and equipment you will need to add to it. A good rule of thumb, is if the workstation can run Windows, it will be able to run Personal NetWare.

Installing Network Interface Controllers

If the workstation has never been networked before, you will have to add a Network Interface Controller (NIC) at the very least. Use the information from the survey to tell you what expansion slots the workstation has available. The survey can also tell you what memory addresses, Interrupt Requests (IRQs), and Input/Output (I/O) Ports are available. You will need this and similar information when you configure your NIC. Check your NIC manuals for more information. The very first thing you should do is *turn the power off*. Open the case of the workstation to gain access to the expansion slots. Check to see if your information is correct and that you have an available slot to accept your card. For example, you will have trouble fitting a 16-bit card into an 8-bit expansion slot.

If your NIC is hardware configurable, you will need to establish the jumper settings at this time. There are banks of pins that can be "jumpered" with small pieces of metal, usually surrounded by plastic, to allow currents of electricity to flow in a specific pattern across the banks of pins. The specific patterns tell the NIC information such as what IRQ, memory address, and I/O port to use. You will have to consult the NIC's manuals again to find out the specific jumper arrangements required to correctly configure the NIC, since these patterns are different for each brand of NIC.

When your NIC's settings are correct, or your NIC is software configurable, place the NIC in the appropriate expansion slot, reseal the workstation case, and attach the cabling system to the NIC. If your NIC is hardware configured and meant to be used on an ISA bus, you should be ready to continue with the Personal NetWare installation.

If the NIC you are installing uses an EISA bus or IBM's proprietary Micro-Channels Architecture (MCA), you will have to boot the workstation with the workstation's configuration utilities. These utilities allow you to configure the EISA or MCA workstation to recognize the fact that a new EISA or MCA card has been added to the system. If you do not do this, you will receive an error when you restart your EISA or MCA workstation, since the workstation will not recognize the new card. (Note, EISA and MCA are not compatible. You can't put an EISA card in an MCA machine or vice-versa.)

If your NIC is software configurable or "jumper-less," you will need to run special configuration utilities provided by the NIC vendor. These utilities set the information the NIC needs to operate with the other workstations hardware such as IRQs, memory addresses, and I/O ports. This information is stored in special memory chips until it is needed by the NIC or altered by you with the vendor-specific utilities.

You should now be ready to continue with the software portion of the Personal NetWare installation procedure. Be sure to add the NIC configuration parameters you used to the workstations documentation. It will be needed when we configure Personal NetWare to talk with the NIC during the installation procedure.

Initial Configuration and Installation

In the previous section, we discussed the preparations necessary to be performed on the network machinery before the networking software could be installed. Personal NetWare consists of several software components that are used to network PCs. The first consists of some DOS Terminate and Stay Ready (TSR) programs that allow the workstation to share its resources with the other authorized members of the workgroup. Additionally, information is kept in a directory off the root, which controls which user accounts have access to which network resources.

The second piece of the Personal NetWare puzzle is the universal client software. This enables the workstation to communicate with the other workstations in the workgroup, and even with networks running other versions of NetWare like 3.12 and 4.01. The universal client consists of four programs that are loaded in the following order: LSL.COM, the specific Open Data-link Interface (ODI) driver for the NIC the workstation is using, IPXODI.COM, and the NetWare DOS Requester.

The final piece of Personal NetWare is the collection of user, administration, installation, and diagnostic utilities. These utilities help Personal NetWare users create and administrate their network. As an added bonus, Novell has included an interactive computer game called NETWARS where up to four members of a workgroup try to destroy each other's spacecraft in a futuristic "dogfight."

Getting Started

The installation utility, INSTALL.EXE, is located on the *Installation + Utilities 1 diskette*. Begin the installation procedure from DOS by switching to the floppy drive that has your Personal NeWare disk and then type **INSTALL**.

The beginning of the installation procedure for Personal NetWare is fairly straightforward. The first screen welcomes you to the installation utility and informs you that help can be obtained with the F1 key throughout the installation procedure (see Figure 4.1). This help is context-sensitive, which means it is applicable to the screen or field you are involved with at the time the help function is invoked. Other options and the corresponding keystrokes are listed at the bottom of the screen. Press Enter to continue to to to the next screen.

Personal NetWare can also be installed from a network drive if you are part of a larger network and want to use Personal NetWare to increase collaboration within a specific workgroup. To do this, simply copy all the files from the Personal NetWare disks to a directory on the network. Any users who wish to install Personal NetWare can run the installation utility by accessing the network directory on which Personal NetWare is kept.

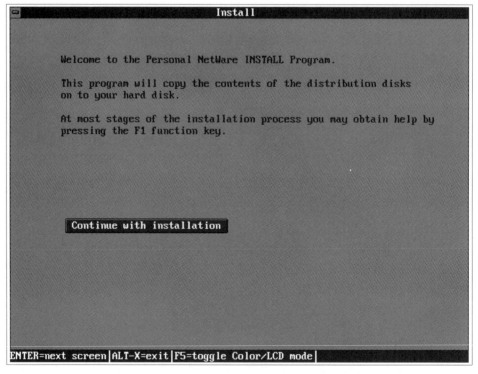

Figure 4.1 Personal NetWare's initial installation screen.

```
┌─────────────────────────────────────────────────────────────┐
│■                            Install                          │
│                                                              │
│                                                              │
│     Please enter your name, company name and product serial  │
│     number below. The serial number can be found on the      │
│     installation diskette label or on the product            │
│     registration card.                                       │
│                                                              │
│                                                              │
│        Name:                    ████████████████████████████ │
│                                                              │
│        Company Name:                                         │
│                                                              │
│        Serial Number:                                        │
│                                                              │
│                                                              │
│                                                              │
│                                                              │
│           ┌──────────────────────────────────┐              │
│           │ Accept the above and continue    │              │
│           └──────────────────────────────────┘              │
│                                                              │
│                                                              │
│                                                              │
│                                                              │
│                                                              │
│                                                              │
│ENTER=select/modify│ESC=previous screen│F1=help│ALT-X=exit│   │
└─────────────────────────────────────────────────────────────┘
```

Figure 4.2   Inserting registration information.

The "Honesty" Screen

The screen following the initial greeting is the "honesty" screen (see Figure 4.2). This screen requires a user name, the company name, and a valid serial number for the installation process to continue. This data will be stored and can be accessed through the help menus of the DOS and Windows user utilities. This information, especially the serial number, will come in handy when you need to make a technical support call; you are asked for a valid serial number before assistance can be rendered. The other reason for entering this information is to make it more difficult to "pirate" a copy of Personal NetWare by requiring a valid serial number for installation.

The INSTALL utility collects data a little bit differently from what you might be used to. The Up and Down arrows as well as the Tab and Shift-Tab keys will still do the expected, and move you from data field to data field; you can also use a mouse to move around. What is unusual is that when you start typing data into a particular field, a small subscreen opens to receive the data. Pressing the Enter key will not move you to the next field as you might expect; it will simply open these subscreens if they are not already open and close them again if they are open.

Fill in the required information and proceed to the next screen by pressing Enter on the "Accept the above and continue" field.

Destination Drives/Directories

The next screen checks your workstation's hard disk to ensure that there is enough room to install Personal NetWare and the Microsoft Windows files necessary to run Windows, as illustrated in Figure 4.3. If you do not wish to install the files necessary to run Personal NetWare with Windows, simply

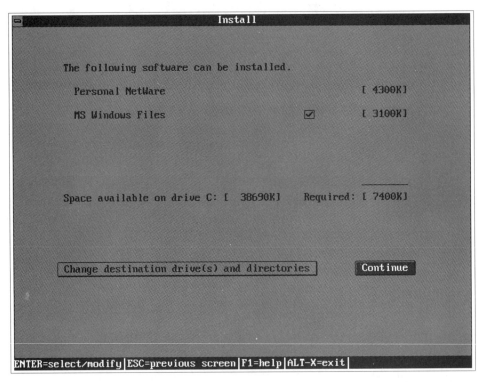

Figure 4.3 Confirming the pathways to Personal NetWare and MS Windows files.

remove the check from the box to the right of the "MS Windows Files" line. The amount of disk space required will be recalculated.

This screen also allows you to determine where the Personal NetWare files will be placed on your workstation's hard drive. The installation utility is going to copy most of the necessary files Personal NetWare needs to run, including all of the client and utility software, to a directory INSTALL will create. The directory will be called C:\NWCLIENT by default.

If you want to place the client and utility software in a different location or give it a different name, move to the "Change destination drive(s) and directories" field and press Enter. A new screen will appear (see Figure 4.4), where you can change the default for the placement of the client and utilities software. You can also change the pathway to your Windows directory with this screen if you are using Windows. By default, INSTALL will look through your directories for a copy of Windows and will grab the first one it comes across.

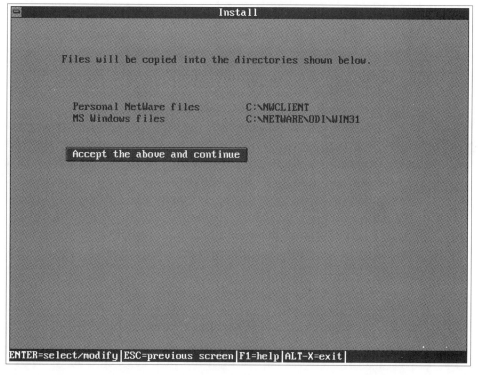

Figure 4.4 Changing the pathways to the Personal NetWare and MS Windows files.

Do Not Modify This Directory

INSTALL will also create a directory where Personal NetWare keeps important information that you are *not* supposed to modify. This directory is located directly off the root and is called C:\NWCNTL. *Do not* try to delete or modify this directory or its files in any way.

Once you are through making any modifications to the pathways to the client/utilities and Windows directories, highlight "Accept the above and continue" and press Enter to return to the hard disk space verification screen. From here, press Enter or the "Continue" button to advance to the next screen.

Windows Concerns

If you are using Windows, the installation procedure will need to make modifications to your workstation's copy of Windows. INSTALL will modify some Windows files and overwrite others with replacements. Only a modified copy of Windows will work when the Personal NetWare software is in use. The net result is that, if you have multiple copies of Windows on your hard disk, you will need to verify that INSTALL has found the correct copy of Windows that you wish to use with Personal NetWare.

A network copy of Windows will also cause some unique problems. A network copy stores the Windows files that you modify on your hard disk. The files that stay the same and therefore can be shared are stored on a network drive. Some of these shared files, however, are also some of the files that INSTALL needs to replace in order for your copy of Windows to work with Personal NetWare. INSTALL will copy these replacement files to the Windows directory on your local hard drive and not where a network copy of Windows will look for them, namely the directory on the network where the shared Windows files are located.

If this is the case, you will need to modify some of the Windows initialization (.INI) files to point to the correct version of the files in question. It is not a good idea to overwrite the shared Windows files on the network because you are probably not the only one to use them. Other users, who rely on this network copy, might not be using Personal NetWare and would not appreciate or understand why Windows suddenly ceased to work properly for them.

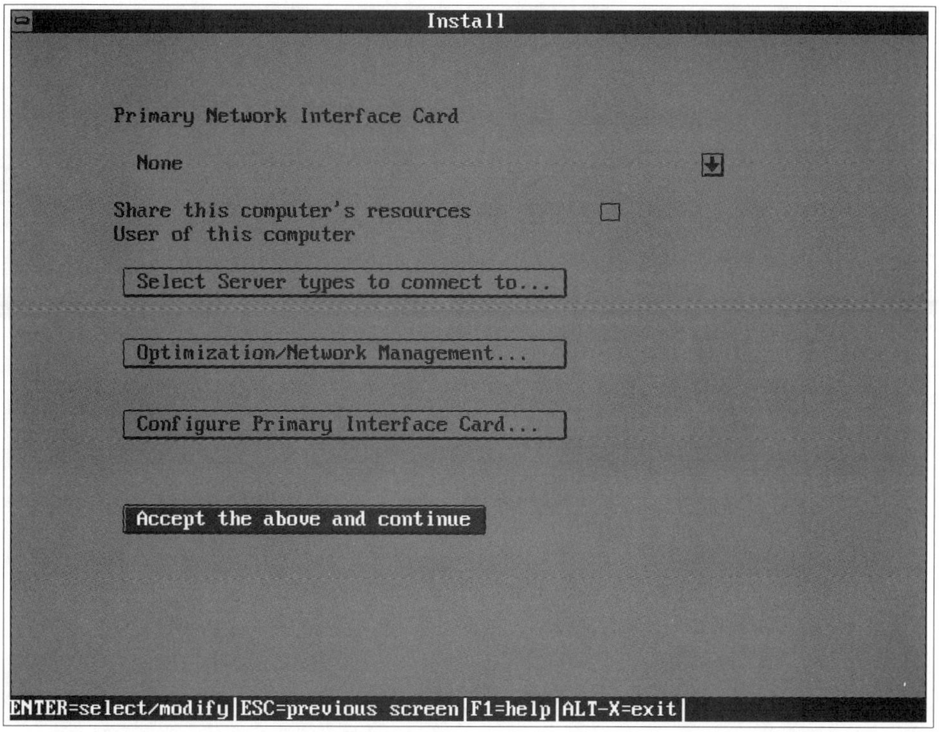

Figure 4.5   INSTALL's main menu.

Select the Primary Interface Card

You now should be at the main menu screen (see Figure 4.5). Your first task is to select the driver for your workstation's network card. Move to the "Primary Network Interface Card" field which should have "None" as the entry, and press Enter. A listing of available network card drivers will appear, as illustrated with Figure 4.6. Select the appropriate driver for your workstation's particular network card.

If your workstation's network card is not listed, you will have to rely on the NetWare ODI driver, which that network card's vendor should have supplied. If the driver is not available, contact your vendor or distributor to obtain it. Often, there are bulletin board services available from which you can download the appropriate driver.

After you have found the correct driver from the vendor, select "OEM supplied driver" which is an option on the list shown in Figure 4.6. You will be queried for

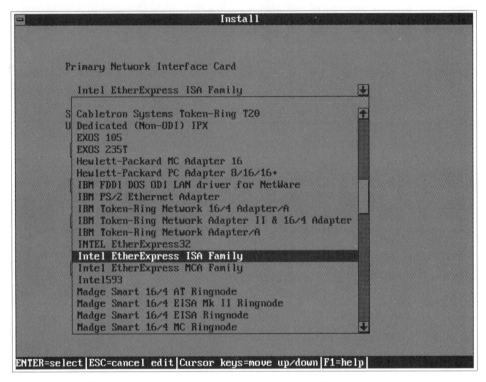

Figure 4.6 Choosing a network interface controller.

the DOS path to the driver (for example, A:\NETWARE\ODI\EXP16ODI.COM). Enter the correct path and press Enter.

Naming Your Server/Workstation

Your next task is to name your PC and designate it as either a Personal NetWare server or simply a workstation on a Personal NetWare network. Recall that a Personal NetWare server is different from a Personal NetWare workstation only in that a server shares resources with other network users. If you will need for other users to have access to this particular PC's resources, such as a hard disk or an attached printer, then you will need to designate this PC as a server. Check the box labeled "Share this computer's resources" to designate your PC as a Personal NetWare server. To designate your PC as only a workstation, leave the box unchecked.

Whether your PC will serve as a workstation or both a workstation and a server, you will need to provide it with a name. This name will be used to identify your PC on the network to other PCs. It will also be used to name any resources that you wish to publish for other network users to access.

The only criteria for the PC's monitor are that the name you choose is unique and a maximum of ten alphanumeric characters with no spaces. A name associating the PC with its owner, department, or location might be your best bet. Some examples could be PAUL, TONY, SMITH35, ROOM205, or CUST-SERV12. The name you assign will be suffixed with "_PC" to form the PC's network name. The previous suggestions would then become PAUL_PC, TONY_PC, SMITH35_PC, ROOM205_PC, and CUSTSERV12_PC.

Workstation/Server Connection Types

After designating server/workstation status and a name for your PC, you will need to tell INSTALL to which types of NetWare servers you will be connecting. Move to the "Select Server types to connect to..." button and press Enter to bring up the screen, as illustrated by Figure 4.7. This screen contains the three types of NetWare servers you can connect with: NetWare 2.x and 3.x, NetWare 4.x, and Personal NetWare Desktop servers. Make sure that only the appropriate boxes are checked. This will save you memory space by not loading VLMs you do not need.

For each type of server, there is also a preferred "access point." For NetWare 2.x and 3.x, it is a preferred server; for NetWare 4.x, it is a preferred tree; and for Personal NetWare, it is a preferred workgroup. More information on Net-Ware 2.x, 3.x, and 4.x can be found in Chapter 10. You do not have to designate a preferred server, tree, or workgroup.

The last item of business on this screen is to choose the first network drive. In a DOS drive table, there are 26 possible drives. Each is designated with a letter of the alphabet. By convention, drives A and B usually refer to floppy drives, while C, D, and E are reserved for local DOS devices such as hard disk and CD-ROM drives. Normally, the first network drive is F, which also happens to be the Personal NetWare default. This means that you can map 21 network drives and designate them with the drive letters F through Z. Designating a later letter in the alphabet such as H will only reduce the number of possible network drives available to you (H through Z).

After you have made your choices for the types of NetWare servers you wish to access and the first network drive, press Enter on the "Accept the above and continue" button to return to the main menu.

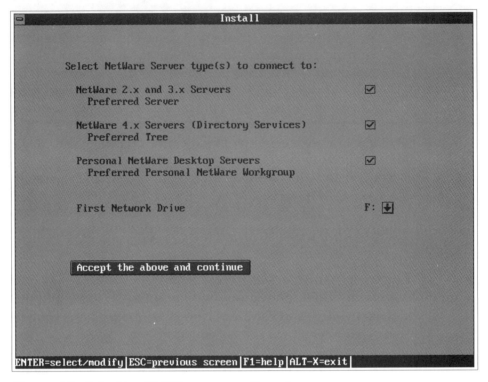

Figure 4.7 Selecting NetWare connections types.

DOS-Protected Mode Services

Following the selection of your NetWare server type connections and the designation of the first network drive, you can use INSTALL to help maximize your workstation/server performance. Highlighting the "Optimization/Network Management..." button and pressing Enter will give you a screen similar to Figure 4.8. The first set of parameters you can set is entitled Optimization and allows you to load the workstation/server performance optimization programs, DPMS.EXE and NWCACHE.EXE.

DPMS.EXE is the driver for the DOS-Protected Mode Services (DPMS) feature that helps you maximize your memory usage. DPMS allows you to conserve conventional memory by giving you the ability to load programs outside of conventional memory while still running in protected mode. The programs that will take advantage of DPMS include DPMS.EXE, SERVER.EXE, NWCACHE.EXE, and any other third-party programs that are designed to use DPMS.

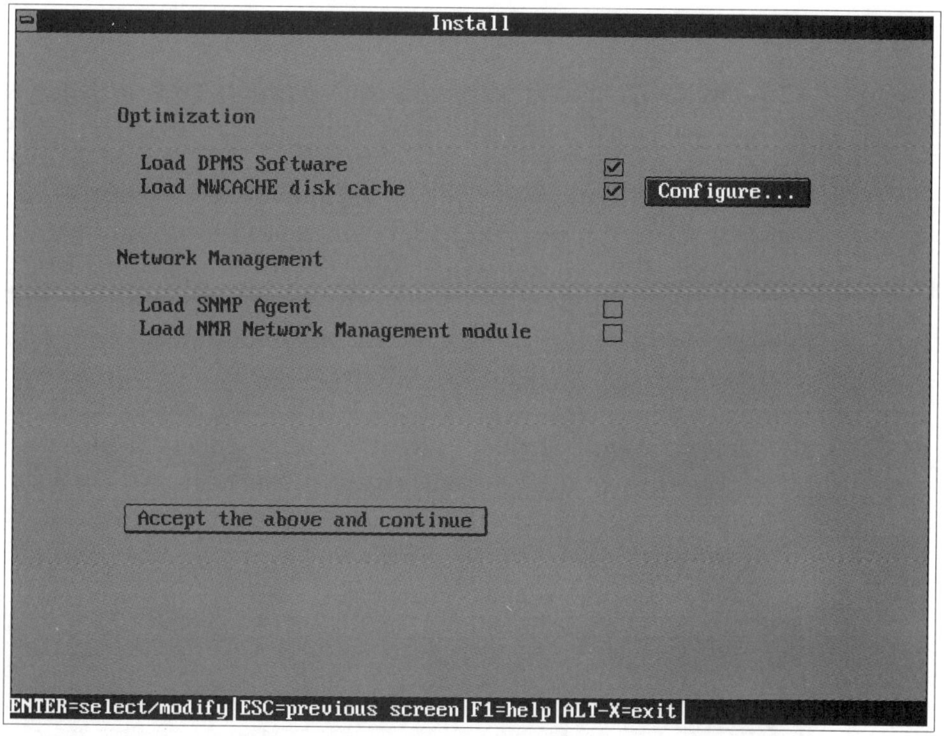
Install
Optimization
Load DPMS Software
Load NWCACHE disk cache
Configure...
Network Management
Load SNMP Agent
Load NMR Network Management module
Accept the above and continue
ENTER=select/modify
ESC=previous screen
F1=help
ALT-X=exit

Figure 4.8 Configuring performance and network management.

If you have chosen to publish your workstation's resources, the Load DPMS Software box will already be checked so that SERVER.EXE can be loaded into nonconventional memory. Do not change this default. You will also need a memory manager so that DPMS.EXE can load.

NWCACHE Disk Caching

The other workstation/server optimization tool available through Personal NetWare is NWCACHE.EXE. NWCACHE.EXE helps reduce the time it takes to access often-used data that DOS requires from hard disks or floppy diskettes by using a process called *disk caching*. Disk caching designates a *cache buffer* (specially defined area) in memory to store this repetitively called data. Data can be read more quickly from memory than a hard drive or floppy diskette, therefore, your performance will improve. When the cache buffer fills up, the least recently used data will be written to the hard disk or floppy diskette to make room for the newer data.

To have INSTALL configure your workstation/server so that NWCACHE is loaded automatically, check the box labeled "Load NWCACHE disk cache" and press Enter on the "Configure..." button located next to it on the Optimization/Network Management... submenu. You will see a screen similar to Figure 4.9. This screen enables you to set parameters for minimum and maximum cache buffer size, to allow write delays, and to allow memory lending.

The last two options require a little explanation. You can cause write requests to be cached in memory for a certain amount of time instead of having every request be written straight through. NWCACHE uses this delay to combine multiple write requests to a hard disk into a single larger one. NWCACHE will also attempt to eliminate duplicate sector write requests. Reducing the number of write requests and the time required for writing them will help your performance more than the write delay will cost you. The default write delay is 5,000 milliseconds.

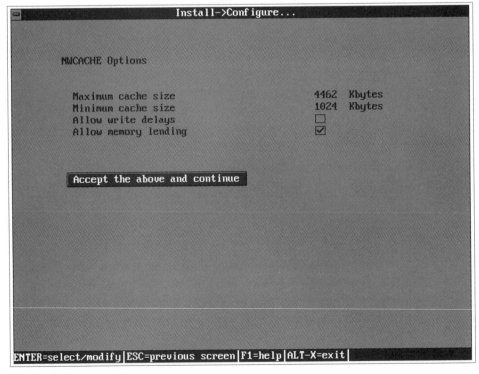

Figure 4.9 NWCACHE.EXE configuration options.

NWCACHE can also lend memory to other applications that may need it. NWCACHE automatically monitors requests for nonconventional memory and can reduce the size of the disk cache buffer it controls and lend this "freed" memory to applications that might need it. However, NWCACHE will not reduce the size of its cache buffer below the designated minimum. When the memory is free again, NWCACHE will reappropriate the memory until the cache buffer reaches the designated maximum size.

Set the NWCACHE options to those you desire and press Enter on the "Accept the above and continue" button to return to the Optimization/Network Management... submenu.

Network Management

Personal NetWare allows for centralized network management through the use of *Simple Network Management Protocol* (SNMP). This industry standard protocol facilitates communication between a network management console and the network devices that the console monitors like routers, hubs, and now Personal NetWare workstations. This feature is only useful, however, if you have a management system in place such as Novell's NetWare Management System, another third-party management system, or an SNMP-based management console.

Activating this feature will add to the STARTNET.BAT file a call to load the *Host Resources Management Information Base* (HOSTMIB.EXE) and the desktop SNMP transport provider (STPIPX.COM). There will also be additions to the NET.CFG file to load the necessary VLMs and set the proper options. If you are attached to another NetWare server, the addresses of the NMS consoles will be automatically added to the NET.CFG file to serve as trap target addresses. Otherwise, you will be prompted for these addresses. The trap addresses serve as a place where a notification can be sent when a situation arises that the management system has been configured to look for, such as the use of invalid passwords. Once again, if you do not have a SNMP- based management system, this feature will be of little use to you.

Configuring the Primary Network Card

The final step involves configuring the network card you will use to access the Personal NetWare network. From the main menu, select the "Configure Primary Interface Card..." and press Enter. You will see a screen similar to Figure 4.10.

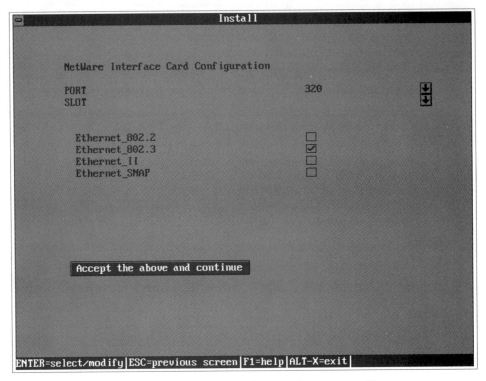

Figure 4.10 Configuring your network interface controller.

The configuration screen for your network interface controller is tailored to the specific type of NIC driver that you chose earlier. For instance, the example that we have been using throughout this chapter is an Intel EtherExpress 16. This means that we have an Ethernet card that is software configurable and is intended for an ISA bus machine. For this particular card, all we need to identify is the *Port* setting and the correct Ethernet frame type(s) that will be used. We do not need to know *Interrupt* values, *Memory* and *Node* addresses, or other information you might have to set for a different type of card.

The information you need to tell Personal NetWare about your NIC configuration should be fresh in your mind before beginning the installation of the Personal NetWare software. If the NIC was installed at an earlier date then the survey that you performed in Chapter 3 should help you obtain the necessary information.

Make the appropriate choices to indicate to Personal NetWare how your NIC is configured. To return to the main menu, highlight the "Accept the above and continue" button and press Enter.

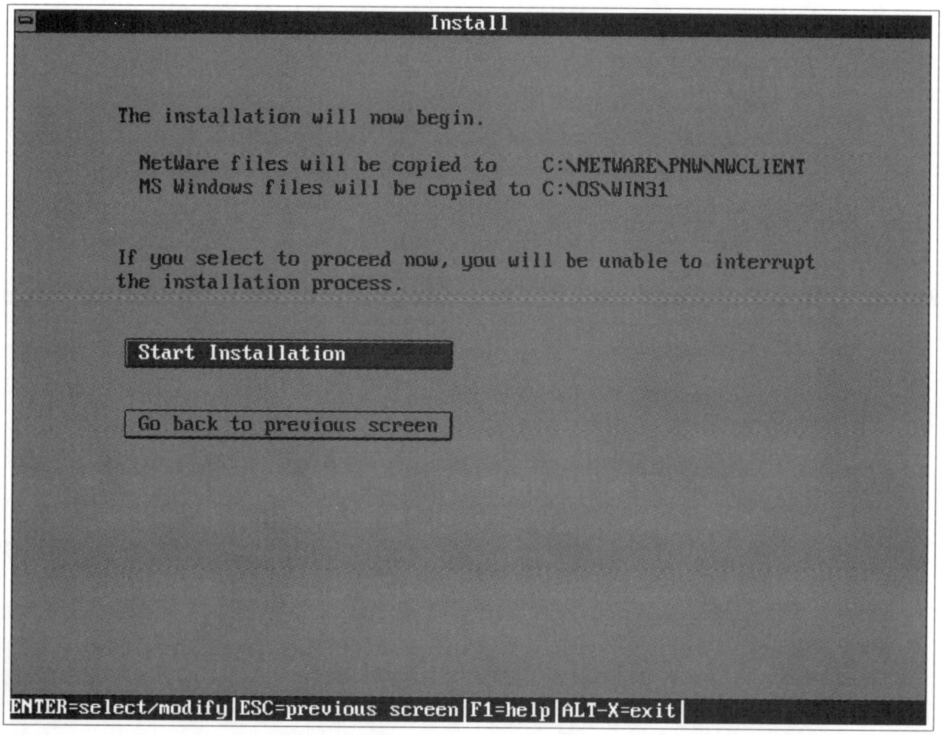

```
┌─────────────────────────────────────────────────────────────┐
│ ▬                            Install                          │
│                                                               │
│                                                               │
│     The installation will now begin.                          │
│                                                               │
│        NetWare files will be copied to     C:\NETWARE\PNW\NWCLIENT │
│        MS Windows files will be copied to  C:\OS\WIN31        │
│                                                               │
│                                                               │
│     If you select to proceed now, you will be unable to interrupt │
│     the installation process.                                 │
│  ┄┄┄┄┄┄┄┄┄┄┄┄┄┄┄┄┄┄┄┄┄┄┄┄┄┄┄┄┄┄┄┄┄┄┄┄┄┄┄┄┄┄┄┄┄┄┄┄┄┄┄┄┄┄┄┄┄┄┄┄ │
│                                                               │
│        ┌──────────────────────┐                               │
│        │  Start Installation  │                               │
│        └──────────────────────┘                               │
│                                                               │
│        ┌────────────────────────────┐                         │
│        │ Go back to previous screen │                         │
│        └────────────────────────────┘                         │
│                                                               │
│                                                               │
│                                                               │
│                                                               │
│                                                               │
│ ENTER=select/modify│ESC=previous screen│F1=help│ALT-X=exit │  │
└─────────────────────────────────────────────────────────────┘
```

Figure 4.11   Proceed with the installation procedure.

Installation of the Software

Your Personal NetWare workstation/server should now be configured. Highlight the "Accept the above and continue" button and press Enter to continue with the installation procedure. You should see a screen similar to Figure 4.11. This screen is sort of a "last chance" to change any of the settings you have just defined before INSTALL actually does its work and sets up the Personal NetWare software.

Once again the paths to which the Personal NetWare and MS Windows (if you are installing the Windows support) files will be copied. You are also given the option to return to the main menu through the "Go back to previous screen" button in order to modify the configuration. Pressing Enter on the "Start Installation" button will begin the actual installation of the software, after which you will be unable to return and modify any of the parameters until the process is complete. If you are ready to proceed, select "Start Installation" and press Enter.

INSTALL performs several more tasks based on information you have already provided it before it will need your attention again. There are modifications to be made to your boot files, configuration files to be created, directories structures to be built to hold the different Personal NetWare files, and all the Personal NetWare files to be copied to those directories. Some of the more important tasks performed at this time will be discussed in more detail in the following sections.

When INSTALL has completed installing the software, you will receive a message informing you of this and asking you to press Enter to continue. You will then see a screen similar to Figure 4.12. This screen has two buttons: Restart Operating System and View READ.ME file. The READ.ME file contains detailed technical information on the installation procedure.

To restart the operating system so that the changes INSTALL has made can take effect, press Enter on the "Restart Operating System" button. When your system reboots, another Personal NetWare utility, SETUP.EXE, will be run

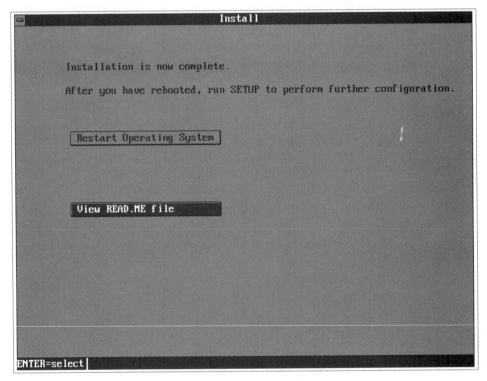

Figure 4.12 Notification of completed installation.

automatically to complete your workstation/server configuration. This part of the installation procedure is described in the Completing the Workstation/Server Installation section.

Basic Modifications to AUTOEXEC.BAT and CONFIG.SYS

INSTALL will make several modifications to the boot files, AUTOEXEC.BAT and CONFIG.SYS. Your PC uses these files to set up the environment when it is turned on or rebooted. Before any modifications are made, however, the original contents of AUTOEXEC.BAT and CONFIG.SYS are saved to the files AUTOEXEC.OLD and CONFIG.OLD as a precaution.

In CONFIG.SYS, a statement declares Z to be the last logical drive letter instead of the default of E. In the AUTOEXEC.BAT file, the path to the Personal NetWare files is added to the PATH statement. If you have designated NWCACHE.EXE for your disk caching, the command implementing SMARTDRV.EXE (if you are using it) in the AUTOEXEC.BAT will be commented out with a REM statement. There will also be a call added to run another batch file, which the installation procedure will create.

The STARTNET.BAT File

The batch file that is executed from AUTOEXEC.BAT is called STARTNET.BAT. STARTNET.BAT contains instructions that call the necessary Personal NetWare programs to establish a session with the network and run the additional features such as disk caching and network management support that you designated earlier. The following is an example STARTNET.BAT with the DPMS and NWCACHE features activated:

```
@ECHO OFF
SET NWLANGUAGE=ENGLISH
C:
CD C:\NETWARE\PNW\NWCLIENT
REM DPMS should be loaded before NWCACHE
DPMS
NWCACHE 4096 1024 /LEND=ON /DELAY=ON
LH SHARE /F:10240 /L:200
LH LSL
LH EXP16ODI
LH IPXODI
LH SERVER
```

```
VLM
CD \
C:\NETWARE\PNW\NWCLIENT\SETUP /FIRST
```

In this example, we wish to take advantage of the optimization features but not the network management support. The STARTNET.BAT begins by setting the machine to the default language of English and then moves us to the proper directory where Personal NetWare programs are stored. DPMS is now loaded so that programs that are able to take advantage of DOS Protected Mode Services may.

NWCACHE is now able to take advantage of DPMS. The cache buffer size is also set to a minimum of 1024 KB and a maximum of 4096 KB. Memory lending is also enabled, as well as a write delay.

SHARE.EXE is a DOS utility that allows multiple access to a file. In essence, a file can be in use by more than one application or user. This can be very important in a network setting where the possibility exists of two users needing to access the same file at the same time. Personal NetWare loads SHARE.EXE here to make sure that it is loaded. SHARE.EXE is also loaded into nonconventional memory to save memory for applications that can only use conventional memory.

Next, the universal client and the Personal NetWare server software are loaded into nonconventional memory. The universal client (consisting of LSL.COM, the NIC driver-EXP16ODI.COM, IPXODI.COM, and VLM.EXE) takes information contained in another file created by the installation procedure, NET.CFG, and establishes a session with the network. The server software, SERVER.EXE, turns the workstation into a Personal NetWare server and publishes resources according to instructions that will be defined later in the installation procedure. At this point, a Personal NetWare server's only real characteristic is the name you have given it.

The last command in STARTNET.BAT is a command to run the Personal NetWare program SETUP.EXE with the /FIRST switch when STARTNET.BAT is first executed. This will complete the basic installation of your workstation/server by allowing you to create or join a workgroup and designate which resources you wish to share if your machine has SERVER.EXE loaded.

The NET.CFG File

NET.CFG is another file that is created from the information that you provided during the previous configuration portion of this installation procedure. NET.CFG does not call other programs, but instead provides information necessary to define the correct capabilities your connection to the network is supposed to have, other than the default settings. An example NET.CFG file might look like this:

```
Link driver EXP16ODI
    PORT 320
    FRAME Ethernet_802.3

Netware DOS Requester
    FIRST NETWORK DRIVE = F
    NETWARE PROTOCOL = PNW,BIND
    SHOW DOTS = ON
    USE DEFAULTS = ON
    VLM = AUTO.VLM
```

One of the high points of the NET.CFG file is the link driver section which defines the configuration for your NIC. The information you provided earlier such as port number, memory address, interrupt number, and frame type is stored here. This information is used to tell Personal NetWare how to interact with your NIC, which driver to use to communicate with it, and what kind of data to expect. In our example, we are using the driver for the Intel EtherExpress ISA Family (EXP16ODI.COM) of Ethernet cards. The only nondefault settings we have chosen are the port setting (320), and the type of data we will be receiving (802.3 Ethernet frames).

The NetWare DOS Requester section defines the universal client's nondefault settings. Information such as the first network drive, the type of NetWare supported, and which VLMs will be used can be found here. Our example shows the first network drive to be F. We also have defined the type of NetWare we expect to deal with. These NetWare Protocols are PNW (Personal NetWare) and BIND (NetWare 2.x or 3.x bindery servers). If we had designated NetWare 4.x as one of the types of NetWare we needed to support, then NDS (NetWare Directory Services) would be listed as well. NetWare does not normally show the DOS entries of "." and "..". If you are using Windows 3.x, this setting needs to be ON. USE DEFAULTS = ON allows VLM.EXE to load its default VLMs. Finally, VLM=AUTO.VLM loads the AUTO VLM, which is not part of the group of default VLMs.

If you had selected network management options, there would have been other VLMs that needed to be loaded as well as another section or two defining the nondefault settings for the network management functions. More will be added to this file when we make a second configuration pass with SETUP.EXE later on.

Completing the Workstation/Server Installation

Once you have used INSTALL.EXE to copy the Personal NetWare files to your workstation/server and perform the initial setup of your workstation/server's characteristics, you will restart your PC so that all the changes can take effect, and the newly installed universal client (NetWare DOS Requester) can establish a session with the network. As was mentioned earlier, SETUP.EXE with the /FIRST switch is run from the STARTNET.BAT at this time to complete your workstation/server's configuration.

Running Personal NetWare for the First Time

When SETUP.EXE is run with the /FIRST switch, you will see a screen similar to Figure 4.13. The idea behind this first time setup is to give you a chance to create a new workgroup or join an existing workgroup. Additionally, you will be able

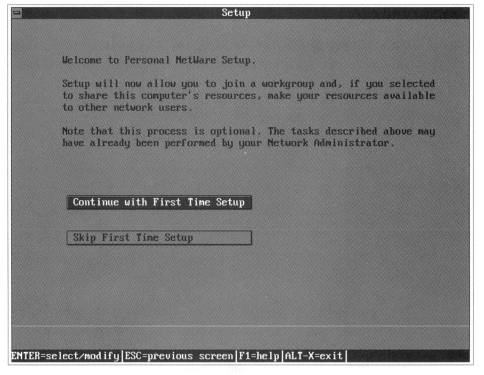

Figure 4.13 SETUP's Welcome screen.

to designate which of your PC's resources you wish to share at this time if your PC is running the SERVER.EXE software.

There are two buttons available: Continue with First Time Setup and Skip First Time Setup. The second button, Skip First Time Setup, allows you to bypass the two operations previously mentioned that SETUP automates and will be discussed in more detail in a later section. If you do not want to skip this automated configuration procedure, press the first button, Continue with First Time Setup to move to the next screen. Two possible screens will appear at this point, depending upon whether this PC is the first workstation or workstation/server on the network.

First Network Workstation/Server

If this is the first workstation or workstation/server to be installed on your network, SETUP will ask you to create the first workgroup (see Figure 4.14). Do

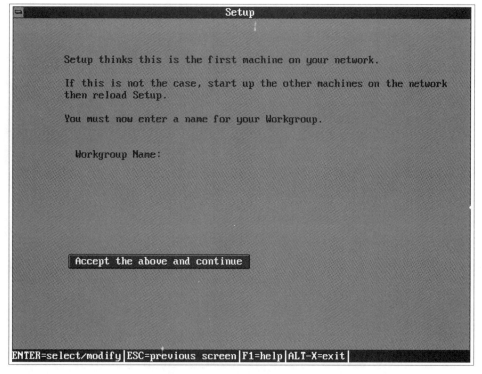

Figure 4.14 Creating the initial workgroup.

so by entering the workgroup name in the "Workgroup Name" field and pressing Enter on the "Accept the above and continue" button. Note that you will also be shown this screen if you have already installed workstations or workstations/servers on your network but the machines in question are not yet turned on for one reason or another.

If you wish to join a workgroup, exit SETUP by pressing **Alt-X**. Boot the workstation/servers that you have already installed, so that they appear on the network. Restart SETUP by typing **SETUP /FIRST** from the NWCLIENT directory. SETUP will now be able to see any workgroups that you have already created during previous installations.

Joining an Existing Workgroup

If there are workgroups in existence and they are currently active on your network, SETUP will show you a screen similar to Figure 4.15. This screen

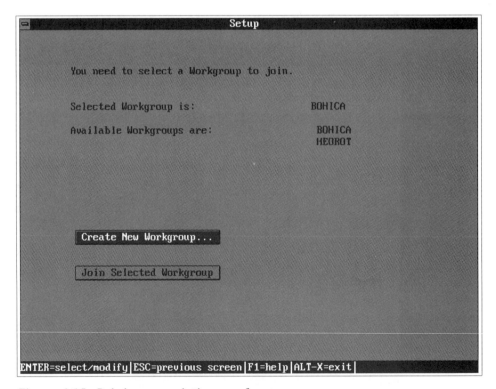

Figure 4.15 Joining an existing workgroup.

contains two buttons: Create New Workgroup... and Join Selected Workgroup. There are also two data fields: The first tells you what the currently selected workgroup is; the second provides you with a list of workgroups that the PC you are setting up can join.

To join an existing workgroup, use the Tab or arrow keys until you are on the list of available workgroups. Select the desired workgroup by highlighting it in the list of available workgroups and pressing Enter. Then, the field for the currently selected workgroup should show the desired workgroup to join. Highlight and press the "Join Selected Workgroup" button to proceed to the next operation that SETUP automates.

If the workgroup you desire to join is not currently active on the network, press **Alt-X** to exit SETUP. Boot the appropriate workstation/server that corresponds to the desired workgroup so it will be active on the network. SETUP will now be able to "see" the workgroup and will list it as one of the available workgroups that you can join. Restart SETUP by typing **SETUP /FIRST** in the NWCLIENT directory, then select the desired workgroup.

If you do not wish to join any of the existing workgroups, you may create another one. Highlight the "Create New Workgroup..." button and press Enter. SETUP provides a small screen to capture the name of the new workgroup. Type in the name of the new workgroup and press "OK" to accept it or "Cancel" to discontinue the operation. Accepting the new workgroup will take you to the next operation that SETUP automates.

Do not create two workgroups on the network with the same name. Although they will both be valid workgroups (because Personal NetWare uses the associated network numbers to differentiate between the two workgroups), users, however, will be unable to easily tell the difference, which will lead to confusion when they try to login.

If the workstation you are installing is *not* a server, then skip to the next section, *Completing the Workstation Setup*. If the workstation you are installing will operate as a server, continue with the next section, *Sharing Resources*.

Sharing Resources

If your workstation will function as a server, the next screen you will see will be similar to Figure 4.16. This screen allows you to designate which of your PC's resources you wish to share with the other users of the network. It lists all the logical disk drives that are available, as well as the printer ports (LPT). Each logical drive and printer port has a name derived from the name you assigned to the workstation during INSTALL's portion of the installation.

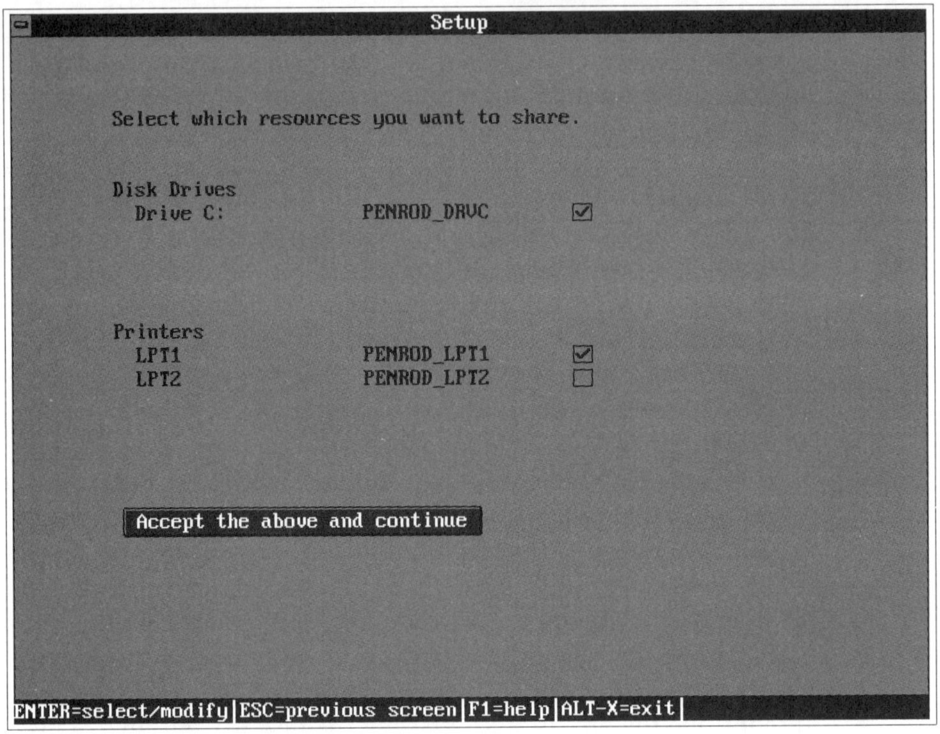

Figure 4.16 Designating shared resources.

For example, the logical drive C would have a name composed of the workstation's name with _DRVC attached to it. Printer ports work much the same way, except _LPT1 would be added to indicate the name of the workstation's printer port one. You can change the names of resources to anything you wish, but be sure to make the names unique and obviously different from the names of other resources in order to avoid confusion.

To alter the names of the resources you intend to share, use the arrow or Tab keys to move to the current name of the resource and begin typing the new name or press Enter. Either action will produce a now familiar data capture window where the name change is entered and accepted by selecting "OK" or the operation is discontinued by selecting "Cancel."

When the names are assigned to the shared resources, highlight the box beside each logical drive and printer port you wish to share with the network and press the Enter key to make a check appear in the box. When you are

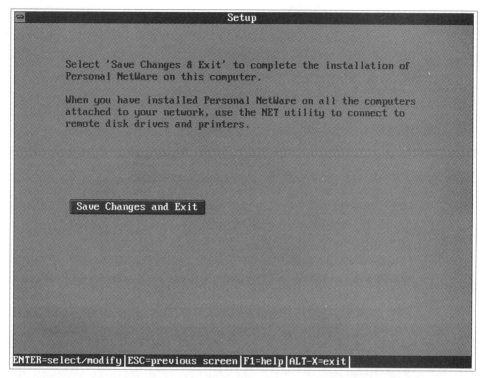

Figure 4.17   SETUP gives a final opportunity to alter data.

finished, highlight the "Accept the above and continue" button to move to the next screen.

Completing the Workstation Setup

Once you have completed creating or joining a workgroup and designating shared resources (if the workstation is a server), SETUP gives you a chance to return to previous screens and modify any of your options. Figure 4.17 illustrates this "last chance" screen. If you are ready to proceed with the completion of the workstation's installation, highlight the "Save Changes and Exit" button and press Enter. If you wish to make a change, press Esc for the previous screen.

When you accept the changes, SETUP will modify several files on your workstation to reflect them including the STARTNET.BAT and the NET.CFG files. You will also receive two more messages. The first will inform you that the setup procedure is complete. Clearing this message will bring up the next, which informs you that you are now logged into the workgroup you chose earlier to join or create. The second message also tells you that your account name is the one you gave as the "User of this computer" during the first part of the installation procedure (INSTALL). This account does not have a password. You will have to add that later with either the NET DOS command line utility or the Windows utilities.

Modifying Workstation/Server Parameters

Modifying the setup parameters for a workstation or workstation/server is a very simple matter. Run SETUP.EXE without the /FIRST option to bring up a screen similar to Figure 4.18.

This screen is very similar to INSTALL's main menu. From here you can modify which network card driver you will use and how it is configured, which server

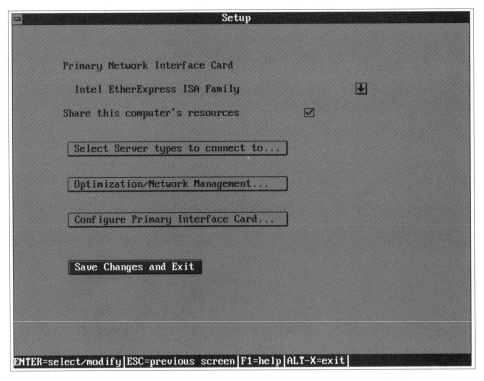

Figure 4.18 SETUP's main screen.

types you can connect to and the associated preferred connection, the workstation optimization and management features, and even whether to share the resources of the workstation.

After you have made the changes that you desire, highlight the "Save Changes and Exit" button and press Enter. SETUP will make the appropriate changes and then give you a message stating that the setup is complete. Clearing the message will give you a new screen with the option to exit to DOS or reboot the machine.

Installing Personal NetWare through Windows

You can also launch the installation utility from Windows by going to the Program Manager, opening the File menu and choosing "Run...". Select the floppy drive with your Personal NetWare diskette, select the program called INSTALL.EXE, and then click the "OK" button to launch the Windows installation utility.

The Windows installation covers the same options and setup features as the DOS installation. Only the screens are different, although the DOS and Windows screens contain the same information. Follow the previous sections pertaining to the DOS installation and use the corresponding Windows screens. Enter the same information just as you would for the DOS installation.

The installation procedure with Windows is also a two-part process. The first part is comprised of assigning the initial settings to the workstation or workstation/server and copying the necessary DOS and Windows files to the client directory you designate. After INSTALL has finished its portion of the procedure, the system will be restarted and SETUP /FIRST will be run to complete the installation procedure.

As before, SETUP allows you to join or create a workgroup and designate which resources will be shared with the network if the workstation will function as a server. When SETUP has finished its portion of the installation procedure, you will be logged into the workgroup you chose to join or create, with the user account name taken from the "User of this computer" field. You will have to configure this account later.

Installing the Personal NetWare Tutorial

Personal NetWare is bundled with a tutorial for both the DOS and Windows utilities. The installation with both is fairly straightforward and simple. For the DOS tutorial, run DOSTUTOR.EXE from the A: or B: DOS prompt. You will see a menu with two options: INSTALL DOS Tutor and Exit. Select INSTALL DOS Tutor to begin the installation process. The only other information required is the location where you would like to install the DOS tutor. The next screen is designed to capture that information. Press Enter when you have the desired DOS path in the "Directory:" field.

The DOS tutorial installation utility will copy all the necessary files to the directory that you chose. DOSTUTOR will inform you when it has completed the installation. You can use the tutorial program as soon as you exit the DOS tutorial installation utility by typing PNWTRAIN in the directory where you installed the DOS tutorial program.

The Windows tutorial program is just as easy to install. You can launch the installation utility from Windows by going to the Program Manager, opening the File menu, and choosing Run. Select the floppy drive that has your Personal NetWare diskette, select the file called WINTUTOR.EXE, and then click the "OK" button to launch the Windows tutor installation utility.

The Windows tutor installation utility works much the same as the DOS utility. The first screen contains a field to capture the DOS path showing where you wish to install the Windows tutor. The first screen also contains two buttons giving you the option to continue with the installation or cancel it. Selecting "Continue" allows the installation utility to proceed with copying the required files to the directory you designated. The "Cancel" button aborts the installation at any time.

When all the required files have been copied to the designated directory, the Windows tutor installation utility gives you the option to view the README.TXT, which contains notes about the tutorial that you might find useful. You will also receive a message stating that the installation procedure is complete.

Conclusion

Now that you have installed a workstation on your Personal NetWare network, you can easily replicate the procedure for as many machines as are necessary. The issues and options that we discussed may be different for each workstation depending on what kind of hardware and software is installed on it. But a little common sense coupled with our discussion of the procedure should make the installation procedure adaptable to the differences.

Chapter 5

Test Driving a New Network

Introduction

You have installed Personal NetWare, and you are sitting at the DOS prompt. Personal NetWare has just opened the door to you into a much larger computing environment than the lone machine sitting in front of you. What is next? It is now time to take a tour of your new surroundings. And, the best way to become familiar with this new environment is to jump right in and do things.

This chapter gives you some exercises to do that will make you much more productive and comfortable navigating the network. We'll cover such notables as:

- Logging in
- Logging out
- Sharing resources
- Sending messages
- Viewing your account
- Starting the tutorial

But first we will take a brief tour of Personal NetWare to get a feel for our surroundings.

Personal NetWare under DOS

Personal NetWare under DOS is accessible through two components:

- DOS prompt commands
- Interactive commands

By providing two different ways of interacting with Personal NetWare in the DOS environment, the system is simpler to use under varying circumstances.

Running Personal NetWare from the DOS Prompt

The DOS prompt commands in Personal NetWare allow users to issue commands to the network directly or through batch files to customize and control their network environment. These commands all start with NET and then supply an argument to identify the kind of action to take. Some of the prompt commands to be covered in this chapter include:

- NET LOGIN
- NET LOGOUT
- NET SHARE
- NET SEND

Running Personal NetWare Interactively

The second method by which you can work with the Personal Netware environment is through the interactive NET, NET USER, and NET ADMIN commands. These commands bring up menu-based programs from which users can choose the functions they wish to perform.

Quick Tour of the NET Menu

From DOS, you can bring up a main menu and display your current connections.

To display the NetWare main menu:

From the DOS prompt, type **NET** and press Enter (see Figure 5.1). Note that the NET USER command will bring up the same screen as the NET command.

Under the File option, you can:

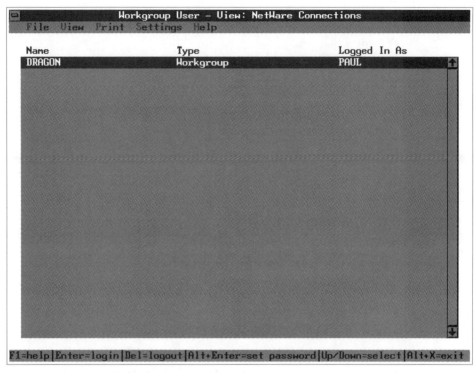

Figure 5.1   The main menu.

- Connect (login) to a workgroup.
- Disconnect (logout) from a workgroup.
- Change properties of printers, shared directories, user accounts, and so on.
- Send messages.
- Save scripts (batch files).
- Edit scripts (batch files).
- Exit the NET or NET USER command.

Under the View option, you can:

- View NetWare connections (default view).
- View logical drive mappings.
- View network printer connections.
- View printer queues.

Under the Print option, you can:

- Print a file.
- Delete a pending print job.
- Change the order of a print job in the queue.
- View or change the print settings for a print job.
- Select a different print queue to look at.
- View or change the printer status and forms.

Under the Settings option, you can:

- Display user account information.
- View or change how users receive messages.
- Assign context settings for NetWare.

Under the Help option, you can:

- Get assistance for using Help.
- View contents of the Help sections.
- Go to a previous Help topic.
- Show the version number of the NET program.

Quick Tour of the NET ADMIN Menu

If you are the network administrator, you can also bring up a main menu and display the available servers in your workgroup.

To see a list of available servers in your workgroup:

At the DOS prompt, type **NET ADMIN** and press Enter (see Figure 5.2).

Under the File option, you can:

- Add a new NetWare object (server, printer, directory, and so forth).
- Delete an existing NetWare object.
- Change the properties of the selected NetWare object.
- Rename the selected NetWare object.
- Show status information about the selected server.
- Back up the selected server's system files.

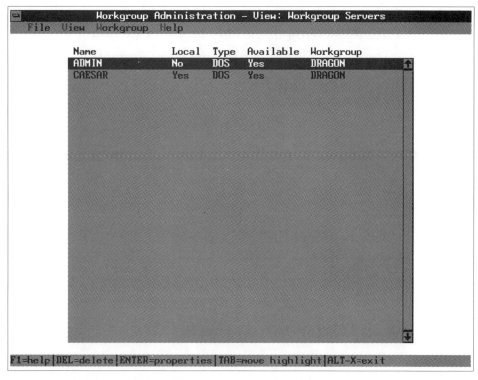

Figure 5.2   A list of servers in your workgroup.

- Restore the selected server's system files.
- Exit the NET ADMIN command.

Under the View option, you can:

- Change the view and administration functions to focus on Shared Directories in the current workgroup.
- Change the view and administration functions to focus on Shared Printers in the current workgroup.
- Change the view and administration functions to focus on Servers in the current workgroup.
- Change the view and administration functions to focus on User Accounts in the current workgroup.

Under the Workgroup option, you can:

- Login to a workgroup.
- Place your server into a different workgroup.
- Create a new workgroup and put your server into it.
- Manage the Audit Log.
- Manage the Error Log.
- Add, change, or delete network routing.
- Synchronize the date and time of all server clocks in the current workgroup.
- Manage local users of your server (security).

Under the Help option, you can:

- Get assistance for using Help.
- View contents of the Help sections.
- Go to a previous Help topic.
- Show the version number of the NET program.

Personal NetWare under Windows

When Windows is first run after Personal NetWare is installed, you will notice the new program group called Personal NetWare. Inside this group are three programs:

- Personal NetWare Setup
- Personal NetWare
- NetWare Diagnostics

This chapter focuses on the Personal NetWare program. The other two programs are covered in other chapters.

Exploring the Personal NetWare Windows Program

The Personal NetWare program is an interactive facility that provides both user and SUPERVISOR functionality all in the same package. When it first starts, (see Figure 5.3) the program displays the main menu, a Control Bar (underneath the main menu), a Status Bar located at the bottom of the window, and three icons representing drive mappings, NetWare connections, and printers. We will look first at the main menu, Control Bar, and the windows represented by the three icons.

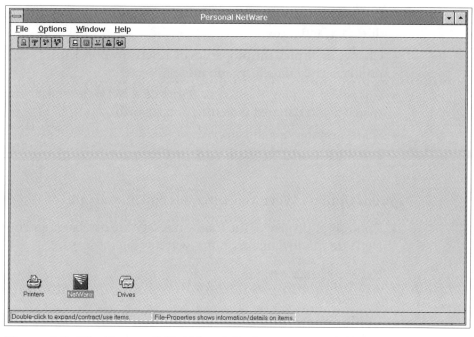

Figure 5.3 The Personal NetWare Windows utility desktop.

The Main Menu

The main menu is composed of four options:

- File
- Options
- Window
- Help

Let's see what each one looks like.

File Option   This is the option where all the real work gets done. When you select this option you can:

- Create a new NetWare object or connection (user account, shared printer, shared directory, and so on).
- Log in
- Log out

- Delete a NetWare object or connection (user account, shared printer, shared directory, and more).

- Change or display the properties of a NetWare object (user account, shared printer, shared directory, and more).

- Change or display the access rights of a NetWare object (user account, shared printer, shared directory, and so forth).

- Share a printer or a directory.

- Exit the Personal NetWare Windows program.

Options Option   When you select this option, you can:

- Control the display of the following NetWare databases and objects in the NetWare window (more on this window later):

  NetWare Databases:

  > Bindery
  > Directory Services
  > Personal
  > Not Connected

  NetWare Objects:

  > Servers
  > Volumes/Disks
  > Queues/Ports
  > Users
  > Groups

- Display or hide the Control Bar.

- Display or hide the Status Bar.

- Save the current display settings when the program exits.

Window Option   When you select this option, you can:

- Cascade the display of the NetWare, Drives, and Printers windows if more than one of them are open at the same time.

- Time the display of the NetWare, Drives, and Printers windows if more than one of them are open at the same time.

- Arrange the icons in the Personal NetWare program window of the Net-Ware, Drives, and Printers windows.
- Refresh the display of the active open NetWare, Drives, or Printers windows.
- Select the Drives window to be open, active, and up front.
- Select the NetWare window to be open, active, and up front.
- Select the Printers window to be open, active, and up front.

Help Option   When you select this option, you can:

- Select a help topic from a table of contents.
- Search for help on a topic.
- Learn how to use Help.
- Read suggestions on how to get started quickly.
- See miscellaneous information about Personal NetWare.

Control Bar

The Control Bar is a tool bar of buttons that resides below the main menu. By default, when the program first starts up, the Control Bar is displayed and all the buttons are depressed, signifying that all display options are turned on for the NetWare window. From left to right the buttons control the display of:

NetWare Databases:

Bindery
Directory Services
Personal
Not Connected

NetWare Objects:

Servers
Volumes/Disks
Queues/Ports
Users
Groups

Place the mouse over the top of each button and look in the status window to see each button's function. This will be helpful when using the NetWare window.

The Heart of Personal NetWare—the NetWare Window

The NetWare window is the one in which those NetWare objects that you have selected from the Control Bar, (user accounts, workgroups, shared printers, shared directories, and so on), are displayed. You also can open the Options option on the main menu and select Views.

The window is divided into two sides, with active objects displayed on the left side and available objects displayed on the right. By default, when the window is opened for the first time after the program is started, the active side shows only the active workgroup icon with the workgroup name printed next to it. If the NetWare Personal Database button is not selected (depressed) from the Control Bar, (third button from the left), then nothing will display in the window (see Figure 5.4).

With the active workgroup highlighted, press Enter or double click on the workgroup with the mouse. The details of the workgroup are displayed in the form of a tree underneath the workgroup icon (see Figure 5.5). By matching icons to the icons on the Control Bar buttons, it makes it easier to identify what

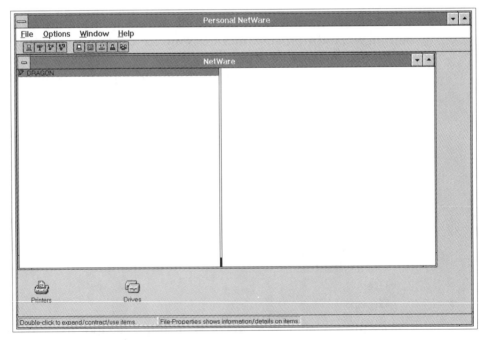

Figure 5.4 The NetWare window.

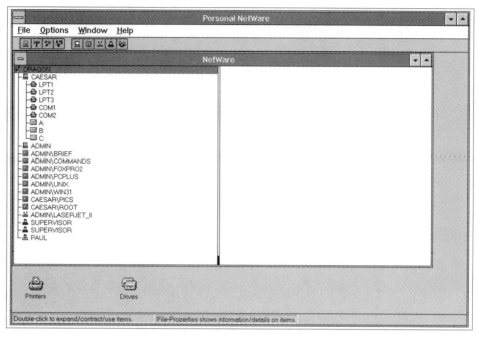

Figure 5.5 Workgroup details.

you are looking at. Using this window to configure accounts and connections will be covered in Chapters 8 and 9.

Where Are My Disks?

The Disks window displays shared directories and mapped drives for your account (see Figure 5.6). The window is split into two sides.

The left side contains the DOS logical drives that are mapped and unmapped. Mapped, or physical drives, have a drive icon next to a letter representing a DOS logical drive. Each kind of drive represented; floppy, hard, logical, and logical mapped each have a unique icon to represent them. Logical mapped drives, both permanent and temporary, contain the name of the shared directory to which they are mapped. Permanent logical mapped drives have a red squiggle on their icon. If a drive is unmapped, there is nothing next to the logical DOS drive letter.

The right side of the window contains a list of the available shared directories that can be mapped. They are displayed with the server they exist on.

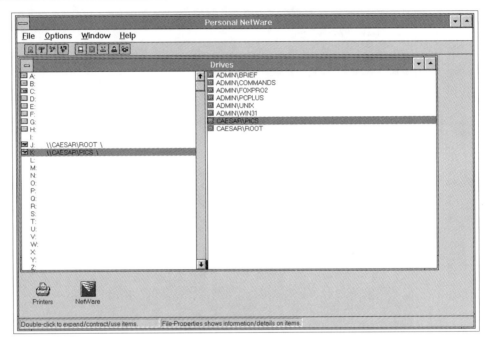

Figure 5.6 Displaying shared directories and mapped drives.

What about Printing?

The Printers window displays shared printers and captured ports for your account, (see Figure 5.7). This window also is split into two sides. The left side displays the printer ports for your workstation. If a port has been captured, the printer icon will be to the left of it; and the shared printer name and the server to which it is attached will be displayed to the right of the port name. If a port has not been captured, then nothing is displayed next to it.

The right side contains a list of the available printers that can be attached to ports on your workstation.

Logging In

The first thing you do when you start Personal NetWare is log in to the network with a valid account. This is the only means by which you can take advantage of the services offered by the network. It may seem a trivial matter to discuss logging in to a network, but there are some things to be aware of, and it is also helpful for first-time users of a network.

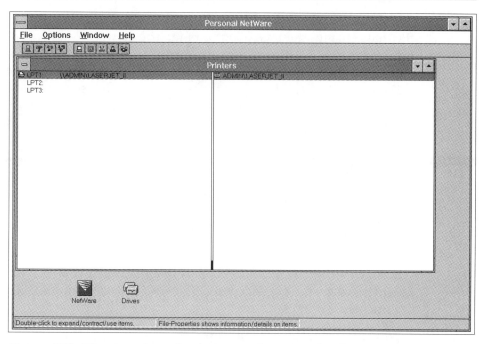

Figure 5.7 Viewing shared printers and captured printer ports.

Before you can log in to Personal NetWare, you must first load it. After Personal NetWare is installed, the default modifies the AUTOEXEC.BAT by placing a call to STARTNET.BAT, so that Personal NetWare is started when you boot your machine. A sample STARTNET.BAT bat file looks like:

```
@ECHO OFF
SET NWLANGUAGE=ENGLISH
C:
CD C:\NWCLIENT
REM DPMS should be loaded before NWCACHE
DPMS
LH SHARE /F:10240 /L:200
LH LSL
LH EXP160DI
LH IPXODI
LH SERVER
VLM
CD\
C:\NWCLIENT\NET LOGIN
```

The last line, C:\NWCLIENT\NET LOGIN, is the command line in the batch file that actually attempts to log you in to the network. Many people prefer to just load Personal NetWare, without logging in to the network every time they reboot their machine. To do this, just remark out or delete the line that calls NET LOGIN. You can log in to the network later by issuing the NET LOGIN command from the DOS prompt. Let's stop and take a look for a moment at the NET LOGIN command.

The NET LOGIN Command

The formats for NET LOGIN look like:

- NET LOGIN *<WORKGROUP/> <USERNAME>*
- NET LOGIN @*<batch file>*

NET LOGIN *<WORKGROUP/> <USERNAME>* is used if you wish to log in to a specific server and user account. The *<WORKGROUP/>* and *<USERNAME>* arguments are optional.

To log in from the DOS prompt:

1. Type **NET LOGIN**, without any optional arguments, and press Enter. You will see the following message:

   ```
   Type your username:
   ```

2. Type your account name, and press Enter. The program will then respond that it is authenticating your account name with the workgroup server to which your machine is currently attached. When it has completed this, you will see this message:

   ```
   Type your password:
   ```

3. Type your account password. If the login attempt is successful, the program will tell you that you are logged in to the workgroup as your account name.

The following test case demonstrates how to use the optional WORKGROUP and USERNAME arguments. Let's say that we have a user account called JOHN, and that his account resides in the workgroup ADMIN. The machine that he is working on is attached to the server ORWELL inside that workgroup. John also has an account, JOHN, in another workgroup called DEVELOP. The server that his account works off of in that workgroup is called RITCHIE.

The following are some sample sessions of what happens when logging in:

```
C:\> NET LOGIN
Type your username: JOHN
Authenticating to server ORWELL.
Type your password:   (John types his password here, but it is not displayed
                       on screen.)
You are logged in to workgroup ADMIN as JOHN.


C:\> NET LOGIN JOHN
Authenticating to server ORWELL.
Type your password:   (John types his password here, but it is not dis-
                       played.)
You are logged in to workgroup ADMIN as JOHN.


C:\> NET LOGIN ADMIN/JOHN
Authenticating to server ORWELL.
Type your password:   (John types his password here, but it is not dis-
                       played.)
You are logged in to workgroup ADMIN as JOHN.


C:\> NET LOGIN DEVELOP/JOHN
Authenticating to server RITCHIE.
Type your password:   (John types his password here, but it is not dis-
                       played.)
You are logged in to workgroup DEVELOP as JOHN.
```

Logging In Using the NET Command

Using our sample account setup, let's see how this can be done interactively using the NET program. For the first pass, we'll log JOHN into his default workgroup ADMIN on server ORWELL. The second time through, we will log JOHN in to his secondary workgroup DEVELOP on server RITCHIE.

Logging into server ORWELL on default workgroup ADMIN:

1. From the DOS prompt, type the command **NET** and press Enter. The screen showing the NetWare view of Personal NetWare will load and display.

2. Select the File option on the main menu. The File menu window will open and display. The Connect... option will be highlighted, since it is the first option.

3. Press Enter to choose the Connect... option. The Login window will appear.

4. Type **JOHN** in the User Name field, and then press the Tab key. Enter John's password here, and press **ALT-O**, or select the OK button with the mouse to start the login process.

Logging into server RITCHIE in workgroup DEVELOP:

1. From the DOS prompt, type the command **NET** and press Enter. The screen showing the NetWare view of Personal NetWare will load and display.

2. Using the arrow keys, highlight the workgroup DEVELOP and press Enter. The Login window will appear.

3. Enter JOHN in the User Name field. Press the Tab key, then enter John's password. Press **ALT-O**, or select the OK button with the mouse to start the login process.

Logging In under Windows

You can also log in to the network from Windows by clicking on the Personal NetWare icon.

To log in to server ORWELL on default workgroup ADMIN:

1. In Windows, double click on the Personal NetWare icon in the Personal NetWare group.

2. Select the Window option from the menu bar. The Window option window is displayed.

3. Select the Netware option. The Netware display window will appear, displaying network connections, workgroups, and users. On the left side of the window is the default, or active network connections, workgroup, and users.

4. Double click on the server icon with the name ADMIN next to it. The Login window will appear (see Figure 5.8).

5. Enter **JOHN** in the User Name field. Press the Tab key, and then enter John's password. Press **ALT-O**, or select the OK button with the mouse to start the login process.

Logging into server RITCHIE in workgroup DEVELOP:

1. From the desktop, double click on the Personal NetWare icon in the Personal NetWare group.

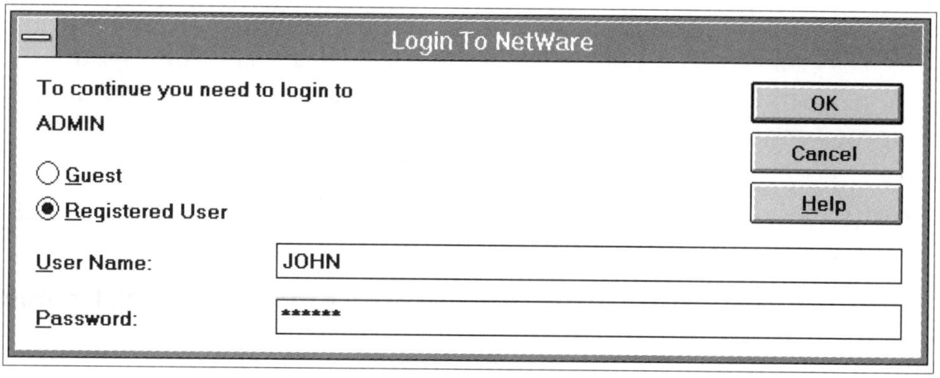

Figure 5.8 The Login window.

2. Select the Window option from the menu bar. The Window option window is displayed.

3. Select the Netware option. The Netware display window will appear, displaying network connections, workgroups, and users. On the left side of the window is the default, or active network connections, workgroup, and users. On the right are the other accessible workgroups.

4. In the right-hand portion of the window, double click on the server icon with the name DEVELOP next to it. The Login window will appear.

5. Enter **JOHN** in the User Name field. Press the Tab key and then enter John's password. Press ALT-O, or select the OK button with the mouse to start the login process.

Logging Out

The final operation you will perform on the network when you are done using network-provided services is logging out. This is the best way to cleanly disconnect from the network. The logout procedure alerts all servers to which you are connected to that you are closing your connections to them. It is important to formally log out, as it gives the administrators on the servers you connect to a way to know when you are on their server and when you are not. This is especially important if they need to take the server down for whatever reason. It prevents data files from being destroyed or corrupted.

Personal NetWare is aware enough to realize when you have dropped off the network. If you reboot, or just shut down the computer, eventually Personal

NetWare gives up trying to get a response from your machine and logs your account off the network. Meanwhile, your account still appears as active to the server to which you last logged in, and this causes headaches for the server owner, as previously stated.

Logging Out from DOS Using the NET LOGOUT Command

The most direct method of logging out is to use the NET LOGOUT command from the DOS prompt. The formats for the NET LOGOUT command are as follows:

To log out of everything:

```
NET LOGOUT
```

To log out of the workgroup:

```
NET LOGOUT /W
```

To log out of NetWare 2.x and 3.x servers:

```
NET LOGOUT /B
```

To log out of a directory tree:

```
NET LOGOUT <name of the tree> /T
```

To log out of a specific Personal NetWare server:

```
NET LOGOUT <name of the server>
```

Logging Out under Windows

You can also log out of the Network from inside Windows.

To log out from Windows:

1. From the desktop, double click on the Personal NetWare icon in the Personal NetWare group.

2. Select the Window option from the menu bar. The Window option window is displayed.

3. Select the Netware option. The Netware display window will appear, displaying network connections, workgroups, and users. On the left side of the window is the default, or active network connections, workgroup, and users. On the right are the other accessible workgroups.

4. From the left side of the NetWare window, choose the workgroup or server icon from which you wish to log out.

5. Press the DEL key. The display will reflect the change in status as Personal NetWare logs you out of the server or workgroup chosen.

Shared Resources

The whole point of being on the network is to share resources. The network provides a playground of things to do and see. And, just like a playground, there are rules attached to the equipment, and you need guidelines for navigating through the place. Let's examine a sample workgroup on a Personal NetWare network to find what's available. Figure 5.9 shows a block representation of resources dedicated to a workgroup called ADMIN.

John, our intrepid user, has an account in the workgroup called DEVELOP. John has just received a brand new account in the workgroup ADMIN and has gone exploring. One of the first things John does is find out what other resources he has access to in the ADMIN workgroup. This knowledge will influence how

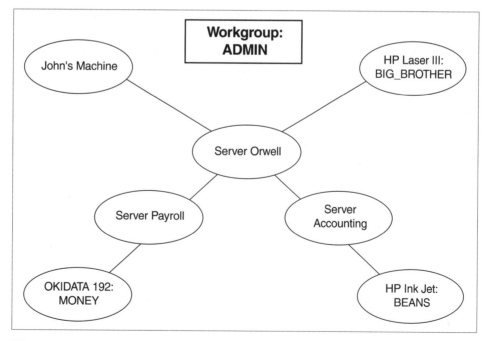

Figure 5.9 The ADMIN workgroup.

he pursues his work within the group and how he organizes his tools for work. The following DOS commands will be discussed in greater detail in Chapter 6.

Finding Workgroups

The first thing John wants to inquire about on his new account is whether he can still see his old workgroup DEVELOP.

To get a list of available workgroups:

At the DOS prompt, he types **NET WGLIST** and presses Enter. The command displays the following to his screen:

```
Available Workgroups
====================
ADMIN
DEVELOP
SHIPPING
MARKETING

Total workgroups: 4
```

The NET WGLIST command will list only those workgroups that are listed in the current workgroup's route statement (in this case, ADMIN's route statement) located in NET.CFG. This means to John that, if DEVELOP shows up on the list, then he can still get to it from his current account.

Finding Available Servers

Next, John wants to know how many servers are available for use within workgroup ADMIN. This will give him some idea as to how big the workgroup is.

To see how many servers are in a workgroup:

At the DOS prompt, he types **NET SLIST** and presses Enter. The command displays the following to his screen:

```
Available Servers       Address
==================      ============
*ORWELL                 0080C70D2413
 PAYROLL                0080C70D2414
 ACCOUNTING             00AA002A488E

Total available servers: 3
```

John sees that he has two other servers besides the one to which he is currently attached that are available within workgroup ADMIN. The names of the servers also indicate the kind of data and programs they currently store and manage. John sees that the information he needs is probably available to him from these other servers. The question here is, does he have any shared directories on these other servers so he can get at that information?

Finding Shared Directories

Next, John tries to locate how many shared directories he can access.

To see how many shared directories exist:

At the DOS prompt, he types **NET MAP** and presses Enter. The command displays the following to his screen:

```
                    Current Drive Mappings

Drive NetWare Volume Server          Your Rights
===== ============= ============== ===========
D:    PERSONNEL     PAYROLL         ALL
E:    RECEIVABLES   ACCOUNTING      ALL
F:    GEN_LEDGER    ACCOUNTING      ALL
G:    SPREADSHEET   ORWELL          READ
H:    WORD_PROCESS  ORWELL          READ
```

From the output, John determines that he has access to the personnel files, accounting information, a spreadsheet program, plus word processing on the other servers in the workgroup. Since the word processing and spreadsheet programs are located on server ORWELL, and the data he needs for reports are located on servers PAYROLL and ACCOUNTING, John does not need to take the time and disk space to load these applications and data on his own machine.

Finding Printers

The next thing John wants to know is where can he print his reports.

To find out what printers are available:

From the DOS prompt, he types **NET PLIST** and presses Enter. The commands displays the following to his screen:

```
NetWare Printer   Server
==============    ==============

BIG_BROTHER       ORWELL
MONEY             PAYROLL
BEANS             ACCOUNTING
```

From the output, John determines that he has access to all the printers in workgroup ADMIN. This is a real convenience for John, since he can generate printed reports at the machine where his information is stored. This also means that his reports will come out of the printer near the people that need to see them, thus saving him time walking from place to place. His other reports and presentation grade materials can be generated from the laser jet printer BIG_BROTHER located on server ORWELL.

Finding Other Users

Next John wants to satisfy his curiosity and find out who is currently logged in to workgroup ADMIN.

To find other users currently on the same workgroup:

At the DOS prompt, he types **NET ULIST** and presses Enter. The command displays the following:

```
Connected Users   Address
===============   ==========

 BERT             0080C70D2414
 ERNIE            0080C70D2415
*JOHN             0080C70D2413
 MARSHA           00AA002A488E
 SUPERVISOR       00AA002A488F

Total connected workgroup users: 5
```

From the output, John can see that five users are currently logged in and using the resources of workgroup ADMIN.

Sending Messages

Sending a message to users on the network can be a real convenience. It allows you to contact many people at the same time and draw their attention to something important. For instance, a server owner who needs to take his or her server off-line for whatever reason can issue a message to everyone to log out of the server, plus warn others on the network that it will be unavailable for use.

On a more personal level, you can send a message to a single person on the network. The advantage to doing this over using the telephone is that you have a much better chance of catching the person right away, no matter what machine they are logged in to, versus depending on them to be within earshot of the telephone.

Sending a Message from DOS with NET SEND

Personal NetWare uses the NET SEND command to issue one-line messages to other users on the network. You can send messages in many different ways, and each has its own format.

To send a message to a single user:

```
NET SEND "message" <username>
```

As an example, let's say that John sees that Marsha is currently logged in to workgroup ADMIN, and decides to send her a message. To do this, John types the command:

```
NET SEND "How's pizza for lunch ?" MARSHA
```

To send a message to several users in a workgroup:

```
NET SEND "message" <user1> <user2> <user3> <user4>
```

Now let's assume that John wants to have a meeting at 2:00 PM with Bert, Ernie, Marsha, and Jane. To do this, John types the command:

```
NET SEND "Meeting @@ 2:00 PM, Room 114" BERT ERNIE MARSHA JANE
```

To send a message to everyone in a workgroup:

```
NET SEND "message" ALL
```

In this case, let's suppose the server ORWELL is going off-line for backups. The SUPERVISOR sends the following message to everyone in the workgroup ADMIN:

```
NET SEND "ORWELL going down in 5 min." ALL
```

To send a message to a user on a specific server:

```
NET SEND "message" <server>/<username>
```

For example, Marsha is logged into server ORWELL and John is logged into server PAYROLL. Marsha wants to specifically send John a message on server PAYROLL. To do this she types:

```
NET SEND "Pizza sounds fine...11:30 ?" PAYROLL/JOHN
```

To send a message to everyone on a specific server:

NET SEND "message" <server>/ALL

For instance, it has been five minutes since the original warning about server ORWELL going off-line for backups and people are still logged in to ORWELL. The supervisor sends a message stressing the need to depart:

```
NET SEND "Log off NOW ! ! !" ORWELL/ALL
```

There are some things to be aware of when sending a message using NET SEND:

- Messages cannot be longer than 30 characters.
- Users who have turned off message reception will not see your message.
- The intended recipient of your message must be logged in to the same workgroup, directory tree, or server as you.

Viewing Your Account

On most networks, users can display information concerning their account status. This information can include:

- Home directories
- Pathways
- Routes
- Access permissions
- Password attributes
- Administrator privileges
- Personal information

Personal NetWare allows you to display details of your own account. These details include:

- Workgroup administrator rights
- Ability to change password
- Is a password required?

- Must the new password be unique?
- Must the password be changed periodically?

Displaying Your Account from DOS

You can get a complete listing of your account from the DOS prompt.

To display your account:

1. From the DOS prompt, type **NET** and press Enter. The screen showing the NetWare view of Personal NetWare will load and display.

2. Press **ALT-S** to select the Settings option of the main menu. The Settings selection menu is displayed.

3. Select the Display account... option. The Account Information window is displayed with the information of your user account (Figure 5.10).

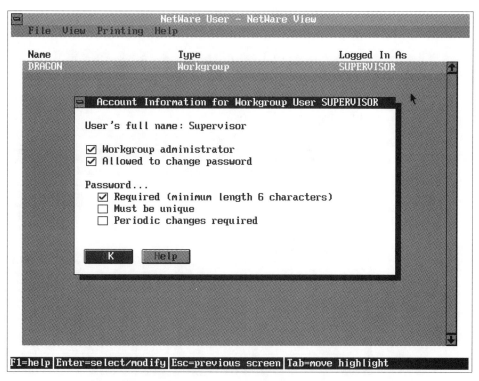

Figure 5.10 The Account Information window (in DOS).

Displaying Your Account from Windows

You can also get a complete listing of your account from Windows.

To display your account:

1. From the desktop, double click on the Personal NetWare icon in the Personal NetWare group.

2. Select the Window option from the menu bar. The Window option window is displayed.

3. Select the Netware option. The Netware display window will appear, displaying network connections, workgroups, and users. On the left side of the window is the default, or active network connections, workgroup, and users.

4. If the user names are not displayed under the active workgroup, double click on the active workgroup icon on the left side of the NetWare window. The user names will be displayed.

5. Select your account name from the list.

6. From the main file menu, choose the Properties... option. The NetWare User Information window will be displayed (Figure 5.11).

7. Choose the Configure button from the window. Your account information will be displayed (Figure 5.12).

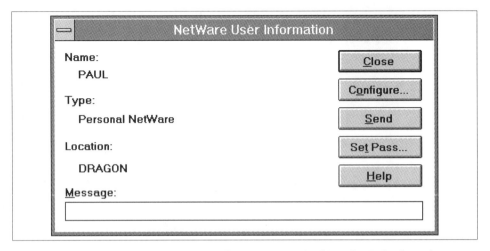

Figure 5.11   The NetWare User Information window (in Windows).

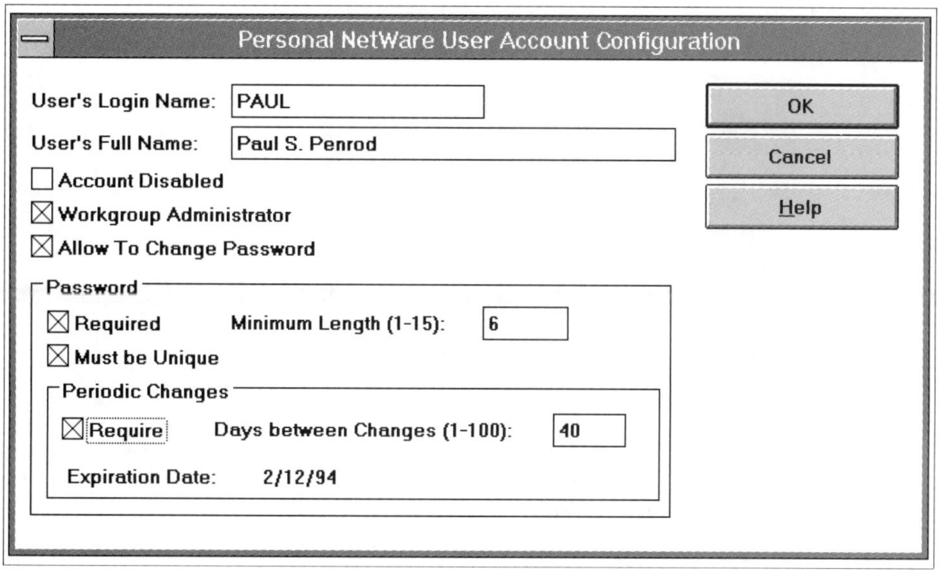

Figure 5.12   The Account Information window (in Windows).

Starting the Tutorial

Need a nap? Read the documentation. Works every time. All kidding aside, vendor documentation, with few exceptions, is not something people look forward to. So what do you do when you don't have time to pull out the manual and spend 20 minutes hunting down that information you wanted to know. If what you are looking for is something you use frequently, there is hope. Enter the tutorial. Personal Netware provides two tutorials; one for DOS, one for Windows. They provide a good general overview of Personal Netware and its use.

Using the DOS-Based Tutorial

You can start the tutorial under DOS by typing **PNWTRAIN** at the DOS prompt and pressing Enter. The main screen for the tutorial will appear (see Figure 5.13). The main screen of the tutorial is divided into two parts. The left displays block graphic items that represent disks, printers, CD-ROMs, and workstations. The right side shows a list of topics that you can select and view.

Let's pick a topic. If you have not played with the arrow keys, the highlight should be over the topic **Overview of networking**. By pressing the Enter key, the first page of the topic is displayed (see Figure 5.14).

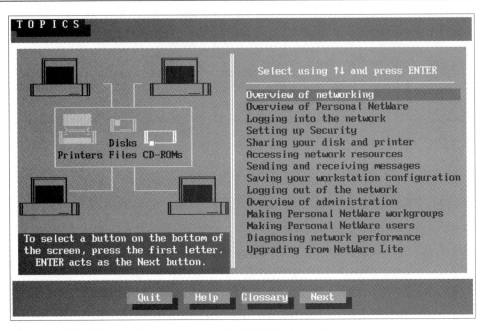

Figure 5.13 The main screen for the DOS tutorial.

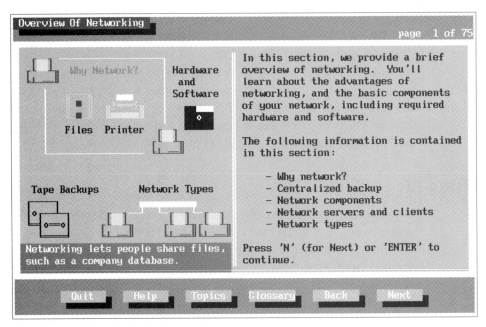

Figure 5.14 View of a selected tutorial topic.

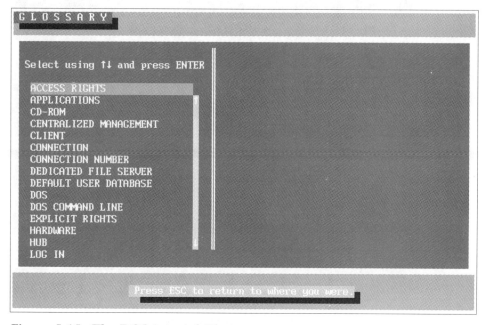

Figure 5.15 The DOS tutorial Glossary screen.

The left side displays block graphic items representing some aspects of networking. The right side starts the discussion. By pressing **N** or Enter, the next page is displayed. Pressing **B** takes you back to the previous screen, (see Figure 5.13). While reading the explanation, if you find a term you do not understand, press **G** and the Glossary screen will come up (see Figure 5.15). You can select the term you want defined with the arrow keys, press Enter, and its explanation will show up on the right side of the window. To return to where you were, press the Esc key.

Using the Windows-Based Tutorial

To start the tutorial under Windows, double click on the Personal NetWare Tutorial icon. The Topics screen for the tutorial will be displayed (see Figure 5.16).

The main screen of the tutorial is divided into two parts. The left displays graphic items that represent disks, printers, CD-ROMs, and workstations. The right side shows a list of topics that you can select and view.

To look for definitions of computer and network terms, select the Glossary button, and the Glossary section of the tutorial will be displayed (see Figure 5.17).

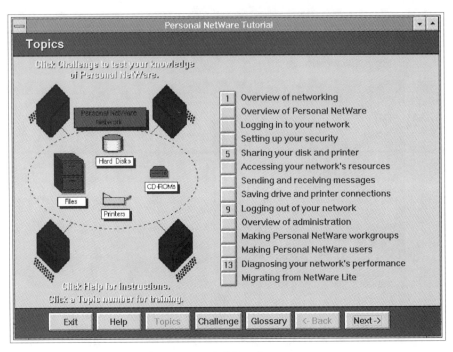

Figure 5.16   The Windows tutorial Topics screen.

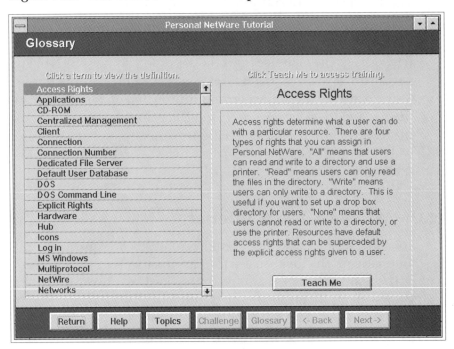

Figure 5.17   The Windows tutorial Glossary.

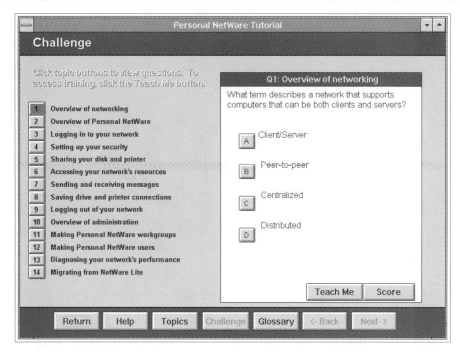

Figure 5.18   Testing your knowledge of Personal NetWare.

The unique thing about the Windows version of the tutorial versus the DOS version is the addition of a Teach Me button. Select this button to see the term defined in context.

Another item that does not appear in the DOS tutorial is the Challenge button. From the Topics screen (Figure 5.16), select the Challenge button, and the testing portion of the tutorial appears (Figure 5.18). This section is used to check your knowledge of Personal Netware topics. A Teach Me button is included to provide additional information on the topic being tested. By pressing the Score button, you can find out how well you are doing with the challenge.

Conclusion

Touring the network in this manner gives you a better understanding about how all the pieces fit together. Locating information and people on the network is a principal activity. Knowing where all the components are and how to find them and use them are the keys to being productive inside the Personal NetWare environment.

Chapter 6

Increasing Productivity with Personal NetWare DOS Utilities

Introduction

Personal NetWare is a complex product that includes many functions, which require only occasional use. Because Personal NetWare stays resident in DOS memory while it does its job, anything that can reduce the amount of memory required is of benefit. It makes sense, therefore, to provide as separate programs those functions that are not necessary for intercommunication. These "functions" or commands are activated by the user only when they are needed and do not remain resident when the task is finished.

Most of Personal NetWare's DOS command line functions, for both the user and the administrator, fall within the NET command set, which further divides into three separate categories of operations:

- Connection commands
- Setting commands
- Function commands

The functions we will discuss in all three categories are primarily user commands, although many can and are used by the SUPERVISOR. Those commands that require almost exclusive SUPERVISOR or administrator knowledge or permissions will be covered in the chapters on network administration.

Connection Commands

Connection commands deal with network connections. But this does not mean just the logical connection of your user account to the network via some computer. They cover a wide range of network resources and objects directly affected by network connections, including:

- Workgroups
- Servers
- User accounts
- Directories
- Printers
- Server extensions

Table 6.1 shows the NET commands that allow you to deal with connections on your Personal NetWare network.

For purposes of this discussion, we will focus on the NET commands in Table 6.1 from a user's perspective. The only exceptions are NET LOGIN and NET LOGOUT, which have already been dealt with in detail in Chapter 5.

Table 6.1	Personal NetWare Connection Commands			
	Listing	**Information**	**Connect**	**Disconnect**
Current Workgroup		NET INFO	NET LOGIN	NET LOGOUT
Any Workgroup	NET WGFIND NET WGLIST		NET JOIN	NET LOGOUT
Servers	NET SLIST	NET CONNECT	NET CONNECT	NET LOGOUT
Directories	NET VLIST	NET MAP	NET MAP	NET MAP DEL
Printers	NET PLIST	NET CAPTURE	NET CAPTURE	NET CAPTURE DEL
Users	NET ULIST			
Server Extensions	NET XLIST			

Connecting to Network Printers

Network printing is an often misunderstood but very necessary feature of efficient networking. Connecting to a network printer entails taking the output to the printer port on your workstation and sending it to another workstation or server that has a printer attached and printing it there. The method by which this is done uses printer queues.

A printer queue is nothing more than a place where printer output from different workstations (called printer jobs) line up and wait their turn to output at a particular printer. Think of it as a collection of reports that make up a presentation; each report is a printer job delivered to you by a separate person. You collect the reports and arrange them in a stack in the order you receive them. As you read each report, you remove it from the stack and discard it when you are done. This is how a printer queue works. But, what does it look like?

Under Personal NetWare, a printer queue is created using the NET SHARE command (covered later in this chapter). At that time, the printer queue is given a unique name that is visible from all the user accounts in the workgroup. Refer back to Figure 5.9. The sample workgroup contained there had three printer queues that were visible from the workgroup ADMIN: BIG_BROTHER, MONEY, and BEANS. When you send your output to these printer queues, it will print at the respective printer to which these queues are attached. For instance, if you want to print a report on the HP Laserjet known as BIG_BROTHER, all you need to do is send it to the printer queue named BIG_BROTHER, and it will output on that printer. You don't need to know where the printer is, or to which machine it is attached. As long as you know the name of its printer queue, you can send it there, and it will find the right printer, even if it is halfway across the state in another office. Making the connection to the printer queue from your workstation is done with the NET CAPTURE command.

The purpose of the NET CAPTURE command is to redirect printing from your workstation to one of the shared printers in the workgroup. This provides a means for everyone in the workgroup to access a printer even if a particular workstation does not have one attached. It is also valuable if you need special print services such as color printing, plotting, drafting, photo slide generation, or any other type of print services requiring special equipment. Often, this specialized printing is done occasionally, and thus is it more cost-effective to share one or two special printers among a group rather than put an expensive printer on everyone's desk.

NET CAPTURE can be used to perform several important functions:

- To list captured printer ports. Format: NET CAPTURE
- To capture a printer port. Format: NET CAPTURE <*LPTn*> <*queue_name*> <*server*> <*options*>
- To stop capturing a port for printing. Format: NET CAPTURE DEL LPT<*n*>

List Captured Printer Ports

Going back to our sample workgroup from Chapter 5 (see Figure 5.9): John is logged in to workgroup ADMIN from his workstation. He has captured LPT1 and pointed it to the printer named BIG_BROTHER on server ORWELL. He wants to check the port and printer settings to make sure he got everything right when he established the connection. To do this, from the DOS prompt, John types the command:

```
NET CAPTURE
```

and presses Enter. The command displays the following to the screen:

```
             Currently Captured Local Ports

    Port NetWare Printer Server          Capture Settings
    ==== =============== =============== ========================

    LPT1 BIG_BROTHER     ORWELL
                         Banner=N Tabs=0  Copies=1 FormFeed=Y
                         Setup=(None) PaperType=DEFAULT
                         Notify=N Direct=N Hold=N
                         Wait=10 Autoendcap=Y
```

John sees that he does indeed have access to the printer BIG_BROTHER, which is attached to the Personal NetWare server ORWELL, so he knows where his reports will end up. He scans the rest of the information and decides to make a few changes. First he decides to print a banner page to identify his printed output from everyone else's, since BIG_BROTHER is shared among several other people. Second, he wants to have his tabs expand to four spaces when the job prints. Let's follow him through the process.

Stop the Capture of a Printer Port

The first thing John needs to do before changing the way Personal NetWare handles his printing is to stop capturing the print jobs intended for the port in question. To do this, John types the command:

```
NET CAPTURE DEL LPT1
```

from the DOS prompt, and presses Enter. The result of the command is:

```
Port LPT1 is no longer captured.
```

It is important to note that NET CAPTURE DEL works for any valid captured printer port (normally LPT1, LPT2, or LPT3).

Capturing and Configuring a Printer Port

Here is where the fun begins. Not only is John going to capture a printer port, but he is going to tell Personal NetWare how to handle all print jobs going through that port. John types the command:

```
NET CAPTURE LPT1 BIG_BROTHER B=Y T=4
```

and presses Enter. The command result is:

```
Port LPT1 has been captured to NetWare Printer BIG_BROTHER on
server ORWELL.
```

Dissecting NET CAPTURE

Let's examine the particular form of the NET CAPTURE command that John typed. Previously, John entered the command:

```
NET CAPTURE LPT1 BIG_BROTHER B=Y T=4
```

to configure his printer port. This command was a form of

```
NET CAPTURE <LPTn> <queue_name> <server> <options>
```

As you can see, there are four sets of arguments attached to NET CAPTURE. We'll discuss each in turn and examine some of the values of these arguments.

<LPTn>   This argument identifies the printer port that will be captured by Personal NetWare. Valid values from DOS are normally LPT1, LPT2, and LPT3.

<queue_name>   This argument identifies the queue associated with the printer within the workgroup to which the printed output is directed. It must be a valid shared printer. If you are unsure that the printer is in the workgroup, or which printers are available in the workgroup, use the NET PLIST command (discussed later in this chapter) to list the shared printers.

<server> This argument identifies the server to which the requested shared printer is attached. This argument is purely optional if the shared printer name is unique. If the shared printer name is duplicated in the workgroup, then enter the server name to tell Personal NetWare to which of the same-named printers you are referring.

<options> This is really a collection of arguments that tell Personal NetWare how to format and control the output destined for the printer. Table 6.2 identifies this collection of arguments and describes how they affect Personal NetWare's handling of printing.

Displaying Network Connection Information

The NET CONNECT command is useful for displaying current connections to any servers, workgroups, and/or any NetWare directory trees. It's also used to connect you to servers and NetWare directory trees.

Returning to our user John, we find that he wishes to map to some data on shared directories. To do this, he needs to know to which servers he is attached. First he types the command:

```
NET CONNECT
```

from the DOS prompt and presses Enter. The command displays this to his screen:

```
Current Connections


==============================================================

ADMIN           John                    Workgroup
ORWELL          v1.20 John              Personal NetWare Server
```

John notices that a connection to server PAYROLL, where his data sits, is not there. John types the command:

```
NET CONNECT PAYROLL
```

from the DOS prompt and presses Enter. The command displays:

```
You are connected to PAYROLL.
```

Table 6.2   NET CAPTURE Print Options

Setting	Argument	Values	Default	Description
Autoendcap	A=	Y or N	Y	Setting this to Y closes open print jobs that were created by an application when it terminates. This takes precedence over the Wait setting, even if it is set to 0 (waits forever to close job).
Banner	B=	Y or N	N	Setting this argument to Y prints a cover sheet that identifies who generated the print request.
Copies	C=	1-250	1	This argument tells Personal Netware how many copies of a print job to reproduce.
Direct	D=	Y or N	Y	Setting this argument to N tells Personal Netware to wait for the entire print request to make it into the print buffer before sending output to the printer. Default is to print any data it receives when it gets it.
Formfeed	F=	Y or N	Y	This argument tells Personal Netware whether to send a formfeed control character to the printer. This will cause the printer to skip to the top of the next page if it is a tractor feed printer, or eject the current printed page if the printer is a sheet feed type. Note: If the printer being used is a PostScript printer, then always set F=N. PostScript output has a formfeed already in it, and it would just waste paper to have Personal Netware send one too.
Hold	H=	Y or N	N	Setting this argument to Y tells Personal Netware to hold the job at the server attached to the requested printer. The job will not print until you release it. By default, Hold is set to N so that all jobs print automatically.
Paper (type)	P=	Must be a valid name	Use default paper type	This argument is useful for printers that use different types of paper and have these types specifically defined for them.
Tabs	T=	0-32	0	This argument tells Personal Netware how many spaces to expand each Tab character. The default is not to expand Tab characters at all.
Setup (string)	S=	Must be a valid init string	Use default printer init string	This argument tells Personal Netware to use this init string to initialize the requested printer, rather than the one it already has. Refer to your printer owner's manual for instructions on what an init string is and how it is used for that printer.
Wait	W=	0-3600	10	This argument tells Personal Netware how long to wait (in seconds) after receiving data from an application before assuming that the print job has completed. Setting W=0 tell Personal Netware to wait forever.

Explicitly Stating the Account

John could also have entered the command as:

```
NET CONNECT PAYROLL/JOHN
```

This version explicitly tells Personal NetWare that the account JOHN is connected to server PAYROLL. By default, Personal NetWare uses the current active account under which the command was issued.

To verify his connection to server PAYROLL, John retypes the first NET CONNECT command. The command displays this to his screen:

```
Current Connections
==============================================================

ADMIN       John              Workgroup
ORWELL      v1.20 John        Personal NetWare Server
PAYROLL     v1.20 John        Personal NetWare Server
```

Displaying Network Information

The NET INFO command is used to display the following list:

- Loaded network software (version numbers)
- User account name
- Workgroup name
- Server name
- Server workgroup

Although software version information may not be immediately useful to a user, the names are. Our user John has access to two workgroups: DEVELOP and ADMIN. If he were to forget to which workgroup he was logged in, John would type the command:

```
NET INFO
```

at the DOS prompt, and press Enter. The command would display something like:

```
Your current username.... JOHN
Current workgroup name... ADMIN
Version of PNW.VLM....... 1.2
```

```
Version of BIND.VLM...... 1.3
Version of NWCACHEX.EXE.. 2.0
Version of NET.EXE....... 1.0

Name of server.......... ORWELL
Server workgroup name.... ADMIN
Version of SERVER.EXE.... 1.20

Machine address.......... 0080C70D2413
```

John would immediately see that he is in workgroup ADMIN, attached to server ORWELL under his account JOHN.

Joining a Different Workgroup

The NET JOIN command allows you to join a different workgroup and use that workgroup as the default each time you log in to the network. The command changes the NET.CFG file so that the newly specified workgroup becomes permanent.

Let's go back to our example user. John has access to two workgroups. Before he received his new account in workgroup ADMIN, his default workgroup was DEVELOP.

To make workgroup ADMIN his default workgroup when he logs in:

1. John types:

   ```
   NET LOGIN ADMIN/JOHN
   ```

   from the DOS prompt, and then presses **Enter**.

2. After completing his login, John then types the command:

   ```
   NET JOIN
   ```

   from the DOS prompt, then presses **Enter**. The command displays this to his screen:

   ```
   Workgroup settings were saved in C:\NWCLIENT\NET.CFG
   You are now in workgroup ADMIN.
   ```

Until John changes it, everytime he logs in to the network, he will be placed in workgroup ADMIN by default.

Mapping Network Logical Drives to Your DOS Drive Table

The NET MAP command under Personal NetWare is one that you will find to be extremely useful. The purpose of this command is to list and connect logical drives to shared directories. This is a very powerful feature because it allows direct access (given proper permissions, of course) to a server's hard disk and mapping of a selected directory or directories to your own DOS drive table as if they were logical hard drives that existed on your system.

There are some things to be aware of when you map drives under Personal NetWare. First, the number of logical drives available under DOS depends on what the LASTDRIVE statement of your CONFIG.SYS was set to. The setup program that installs Personal NetWare sets the value of LASTDRIVE to Z, so that logical drives A: through Z: are available for use by DOS. If you change the LASTDRIVE statement to a letter between A and Z, then you will have fewer drives to map with.

The second item of importance concerns the logical drives already in use. For most computer systems running DOS, drives A:, B:, and C: are typically occupied by a real disk drive. If you map one of these drives while running Personal NetWare, then DOS cannot see your real hard device. It will reference the shared directory to which the mapping now points the logical drive. If you are running on a server, don't map drive C: to something else. The reasons and results should be obvious.

The third item to be aware of is that all mappings are lost when you log out of your account, unless you use the NET SAVE command. But more about this later.

The formats for the NET MAP command are as follows:

- To list all drive connects:

  ```
  NET MAP
  ```

- To connect to a shared directory or NetWare volume:

  ```
  NET MAP [<drive> or <NEXT>] <server>/<directory or volume>
  ```

- To connect to a shared directory or NetWare volume and select a default path:

  ```
  NET MAP [<drive> or <NEXT>] <server>/<directory or volume>:path
  ```

- To connect to a shared directory or NetWare volume and identify a directory as root for this logical drive:

```
NET MAP [<drive> or <NEXT>] <server>/<directory or
volume>:path\
```

- To disconnect a mapped logical drive from a shared directory or NetWare volume:

```
NET MAP DEL <drive>:
```

Let's follow John as he sets up his new account and see what all these cryptic formats mean. John has a new account in workgroup ADMIN (see Figure 5.9). He has identified his servers ORWELL, PAYROLL, and ACCOUNTING. Now, John wants to know which directories on those servers are public for his use. To do this John types the command:

```
NET VLIST
```

and presses Enter. The command displays to his screen:

```
NetWare Volume   Server
===============  ===============
BENEFITS         PAYROLL
CUSTOMERS        ACCOUNTING
DBASE            PAYROLL
EXCEL            ADMIN
EXPENSES         PAYROLL
FOXPRO2          ADMIN
FREELANCE        ACCOUNTING
LOTUS            ACCOUNTING
PERSONNEL        PAYROLL
POLICY           ADMIN
RECEIVABLES      ACCOUNTING
RESUMES          PAYROLL
SALES            ACCOUNTING
WINDOWS          ADMIN
WINWORD          ADMIN
```

From the list of available shared directories, John chooses to access these:

- FOXPRO2
- LOTUS
- PERSONNEL
- SALES
- WINDOWS
- WINWORD

Now the fun begins: mapping the drives. John maps the FOXPRO2 directory by typing the command:

```
NET MAP D: ADMIN/FOXPRO2
```

and pressing Enter (he could also have typed NET MAP D: FOXPRO2).

Since there is no other shared directory named FOXPRO2 in this workgroup, Personal NetWare resolves the server reference back to server ADMIN. Now, if John knew that the suggested logical drive assigned to shared directory FOX-PRO2 was D:, then he could have entered the command this way:

```
NET MAP ADMIN/FOXPRO2
```

or

```
NET MAP FOXPRO2
```

Or he could have let Personal NetWare choose the drive for him by entering the command this way:

```
NET MAP NEXT ADMIN/FOXPRO2
```

The NEXT option of the NET MAP command tells Personal NetWare to use the next available logical drive letter that is unused. This is convenient when you don't know what the next available drive letter is, or you do not have another batch file or program that depends on the data or program referenced to be on a certain logical drive. In John's case, it is important for him to keep things assigned to one particular drive so that his batch files work properly every time. If you need to have your reference programs or data in one particular spot at all times, then *do not* use the NEXT option when mapping logical drives; instead, explicitly assign them to a logical drive, as demonstrated below.

John continues to map his drives by typing the following commands:

```
NET MAP E: ADMIN/WINDOWS
NET MAP F: ADMIN/WINWORD
NET MAP G: PAYROLL/PERSONNEL:STAFF
NET MAP H: ACCOUNTING/LOTUS
NET MAP I: ACCOUNTING/SALES:CURR_Q1\
NET MAP J: ACCOUNTING/SALES:CURR_Q2\
NET MAP K: ACCOUNTING/SALES:CURR_Q3\
NET MAP L: ACCOUNTING/SALES:CURR_Q4\
```

Now, we need to stop and look at two of the last set of commands that John entered, particularly:

```
NET MAP G: PAYROLL/PERSONNEL:STAFF
NET MAP I: ACCOUNTING/SALES:CURR_Q1\
```

NET MAP G: PAYROLL/PERSONNEL:STAFF

Notice :STAFF at the end of the NET MAP command. This tells Personal NetWare to use the PERSONNEL shared directory as G:'s root directory but to change to the STAFF subdirectory underneath the PERSONNEL shared directory. Thus, when John first changes to G: he will see this:

```
G:\STAFF>
```

instead of

```
G:\>
```

John can backtrack to G:\ by issuing the change directory command from DOS. This places him in the PERSONNEL shared directory and not the subdirectory STAFF underneath it.

NET MAP I: ACCOUNTING/SALES:CURR_Q1\

This and the previous command have the same syntax, NET MAP G: PAYROLL/PERSONNEL:STAFF with the exception of the \ at the end. This backslash has special significance to Personal NetWare when mapping a drive. In this case, it tells Personal NetWare not to make the SALES shared directory the root directory for drive I:, but the CURR_Q1 subdirectory underneath it. When John later changes to I: he will see:

```
I:\>
```

instead of

```
I:\CURR_Q1>
```

as in the previous case. Another difference is that he will only be able to see what is in the CURR_Q1 subdirectory and anything underneath it. John will not be able to see the SALES shared directory itself.

Satisfied that he is almost finished, John needs to make sure that he has everything mapped the way he wants it. He types the command:

```
NET MAP
```

from the DOS prompt and presses Enter to display on his screen:

```
               Current Drive Mappings

Drive   NetWare Volume   Server            Your Rights
=====   ==============   ==============    ===========
D:      FOXPRO2          ADMIN             ALL
E:      WINDOWS          ADMIN             ALL
F:      WINWORD          ADMIN             ALL
G:      PERSONNEL        PAYROLL           READ
H:      LOTUS            ACCOUNTING        ALL
I:      SALES            ACCOUNTING        READ
J:      SALES            ACCOUNTING        READ
K:      SALES            ACCOUNTING        READ
L:      SALES            ACCOUNTING        READ
```

As a check, John changes to L: to look at the fourth-quarter sales figures. The directory is empty. Realizing that those numbers will not be there for some time yet, he decides to drop the mapping of that drive until he needs it. To delete his mapping of L: John types the command:

```
NET MAP DEL L:
```

at the DOS prompt and presses Enter. The command result is:

```
Mapping for driver letter L: has been deleted.
```

Listing the Available Network Printers

The NET PLIST command lists printers that are available and the servers they are attached to. John now wants to find out which printers are available within his workgroup. He types the command:

```
NET PLIST
```

from the DOS prompt and presses Enter. The following is displayed to his screen:

```
NetWare Printer   Server
==============    ==============
BEANS             ACCOUNTING
BIG_BROTHER       ORWELL
MONEY             PAYROLL
```

If the list of network printers is too large to fit on his screen, John would type the command this way:

```
NET PLIST /P
```

The /P option tells NET PLIST to page the output so that John can read through it without missing anything. Let's say that he wants to look through this very long list of printers for all those beginning with HP. To do this, he types the command:

```
NET PLIST HP*
```

using the asterisk (*) as the wildcard symbol for pattern matches. Now NET PLIST will display all printers whose names begin with HP.

Listing the Available Servers

The NET SLIST command lists servers that are available along with their addresses. John wants to find out which servers are available within his workgroup. He types the command:

```
NET SLIST
```

from the DOS prompt and presses Enter. The following is displayed to his screen:

```
Available Servers          Address
========================   ==========
 *ORWELL                   0080C70D2413
  PAYROLL                  0080C70D2414
  ACCOUNTING               00AA002A488E

Total available servers: 3
```

If John wants to narrow the amount of information reported back by NET SLIST, he could add another parameter to specifiy a server name. To do this he would type the command in this format:

```
NET SLIST <name of server>
```

The name can include the wildcard asterisk (*) and question mark (?) symbols to do pattern matches. If there is too much information reported to fit on the screen, John can append a /P to the end of the command so that it displays the information one page at a time. For example, let's say that John wants to look through this long list of servers for all those beginning with S. To do this, he types the command:

```
NET SLIST S*
```

Now NET SLIST will display all servers whose names begin with S.

Listing the Current Network Users

The NET ULIST command is used to display the names and addresses of all users logged in to the current workgroup. The list is useful when you want to send messages or see who is currently logged in to the network. The addresses also are sometimes used to diagnose problems on the network. For example, John wants to know if Marsha is logged in to his current workgroup ADMIN. From the DOS prompt, he types the command:

```
NET ULIST
```

and presses Enter. The following is displayed to his screen.

```
Connected Users    Address
================   ==========
  BERT             0080C70D2414
  ERNIE            0080C70D2415
*JOHN              0080C70D2413
  MARSHA           00AA002A488E
  SUPERVISOR       00AA002A488F

Total connected workgroup users: 5
```

If John wants to narrow the amount of information reported back by NET ULIST, he could add another parameter to specifiy a server name and a user name. To do this he would type the command in this format:

```
NET SLIST <name of server>/<user name>
```

The user name can include the wildcard * and ? symbols to do pattern matches. If there is too much information reported to fit on the screen, John can append a /P to the end of the command so that it displays the information one page at a time. If John wants to see who is on server ORWELL, he would type the command this way:

```
NET ULIST ORWELL
```

If John wants to see if MARSHA is logged in to server PAYROLL, he would type the command this way:

```
NET ULIST PAYROLL/MARSHA
```

To do a specific name search for all accounts logged into server ORWELL that begin with B, John would type the command this way:

```
NET ULIST ORWELL/B*
```

Listing Available Shared Directories

The NET VLIST command is used to display the available list of shared directories, the active workgroup, and the server on which they reside.

John now wants to access data within his active workgroup ADMIN. The data and programs he needs reside on other servers inside the workgroup. To find out what is available, John types:

```
NET VLIST
```

at the DOS prompt and presses Enter. The command displays the following to his screen:

```
NetWare Volume   Server
===============  ===============
BRIEF            ADMIN
COMMANDS         ADMIN
EXCEL            ACCOUNTING
FOXPRO2          ADMIN
LOTUS            ACCOUNTING
PEACHTREE        ACCOUNTING
PICS             PERSONNEL
RESUMES          PERSONNEL
WINDOWS          ADMIN
WINWORD          ADMIN

Total NetWare Volumes: 10
```

If John wants to narrow the amount of information reported back by NET VLIST, he could add another parameter to specifiy a shared directory name. To do this he would type the command in this format:

```
NET VLIST <name of shared directory>
```

The name can include wildcard * and ? symbols to do pattern matches. If there is too much information reported to fit on the screen, John can append a /P to the end of the command so that it displays the information one page at a time.

As another example, let's say John needs to find out if he has access to Word for Windows from the network, so he can save some disk space by not having to load it on his hard disk. He doesn't remember what the directory is called, but he thinks it is WINWORD. Fortunately, he can do a search for it. To do this, John can type the NET VLIST command in one of the following ways:

```
NET VLIST W*
```

which lists all shared directories starting with W;

```
NET VLIST WIN????
```

which lists all shared directories that start with WIN and have four subsequent characters in their names;

```
NET VLIST WINWORD
```

which lists the shared directory WINWORD if it exists in the workgroup.

Identifying the Available Workgroups on the Network

The NET WGFIND command lists all the workgroups that exist on the network. NET WGFIND gives you the option to set up your account to log in to one of them. John wants to know which workgroups exist on the network where he is logged in. To do this, he types:

```
NET WGFIND
```

at the DOS prompt and presses Enter. The command displays this to his screen:

```
Workgroups Found
================================================
  1 ADMIN              Local Workgroup
  2 DEVELOP            Local Workgroup


Total workgroups: 2
 0 networks found.


Looking for workgroup [*]

Workgroups Found
================================================
  1 ADMIN              Local Workgroup
  2 DEVELOP            Local Workgroup

Total workgroups: 2
Type the number corresponding to the workgroup to select OR
Type a filename to save the list (Enter to exit):
```

At this point, John is faced with a decision. If he selects workgroup ADMIN by typing a **1** at the prompt, the result is:

You are now set up to get to workgroup ADMIN.

If John wants to save the list to a file, he enters the filename

```
C:\TEMP\LIST.NET
```

and presses Enter. The result is:

```
Workgroup list saved in C:\TEMP\LIST.NET
```

If John just wants to exit the commands, he presses the Enter key without typing anything at the prompt. He is then returned to the DOS prompt. The NET WGFIND command can also list specific workgroups with a search string. To do this, enter the command this way:

```
NET WGFIND <workgroup name>
```

For example, to see if there is a workgroup called DEVELOP, type the command:

```
NET WGFIND DEVELOP
```

To list all workgroups beginning with the letter D, type the command:

```
NET WGFIND D*
```

To list all workgroups with six characters in their names and start with WIN, type the command:

```
NET WGFIND WIN???
```

Another point to consider is that NET WGFIND causes a lot of network traffic, which can really slow things down. Where possible, use the next command to be discussed, NET WGLIST.

Listing the Available Workgroups

The NET WGLIST command differs from the NET WGFIND command in two ways. First, it does not cause a lot of network traffic. Second, it lists only the workgroups that are in your route statements that appear in the NET.CFG file. For example, John wants to know which workgroups he can see from his account on the network. To do this, he types:

```
NET WGLIST
```

at the DOS prompt and presses Enter. The command displays this to his screen:

```
Available Workgroups
=====================
ADMIN
DEVELOP


Total Workgroups: 2
```

If John wants to narrow the amount of information reported back by NET WGLIST, he could add another parameter to specifiy a workgroup name. To do this he would type the command in this format:

```
NET WGLIST <name of workgroup>
```

The name can include wildcard * and ? symbols to do pattern matches. If there is too much information reported to fit on the screen, John can append a /P to the end of the command so that it displays the information one page at a time.

If John wants to further narrow his search to only those workgroups that begin with the letter D, he could type:

```
NET WGLIST D*
```

If he wants to narrow his search still further to include only those workgroups with names six characters long and starting with DEV, he would type:

```
NET WGLIST DEV???
```

Then, if John wants to see if the workgroup DEVELOP is visible from his account, he would type the command:

```
NET WGLIST DEVELOP
```

NET XLIST

The NET XLIST command is used to list service extensions. To use this command type:

```
NET XLIST
```

from the DOS prompt and press Enter. The service extensions will be listed. If you want to list a specific extension, type the command this way:

```
NET XLIST <name of extension>
```

The name can include wildcard * and ? symbols to do pattern searches. If there is too much information to fit on one screen, you can append a /P to the end of the command so that it displays the information a page at a time.

Setting Commands

Setting commands are those that cause a change to stored information, which influences the behavior of Personal NetWare and your user account. They are different from the connection commands in that they do not establish communications between devices, but regulate their behavior. The commands to be covered here are:

- NET CONTEXT
- NET LINK
- NET RECEIVE
- NET SETDOG
- NET SETPASS

Viewing or Changing Your Current Context (4.x)

The NET CONTEXT command is useful only if you are connected to NetWare 4.x. It allows you to view your current context or change it. To view your current context, type the command:

```
NET CONTEXT
```

from the DOS prompt and press Enter. Personal NetWare will display it for you. To change you current context type the command:

```
NET CONTEXT <new context>
```

from the DOS prompt and Personal NetWare will switch the context for you.

Setting Network Link Connection Timings

The NET LINK command is used to set the number of link retries, the amount of time to wait (in clock ticks) after broadcasting, and amount of to wait time between each send. The formats for the NET LINK command are shown next.
To display current link settings:

```
NET LINK
```

To change link settings:

```
NET LINK <number of retries> <timeout value> <send delay value>
```

To save link settings:

```
NET LINK SAVE
```

Some explanation is in order. The number of retries refers to the number of times Personal NetWare will attempt to deliver from point to point on the network. The default setting is 3, but conditions change. If there is a lot of network traffic and/or a large number of servers, then you will want to raise the number of retries to lower the failure rate of delivery.

The time-out value refers to the number of ticks of your workstation's internal clock (which runs much faster than the clock/calendar) to wait after broadcasting something to the network. On networks where there are many routers or long runs of cable between machines, this number may have to increase from its default value of 2 to reduce broadcast failure rate. The send delay value refers to the number of ticks of the workstation's internal clock to delay before sending the next packet. The default value is 0. If there seems to be a lot of sending failures from the workstation due to heavy traffic or high process overhead on the machine itself, the number may have to increase to reduce the failure rate. To view your current settings, type:

```
NET LINK
```

from the DOS prompt and press Enter. The command will display this to your screen:

```
Link settings are currently set to:
     Retries: 3
     Timeout: 3
     Send Delay: 0
```

Let's say that your workstation is showing a high failure rate on packet transmission. To combat that, it has been determined to change your retry count to 5, your time-out value to 4, and your send delay to 1. To do this type the command:

```
NET LINK 5 4 1
```

from the DOS prompt and press Enter. The command displays this to your screen:

```
Link settings are now set to:
     Retries: 5
     Timeout: 4
     Send Delay: 1
```

After testing the workstation, you are satisfied with the results and want to make the settings permanent. To do this, type the command:

```
NET LINK SAVE
```

at the DOS prompt and press Enter. The command displays:

```
Your current broadcast settings were saved to
C:\NWCLIENT\NET.CFG
Link settings are currently set to:
     Retries: 5
     Timeout: 4
     Send Delay: 1
```

Handling Received Messages

The NET RECEIVE command controls how messages you receive from others will be handled. You can check your message receive status, turn it on or off, and set a delay that will remove a received message from your screen after so many seconds. By default, any received message will stay on the screen until you physically remove it by pressing CTRL-Enter.

To view your receive status:

Type

```
NET RECEIVE
```

and press Enter. If your message receive status is turned on, the command will display:

```
Messages sent to your workstation will appear on your monitor.
```

If your message receive status is turned off, the command will display:

```
Messages sent to your workstation will NOT appear on your monitor.
```

To turn on message receiving:

Type

```
NET RECEIVE ON
```

from the DOS prompt and press Enter. The command will display:

```
Messages sent to your workstation will appear on your monitor.
```

To turn off message receiving:

Type

```
NET RECEIVE OFF
```

from the DOS prompt and press Enter. The command will display:

```
Messages sent to your workstation will NOT appear on your monitor.
```

Let's say that you don't want to manually remove messages each time you receive one. Set a time delay and let Personal NetWare do it for you. To set a delay of 30 seconds, type the command:

```
NET RECEIVE 30
```

from the DOS prompt and press Enter. The command will display:

```
Messages sent to your workstation will appear on your monitor
for 30 seconds.
```

After 30 seconds, the message will be removed from the screen automatically if you have not already done so. Currently, Personal NetWare allows up to 1,500 seconds of delay (25 minutes). To disable the delay, set the timeout value to 0.

Using the Network Watchdog Program

The NET SETDOG command starts a program known as a "watch dog." This type of program runs on servers and periodically checks to make sure that all the clients the server thinks are active really are. If the watch dog program does not get a response within a specific period of time, it automatically closes the connection to that client. In essence, it logs you off if your workstation does not automatically respond to its query. By default, Personal NetWare sets its watchdog query to every 15 minutes. The watchdog program can be invoked as often as once a minute or as long as once every 4,083 years (2,147,483,647 minutes). To disable it, set the watchdog timer to 0 minutes. The NET SETDOG command format is:

```
NET SETDOG <timeout_in_minutes> <server_name>
```

Referring back to user John's workgroup ADMIN (see Figure 5.9), let's say the SUPERVISOR on server ORWELL has received some complaints that users are being logged off because their new workstations have a power-saving feature that puts their computers to sleep when they are not being used. To combat this, the SUPERVISOR changes the watchdog time-out from the default 15 minutes to 2 hours. To do this he types:

```
NET SETDOG 120 ORWELL
```

and presses Enter. The command result is:

```
Watchdog has been set on server ORWELL for 120 minutes.
```

Because ORWELL is his default server, the SUPERVISOR also could have typed the command this way:

```
NET SETDOG 120
```

Setting Your Account Password

The NET SETPASS command allows you to change your password in one of three locations: your workgroup, on a NetWare bindery server, or on a NetWare 4.x directory tree.

- To change your workgroup password, type the command:
  ```
  NET SETPASS
  ```
- To change your password on a NetWare server, type the command:
  ```
  NET SETPASS <server name>
  ```
  where *<server name>* is the name of the server on which you wish to change your password.
- To change your password on a NetWare directory tree, type the command:
  ```
  NET SETPASS /T
  ```

In any case, you will be prompted for a new password twice to verify the new password. John, our intrepid user wants to change his password. To do this he types

```
NET SETPASS
```

at the DOS prompt and presses Enter. He is prompted:

```
Type new password:
```

John types his new password, which is not displayed. When he finishes, he sees the following prompt:

```
Retype new password:
```

John enters in his new password a second time. The program verifies both instances and responds:

```
Your password has been changed.
```

Function Commands

The function commands are those NET commands that cause some action to be taken on the network. The function commands covered here are:

- NET AUDIT
- NET DOWN
- NET HELP
- NET PRINT
- NET SAVE
- NET SHARE
- NET WAIT

Using the Audit Log

Any network usually has more than one user. Because there is more than one person doing things on the network, it becomes necessary to track some of the functions users perform while on the network. This is a necessity borne out of the need to keep things running. Users delete files inadvertantly; log in to places they probably should not be in; change settings on their accounts, or permissions on files, shared directories, and other resources without telling anyone. This can lead to chaos. The Audit Log is designed to track these kinds of activities, plus entries specifically put there by users so the SUPERVISOR has a record of what has transpired over a period of time.

By reading this information, a SUPERVISOR can tell if a user needs help, or is trying to create problems by doing things he or she should not. It also tells the SUPERVIOR what caused the network and its resources to be in its current operating state.

The NET AUDIT command is used to display the status of network auditing and to enter an audit entry if auditing is turned on. If auditing is turned on, each time you make an entry in the audit log, the following information is recorded:

- The date and time when NET AUDIT was invoked
- Who invoked the NET AUDIT command
- Any entry message attached to the NET AUDIT command

To check if auditing is on, type the command:

```
NET AUDIT
```

from the DOS prompt and press Enter. If auditing is allowed, the response will be:

```
Auditing is on.
```

If auditing is not allowed, the response will be:

```
Auditing is off.
```

To make an entry into the AUDIT LOG, type the command:

```
NET AUDIT "message"
```

where "*message*" is any text entry up to 80 characters long inside quotation marks. The text string may not contain any control characters or imbedded quotation marks. If auditing is enabled, the following will appear onscreen:

```
The AUDIT message was added to the workgroup audit log.
```

If auditing is turned off, the message will be:

```
The AUDIT message was NOT added to the workgroup audit log.
```

Removing a Server from the Network

The NET DOWN command closes down a server and drops all user connections to it. It is important to note that, in order to use this command, you must have the rights to manage the server you are trying to shut down.

The SUPERVISOR who owns server ORWELL wants to shut down the sever for backups. To do this he or she types the command:

```
NET DOWN ORWELL
```

from the DOS prompt and presses Enter. If there is no one else connected to the server, it will shut down. If there is someone logged in, the SUPERVISOR will be asked if he/she wishes to continue anyway. Answering N for NO aborts the shutdown.

If the SUPERVISOR's default server is ORWELL, then he/she could also enter the command this way:

```
NET DOWN
```

If the SUPERVISOR doesn't care who is attached to ORWELL and wants to bring it down right now, he/she would type the command:

```
NET DOWN ORWELL NOW
```

The server would shut down, and the users would be disconnected without any debate.

Displaying Help for the NET Commands

The NET HELP command displays help on the NET commands themselves. There are several ways to use this command. To display a list of all the commands covered by NET HELP type:

```
NET HELP /?
```

or

```
NET HELP ?
```

at the DOS prompt and press Enter. A list of the commands will be displayed to the screen.

To get help on a specific topic, let's say the NET MAP command, type:

```
NET HELP MAP or NET ? MAP or NET MAP ?
```

at the DOS prompt and press Enter. The help text for NET MAP will be displayed on the screen.

Printing to a Network Printer

Most of the time, people will send output to the printer by way of the application they are using, but there are occasions when it is necessary to send something to a printer from the DOS command line, and this is when the NET PRINT command comes in handy.

The NET PRINT command is used to print files to a network printer. If you have a shared printer on your workstation or server, then you must use the NET PRINT command rather than send the file directly to the port. Personal NetWare now controls the port through the NET CAPTURE command, so it is important to send the files this way, so that the network can resolve where it needs to go.

To use the NET PRINT command type:

```
NET PRINT <filename> <printer name>
```

For example, John wants to send some reports to the LaserJet called BIG_BROTHER on server ORWELL. To do this he types:

```
NET PRINT REPORT.DOC BIG_BROTHER
```

If he had multiple reports to send, he could type something like:

```
NET PRINT REPORT??.DOC BIG_BROTHER
```

or

```
NET PRINT *.DOC BIG_BROTHER
```

Saving Your Current Connection Settings

The NET SAVE command saves the network connections and environment variables that are active for your account in a batch file that can be run later so that you can reestablish them when you log back in. To use the command, type:

```
NET SAVE
```

from the DOS prompt and press Enter. The command result is:

```
Your network and environment settings were saved to
C:\NWCLIENT\PNWLOGIN.BAT
```

You can pick a specific filename to send the information to by typing:

```
NET SAVE C:\TEMP\MYLOGIN.BAT
```

which will cause the file MYLOGIN.BAT to be created in the directory C:\TEMP with the network and environment information. Saving connection settings this way allows you to set up a custom login file that you might want to use on occasion, or if you have an account on a second workgroup that requires different settings from the account you use regularly.

Sharing Printers and Directories

The NET SHARE command serves as the mean by which printers and directories can be used as shared resources on the network. In order for you to take advantage of this command, you must meet three requirements:

1. The workstation in question must be a Personal NetWare server.

2. You must be logged in to the same workgroup as the server in question.

3. You must have the permissions to manage the server.

Now, here is how the command works. John wants to share a directory C:\JOHN\REPORTS on sever ORWELL with the rest of the workgroup. To do this, (he has already met the three requirements), he types the command:

```
NET SHARE C:\JOHN\REPORTS JOHNS_REPORTS
```

from the DOS prompt and presses Enter. The shared directory JOHNS_REPORTS is now visible to all users in the workgroup, and they can now use the NET MAP command to assign a logical drive to access it.

John also wants to share a new HP Deskjet 500C, attached to server ORWELL on LPT2, with the workgroup. To do this he types the command:

```
NET SHARE LPT2 LITTLE_BRO
```

The new printer is now visible to the rest of the workgroup, and each user can use the NET CAPTURE command to direct one of their printer ports to use the new printer.

There are two points to be aware of here. First, any name chosen for a shared object, such as a printer or directory, cannot be longer than 15 characters and cannot have embedded spaces. Second, for shared printers, the only ports that will be recognized from DOS for sharing are LPT1, LPT2, LPT3, COM1, and COM2.

Suspending Operation

The NET WAIT command causes the workstation executing the command to "go to sleep" for a period of time specified in seconds. The maximum time you can pause the workstation for is 32,767 seconds, or a little more than nine hours. To use the NET WAIT command, type:

```
NET WAIT <seconds to wait>
```

from the DOS prompt and press Enter. The command will display a countdown of how many seconds remain until it reaches zero.

Conclusion

Personal NetWare provides a good set of utility functions that make managing and using the network a much simpler task. The functions described in this chapter can all be run from the DOS command line, but they really shine in batch files. By using these commands in batch files, it is possible to customize your environment and automate many of the tasks necessary to work efficiently in Personal NetWare.

Chapter 7

Increasing Productivity with Personal NetWare Windows Utilities

Introduction

Personal NetWare is an extensive product. Because of the multiplicity of functions presented in the Windows environment, this chapter will focus on those that are most important to the average person. We will cover these areas:

- Printers
- Disks

Those functions that apply to system administration are covered in the chapters on system administration.

Once I Find My Printer, Then What?

When first introduced to a new network, one of the first questions users ask is, "How do I print?" "Like this," the system administrator will usually respond, and then proceed to amaze, delight, and confuse the new user with rapid-fire instructions and use of the mouse.

137

Printing under Personal NetWare is not complicated to set up or use under Windows. It comes in two parts: sharing the printer and capturing the port. You cannot capture a port unless you have a printer to send it to, and you cannot have a printer to send it to unless you share a printer attached to your server. Therefore, let's trace the steps that establish the printing process on a network.

Sharing the Printer

The first requirement of sharing a printer is that it must be on a Personal NetWare server that is actively running the server software. The second is that your account must have READ/WRITE permissions on the server. When those preliminaries are out of the way, here is what happens next.

To give a user access to a printer:

1. From the desktop, double click the mouse on the Personal NetWare icon in the Personal NetWare group.

2. Select the Window option from the menu bar. The Window option window is displayed.

3. Select the Netware option. The Netware display window will appear showing network connections, workgroups, and users. On the left side of the window is the default or active network connections, workgroups, and users (see Figure 7.1).

4. Double click on the icon of the server that has the printer you wish to share with the workgroup. A tree list of all the disk drives, printer ports, and serial ports will appear.

5. Select the printer port that has the printer you want to share attached to it.

6. Select the File option from the menu bar. The File window will be displayed.

7. Select the Share option. The NetWare Share dialog window appears (see Figure 7.2).

8. Type a name for the printer, and press Enter. The Personal NetWare Rights dialog window appears (see Figure 7.3).

9. Set the default and explicit rights to the printer, if necessary, and then choose the Close button.

10. Configure the Printer Queue. The details of this will be contained in the chapters on administration.

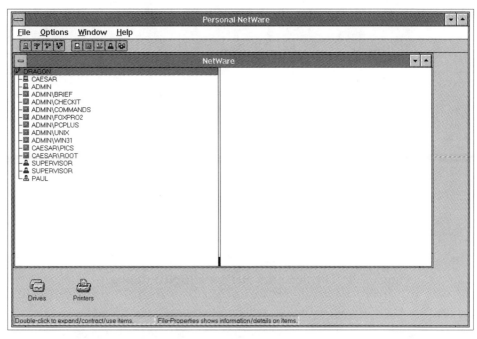

Figure 7.1 The NetWare display window.

Figure 7.2 The NetWare Share dialog.

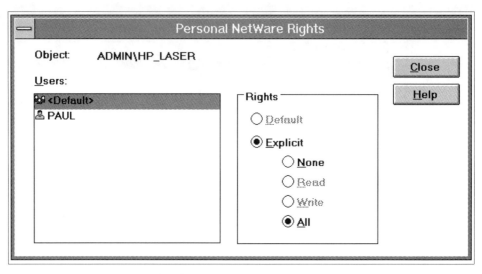

Figure 7.3 The Personal NetWare Rights dialog.

Deleting a Printer Connection   Sometimes it is necessary to drop a shared printer from a server. The printer could need repairs, or maybe it just moved to another computer.

To drop a printer from the network:

1. From the desktop, double click the mouse on the Personal NetWare icon in the Personal NetWare group.
2. Select the Window option from the menu bar. The Window option window is displayed.
3. Select the NetWare option. The NetWare display window will appear showing network connections, workgroups, and users. On the left side of the window is the default or active network connections, workgroups, and users.
4. Select the icon representing the shared printer you wish to discontinue.
5. Select the File option from the menu bar. The File window will be displayed.
6. Select the Disconnect option in the File window. The connection to the printer will be dropped. The Printers window will be updated to show that the printer is no longer available.

Capturing the Port

The next thing to do after making sure you have the right printer shared on the network is to capture a port on your workstation and direct it to the selected printer through Personal NetWare. You can do this by two methods.

To capture a port by drag-and-drop:

1. From the desktop, double click the mouse on the Personal NetWare icon in the Personal NetWare group.

2. Select the Window option from the menu bar. The Window option window is displayed.

3. Select the Printers option. The Printers display window will appear showing printer connections, ports, and shared printers (see Figure 7.4). On the left side of the window is the printer ports and active printer connections. On the right side are the shared printers visible to the account on this workstation.

4. With the mouse, choose the shared printer you wish to connect to. The selected printer will be highlighted.

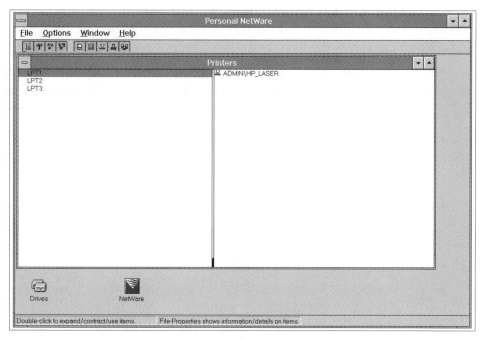

Figure 7.4   The Printers display window.

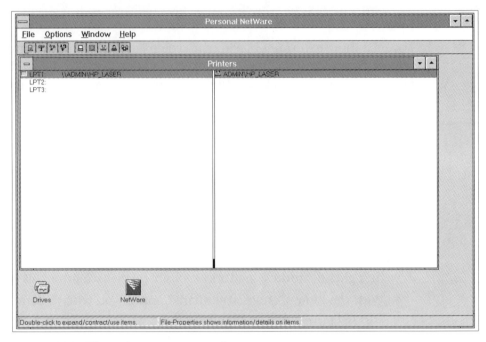

Figure 7.5   The printer connected to a port.

5. Holding down the left mouse button, drag the mouse pointer from the printer icon over to the left side of the window and release the mouse button (drop) over the printer port icon you wish to capture. The window will now show the connection of the printer to the port (see Figure 7.5).

6. To make the connection permanent, Select the File option from the menu bar. The File option window will appear.

7. Select the Permanent option from the File option window. The captured printer port icon will change to reflect the permanent status. You can also look at the Netware window and see the newly established printer port as one of the displayed resources.

Capturing a port the hard way:

1. From the desktop, double click the mouse on the Personal NetWare icon in the Personal NetWare group.

2. Select the Window option from the menu bar. The Window option window is displayed.

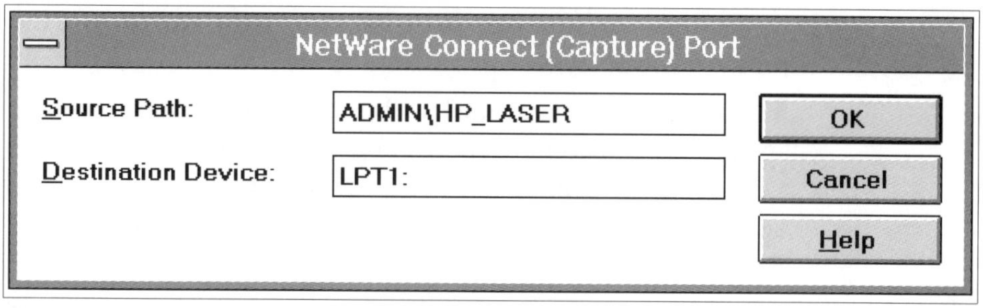

NetWare Connect (Capture) Port		
Source Path:	ADMIN\HP_LASER	OK
Destination Device:	LPT1:	Cancel
		Help

Figure 7.6   The NetWare Capture Port.

3. Select the Printers option. The Printers display window will appear showing printer connections, ports, and shared printers. On the left side of the window is the printer ports and active printer connections. On the right side are the shared printers visible to the account on this workstation (see Figure 7.4).

4. On the right side, select the printer you wish to attach to the printer port.

5. On the left side, select the port you wish to capture.

6. Select the File option from the menu bar. The File option window will appear.

7. Select the Connect option. The Netware Connect (Capture) Port dialog window appears (see Figure 7.6).

8. Choose the OK button from the Netware Capture Port dialog box to connect the port to the printer.

9. To make the connection permanent, Select the File option from the menu bar. The File option window will appear.

10. Select the Permanent option from the File option window. The captured printer port icon will change to reflect the permanent status. You can also look at the Netware window and see the newly established printer port as one of the displayed resources.

Freeing a Captured Port   Connecting to a printer is important, but what do you do if you need to drop a printer port connection?

To free a captured port:

1. From the desktop, double click the mouse on the Personal NetWare icon in the Personal NetWare group.

2. Select the Window option from the menu bar. The Window option window is displayed.

3. Select the Printers option. The Printers display window will appear showing printer connections, ports, and shared printers. On the left side of the window is the printer ports and active printer connections. On the right side are the shared printers visible to the account on this workstation (see Figure 7.4).

4. Select the printer port with the connection you wish to discontinue.

5. Select the File option from the menu bar. The File window will be displayed.

6. Select the Disconnect option in the File window. The connection to the printer port will be dropped. The Printers window will be updated to show that the port is now available.

Mapping Disks and Sharing Directories

The second important resource that comes to you via the network is shared disk space. This one feature lets you share programs, data, and disk space, all from the comfort of your keyboard. Sharing disk resources and their contents is one of the factors in increased productivity in a network environment. It also saves money because every computer does not need to have extra or bigger disks installed along with multiple copies of the same program. A less expensive site license handles the multiple use of a single copy of software.

Before you can enter this state of wedded bliss, however, you must first do two things: share your directories and map drives to other shared directories.

Sharing a Directory

In order to accomplish these tasks, though, there are some prerequisites. First, the directory to be shared must reside on a Personal NetWare server, with the server software running. Second, the number of configured network directories must be greater than the number of current network directories (shared directories). Third, your account must have READ/WRITE permissions on the server.

To share a directory:

1. From the desktop, double click the mouse on the Personal NetWare icon in the Personal NetWare group.

2. Select the Window option from the menu bar. The Window option window is displayed.

3. Select the NetWare option. The NetWare display window will appear showing network connections, workgroups, and users. On the left side of the window is the default or active network connections, workgroups, and users.

4. Double click on the icon that represents the disk on the server where the directory you wish to share is located. A tree will be displayed that shows the first level subdirectories on that disk (see Figure 7.7). If the directory you want is not there, keep going until you find it.

5. Select the directory you wish to share from the displayed directory tree.

6. Select the File option from the menu bar. The File window is displayed.

7. Select the Share option in the File window. The NetWare Share dialog box will appear (see Figure 7.8).

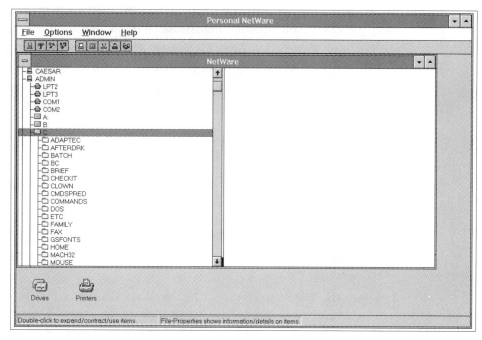

Figure 7.7 A directory tree.

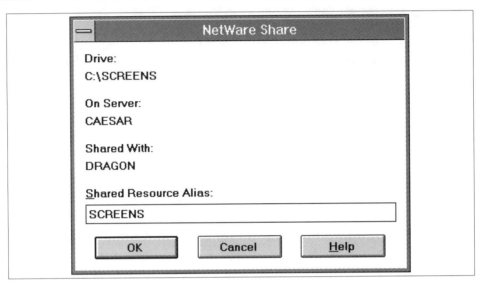

Figure 7.8 The NetWare Share dialog box.

8. Type in a name for the directory to be identified as on the network, and press Enter. The NetWare Rights dialog box will appear.

9. Set the default and explicit access rights for the directory, if necessary.

10. Choose the Close button. The NETWARE window will be updated to show the new shared directory as an available resource on the network.

Dropping a Shared Directory   Sometimes it becomes necessary to remove a shared directory from the network.

To drop a shared directory:

1. From the desktop, double click the mouse on the Personal NetWare icon in the Personal NetWare group.

2. Select the Window option from the menu bar. The Window option window is displayed.

3. Select the NetWare option. The NetWare display window will appear showing network connections, workgroups, and users. On the left side of the window is the default or active network connections, workgroups, and users.

4. Select the icon representing the shared directory connection you wish to delete.

5. Select the File option from the menu bar. The File window will be displayed.

6. Select the Delete option in the File window. The connection to the directory will be dropped. The Drives window will update to show that the directory is no longer available.

It is important to check and make sure you have made no permanent connections to the deleted shared directory. Attempting to access the shared directory after it has been removed from the system will cause an error to be displayed.

Can I Do Anything with the Directory?

Before mapping a drive to a shared directory, it is sometimes helpful to know something about that directory. You should know the answers to these questions: Can I read or write to this directory? Does the directory have space for me to write files to it without filling up the disk? To answer those questions, Personal NetWare provides the a couple of functions.

To determine how much free space is left on the drive containing a shared directory:

1. From the desktop, double click the mouse on the Personal NetWare icon in the Personal NetWare group.

2. Select the Window option from the menu bar. The Window option window is displayed.

3. Select the NetWare option. The NetWare display window will appear showing network connections, workgroups, and users. On the left side of the window is the default or active network connections, workgroups, and users.

4. Select the shared directory icon or the NetWare volume icon the shared directory resides on.

5. Select the File option from the menu bar. The File window will be displayed.

6. Select the Properties option in the file window. A dialog box appears showing the disk size and the free space left on it (see Figure 7.9).

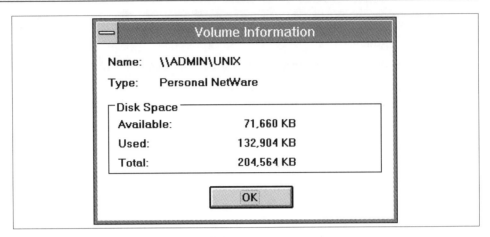

Figure 7.9 Free disk space display.

To see what access rights you have to a shared directory, do the following:

1. From the desktop, double click the mouse on the Personal NetWare icon in the Personal NetWare group.

2. Select the Window option from the menu bar. The Window option window is displayed.

3. Select the Drives option. The Drives display window will appear showing the logical drives for your workstation on the left, and available shared directories on the right (see Figure 7.10).

4. Select the shared directory you are interested in. If it is connected to a logical drive on the left side of the window, you can select that logical drive instead.

5. Select the File option from the menu bar. The File window will be displayed.

6. Select the Rights option in the file window. A Drive Info dialog box will appear (see Figure 7.11). This box shows to which server the shared directory is connected, the version of NetWare that is currently running on it, and your access rights to that directory or volume.

Mapping the Drive

If there are shared directories available, you can map them to DOS logical drives by these two methods.

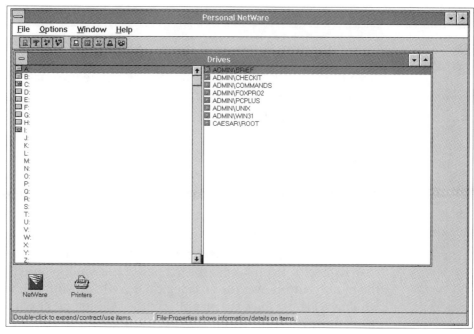

Figure 7.10   The Drives display window.

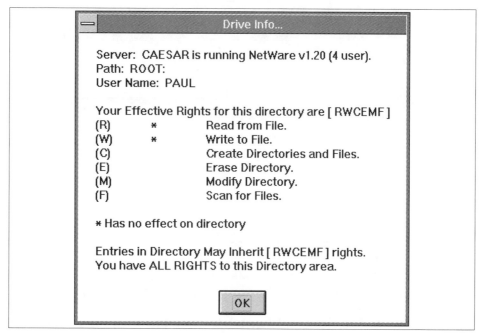

Figure 7.11   The Drive Info dialog box.

To map a directory by drag and drop:

1. From the desktop, double click the mouse on the Personal NetWare icon in the Personal NetWare group.

2. Select the Window option from the menu bar. The Window option window is displayed.

3. Select the Drives option. The Drives display window will appear showing the logical drives for your workstation on the left, and available shared directories on the right side.

4. With the mouse, choose the shared directory you wish to map. The selected directory will be highlighted.

5. Holding down the left mouse button, drag the mouse pointer from the shared directory icon over to the left side of the window and release (drop) the mouse button over the DOS logical drive letter you wish to map. The window will now show the mapping of the DOS logical drive to the shared directory (see Figure 7.12).

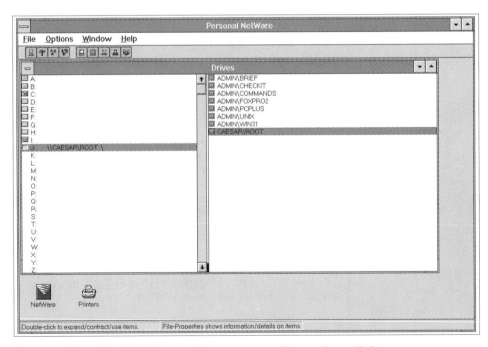

Figure 7.12 The DOS logical drive mapped to a shared directory.

6. To make the connection permanent, select the File option from the menu bar. The File option window will appear.

7. Select the Permanent option from the File option window. The mapped logical drive icon on the left of the Drives window will change to reflect the permanent status.

To map a drive the long way:

1. From the desktop, double click the mouse on the Personal NetWare icon in the Personal NetWare group.

2. Select the Window option from the menu bar. The Window option window is displayed.

3. Select the Drives option. The Drives display window will appear showing the logical drives for your workstation on the left, and available shared directories on the right.

4. On the right side, select the shared directory you wish to map to a DOS logical drive.

5. On the left side, select the DOS logical drive you wish to map.

6. Select the File option from the menu bar. The File option window will appear.

7. Select the Connect option. The NetWare Connect (Map) Drive dialog box appears (see Figure 7.13).

8. Choose the OK button from the NetWare Connect (Map) Drive dialog box to map the shared directory to the DOS logical drive.

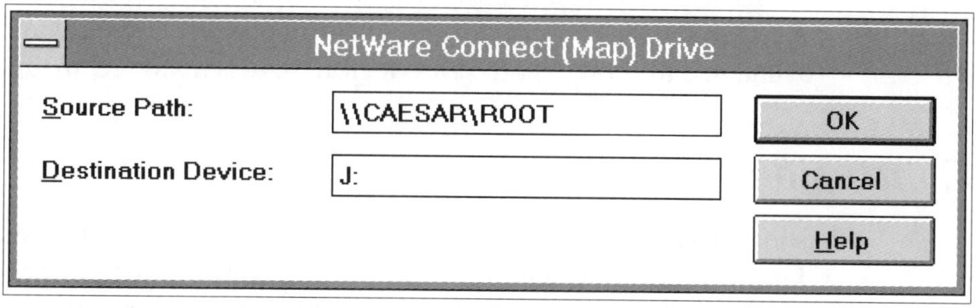

Figure 7.13 The NetWare Connect (Map) Drive dialog.

9. To make the connection permanent, select the File option from the menu bar. The File option window will appear.

10. Select the Permanent option from the File option window. The mapped logical drive icon on the left of the Drives window will change to reflect the permanent status.

To remove a drive mapping:

1. From the desktop, double click the mouse on the Personal NetWare icon in the Personal NetWare group.

2. Select the Window option from the menu bar. The Window option window is displayed.

3. Select the Drives option. The Drives display window will appear showing the logical drives for your workstation on the left, and available shared directories on the right.

4. Select the DOS logical drive you want to disconnect from the shared directory.

5. Select the File option from the menu bar. The File window will be displayed.

6. There are three ways to complete the final step. You can select the Disconnect option in the File window. The connection to the directory will be dropped. The Drives window will be updated to show that the DOS logical drive is no longer mapped. Or, highlight the DOS logical drive with the mouse, and press the Del key. The connection to the directory will be dropped. The Drives window will update to show that the DOS logical drive is no longer mapped. Finally, you can, while holding down the left mouse button, drag the mouse pointer from the DOS logical drive icon over to the right side of the window and release the mouse button. The connection to the directory will be dropped. The Drives window will be updated to show that the DOS logical drive is no longer mapped.

Conclusion

Personal NetWare provides a good set of utility functions that make managing and using the network a much simpler task. The use of the mouse, icons, plus drag and drop features of some of these functions makes using Personal NetWare a more enjoyable task.

Chapter 8

Network Security

Introduction

Most people who work with, maintain, or use a network, have some kind of opinion as to what network security is and how it should be implemented. Without going into a lot of detail, network security can be described as the means to limit access by users to information, and prevent them from performing certain actions on equipment attached to the network. Network security is a tool to help information flow in an orderly manner. It is not a tool to exercise dominion over another person; nor is it there to build empires. Too many people act very immaturely when security issues arise. In the next few pages, we will explore some ideas that express the purpose of security on a network.

By design, a network is a public forum, a place to share information with other people. Security is not an inherent quality of networks; therefore, it must be added on top of the basic structure as a means of guiding and restricting user activities.

Any person who acts in the capacity as a system administrator must realize that efficient flow of information within a network is what keeps the user community working and productivity up. The network itself is a means of accomplishing this, not an end unto itself. Anytime management or the system

153

administrator(s) impose themselves unnecessarily on the flow of information through the use of security measures it impedes progress and creates friction in the user community.

A system administrator should be a person who is not only technically competent at network administration, but a level headed individual who can effectively communicate with both management and the user community. A system administrator should also realize that the responsibility of the position is one of service to the user community, not control over it. Such a person will educate his or her users in what is acceptable behavior on the network and encourage them to cooperate to take advantage of what the network has to offer.

Security Planning Issues

By design, a network is available for use by more than one person, which makes people think about the kind of information they keep there, how many people will be able to see it, and whether it is possible to maintain the confidentiality of "sensitive" material. When planning for network security, common sense dictates that you ask yourself a few pertinent questions.

What Kind of Information Is Sensitive?

Information can be considered sensitive if it needs to be restricted to only certain people in a group. This "need to know" basis can be very limited; i.e., a single item such as the name of a person or company. It also can be very broad in scope, such as accounting and payroll figures. Some examples of sensitive information may include:

- Accounting records
- Classified documents
- Client lists
- Court records
- Credit histories
- Employee files
- Medical records
- Payrolls
- Personnel information

- Phone lists and records
- Tax information
- Technical information
- Vendor lists

Should I Keep This Information on the Network?

If the information needs to be shared with someone, and it would be inconvenient or impossible to do so without the network, then it probably needs to be kept there. *Don't* keep things such as:

- Personal correspondence
- Personal diaries
- Personal financial information
- Personal phone list
- Personal tax statements
- Work for another company

Many people think of the network as a cubby hole in which to put things, only to find out later that their private lives have been made public. A good rule of thumb is if no one else should see it, don't store it on the network.

Where Should I Keep Sensitive Information?

Networks should be designed and constructed in sections so that common information and usage can be grouped together. Restricted or sensitive information should be separated from the rest of the network.

Sensitive information is sometimes placed in a separate computer, away from the computer that handles many other types of activities and data. For example, let's say that financial records and functions are kept on a sizable network with several machines dedicated to act as servers. Since the financial information should not be distributed among the user community at large, the system administrator will probably store all of it on one server and then limit the access to the programs and data stored there to those who need it.

When there is a single computer serving many users, sensitive information is usually placed on a separate disk if the computer has multiple hard drives. Going back to our example network, let's say that it now is much smaller and has only one machine acting as a server. This server has several hard drives available to store programs and data, such as financial information. The system administrator, in this case, will most likely place the financial data and programs on a separate hard drive, and then allow access to only those users who need it.

Let's reduce our example network even further and remove all but one hard drive from the single server. Financial information can then be kept in a separate partition or subdirectory tree. In this case, the system administrator will limit access to that partition or subdirectory tree to only those users who need the information or functions.

Some circumstances render network resources inadequate for storage, or the information is so sensitive that it cannot be kept there full time. In such circumstances, the information is only loaded when needed. In these cases, sensitive information is kept on removable media such as floppies, tape, removable hard drives, CD-ROM, WORM, or optical disks.

Who Needs Access to Sensitive Information?

Assigning access to sensitive information is a judgment that usually is made by the person responsible for maintaining that information. In business, it generally falls to the department manager to decide who needs to see information private to his or her department. However, the system administrator and the owner of the machine on which the information resides are usually the ones who have the final say in the matter. The system administrator (if one exists) has this distinction since he or she is ultimately responsible for all the information and resources on the network as a whole. The owner of the PC on which the information resides also shares this responsibility since the owner has physical access to the machine.

Here is a practical example: John manages the financial department for a small company. Within the department, his company has given him charge over payroll, accounts receivable, accounts payable, contracts, and other monetary functions. Each section has a person responsible for maintaining each function, which is accomplished by using applications stored on his or her computer network.

Marsha, the system administrator for the computer network, maintains the accounts of all the people allowed on the network. She controls what they can do on the network by granting permissions to their accounts.

In order to control access to financial information, Marsha blocks everyone outside of John's department from seeing that information or using the programs to access it. John can handle the details of the people in his department in two ways. First, he can submit a list of people to Marsha, telling her what financial information and functions they need to access, and let her grant permission. The second option is for Marsha to grant special function permission to John's account, thereby giving him the ability to allow people access to the data and programs for which he is responsible.

Implementing Network Security

Now that you've pondered these few broad yet important issues regarding what must be kept secure on your network and who needs to access that information, you are ready to begin to implement a scheme that will protect your important data, but not hinder your productivity. To do this, we again need to answer several questions.

- What functions on the network are privileged?
- Who should have these privileged functions?
- How are they assigned to the users who need them?
- What should you consider when organizing your users and workgroups?
- What access rights to files and directories can be restricted or granted?
- Who needs access to the network, and how much do they need?
- What policies can and should you enforce when dealing with account passwords?

Answering these questions will help you implement a reasonably effective security policy, which will facilitate, not hinder, your office productivity.

What Functions on the Network Are Privileged?

Privileged functions on the network are those that should be restricted to a small group of people, for two reasons. First, using these functions indiscriminately could damage or destroy data, programs, or network functionality. Second, privileged functions are installed to maintain orderly use and control of network resources and accounts. Some of the functions that should be blocked or limited to general use on the network include:

- Changing user accounts
- Creating directories
- Creating user accounts
- Deleting directories

- Deleting files
- Deleting user accounts
- Formatting hard drives
- Installing applications
- Mapping hard drive connections
- Mapping network connections
- Mapping printer connections
- Removing applications

Who Should Have Access to These Privileged Functions?

As was alluded to previously, these privileged functions should be restricted to a small group of people to maintain an orderly network. There should be at least one person with the ability to do anything and everything on the network. This person is designated as the "super user" or system administrator.

Now, we need to make an important distinction. Anyone can be a "super user," but not everyone can be a system administrator. There should be only one system administrator (if possible) responsible for the network. The administrator can and should delegate a portion of his or her authority to others, or give them "super user" status that allows them to help maintain and have responsibility for a portion of the network. If your network is too small to warrant a full-time administrator, then competent users working together to manage different portions of the network can work almost as well.

Let's say, for example, that a network has been established with several sections or workgroups, including:

- Accounting
- Administration
- Development
- Production

Each section also contains several workstations. Let's also say that the company is in full operation from 6:00 A.M. to 6:00 P.M. because customers exist across three time zones, and that all computing services are available for use to some extent during off hours so that development work, production, accounting, and shipping and receiving can catch up from the previous day's business. This scenario is fairly typical of many small businesses.

Now, the question of how to manage the network comes into focus. One person cannot be available 24 hours a day to make sure that any and all problems on the network are dealt with. There needs to be a delegation of responsibility.

Practicality suggests that there be one system administrator. The system administrator should be available during peak use hours to handle problems with applications and the network. Along with the system administrator, there should be at least one person in each section or department who can handle the problems directly related to that department's data and applications. These people usually are granted privileged functions that let them act in behalf of the system administrator, but with respect to their respective sections only. This usually includes user accounts and access to programs and data within their sections or workgroups. Normally, they are not able to change the structure of the network, access to shared resources such as printers, or access to resources outside their sections or workgroups. These functions are reserved for the system administrator.

If the network is big enough, the system administrator may give one or more people full system administrator privileges to handle the workload during peak hours. The administrator can be on call during off hours, or there can be another person available to manage the care and feeding of the network.

If the network is too small for a company to spare an individual to serve as a full-time administrator, the duties will fall more heavily on the backs of the users in charge of the separate domains. More often than not in a peer network, administrative duties turn into everyone's responsibility. But, to ensure that work is disrupted as little as possible, someone who has the ability to keep applications running on the network needs to be available.

Using Personal NetWare's Privileged Functions

In Personal NetWare, the SUPERVISOR account, or any user account that has workgroup manager privileges, can use the privileged functions. This does not necessarily mean that the SUPERVISOR account, or any other account with workgroup manager privileges, can modify all resources.

For instance, a server has a set of access permissions, in addition to user account permissions, when it comes to modifying the server's configuration. In order to modify any server settings, a user account must either own the server or have the rights to manage the server. However, in the default settings, any user account with workgroup manager privileges can generally modify any resources in the workgroup.

To modify an account to have workgroup manager privileges in Personal NetWare, do the following (you must be logged in as SUPERVISOR for this procedure).

From DOS:

1. From the DOS prompt, type **NET ADMIN**, and the main network administration screen will appear (Figure 8.1).

2. Select the View menu item by pressing **ALT-V**. The View menu selection window will appear (Figure 8.2).

3. Select the users option by pressing **ALT-U**. The users screen will appear with all accounts displayed.

4. Using the arrow keys, select the user account to modify, and press Enter. The Properties window for the selected user account will be displayed.

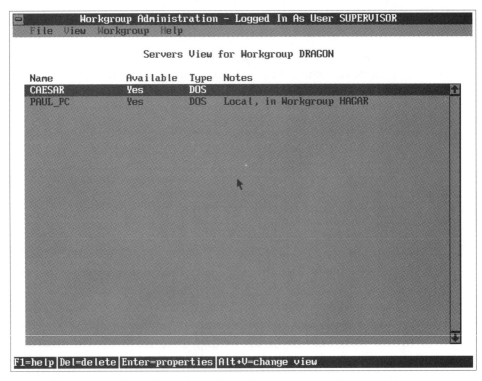

Figure 8.1 The Main Network Administrator screen.

5. If there is not a check mark in the box located next to the Workgroup Manager option, then press **ALT-W** to place one there and activate these privileges for this account.

6. Highlight the OK button and press Enter, or press **ALT-O**.

From Windows:

1. From the desktop, double click on the Personal NetWare icon in the Personal NetWare group.

2. Select the Window option from the menu bar. The Window option window is displayed.

3. Select the NetWare option. The NetWare display window will appear, displaying network connections, workgroups, and users (Figure 8.3).

4. Double click on an existing workgroup icon to display the shared directories, if they are not already displayed.

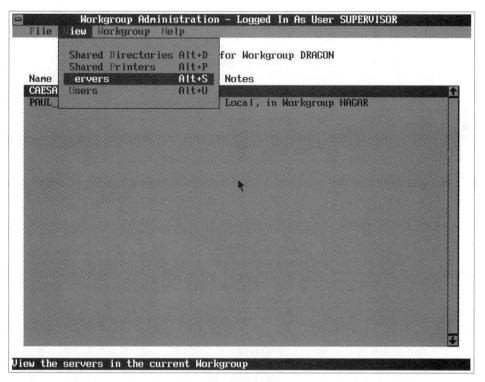

Figure 8.2 The View Menu Selection screen.

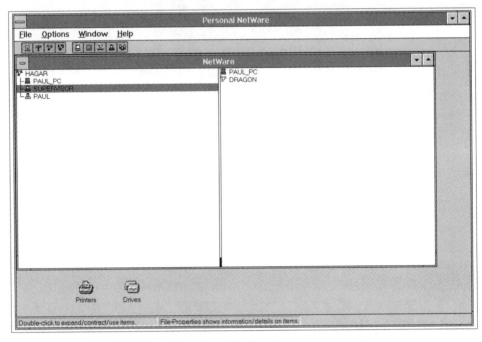

Figure 8.3   The NetWare Display window.

5. Highlight the user account to modify user access rights, and press Enter. The NetWare User Information window is displayed.

6. Select the Configuration button. The Personal NetWare User Account Configuration window is displayed.

7. If there is not an X in the box next to the Workgroup Administrator option, select the box to activate these privileges (Figure 8.4).

8. Select the OK button to save the changes. This closes the Personal NetWare User Account Configuration window.

9. Select the Close button. This closes the NetWare User Information window.

10. Exit the Personal NetWare application.

Segmenting Your Personal NetWare Network

As we discussed earlier in the chapter, data that needs to be secure should be separated from the more public data. Personal NetWare allows you two ways to separate sensitive data through segmenting your network:

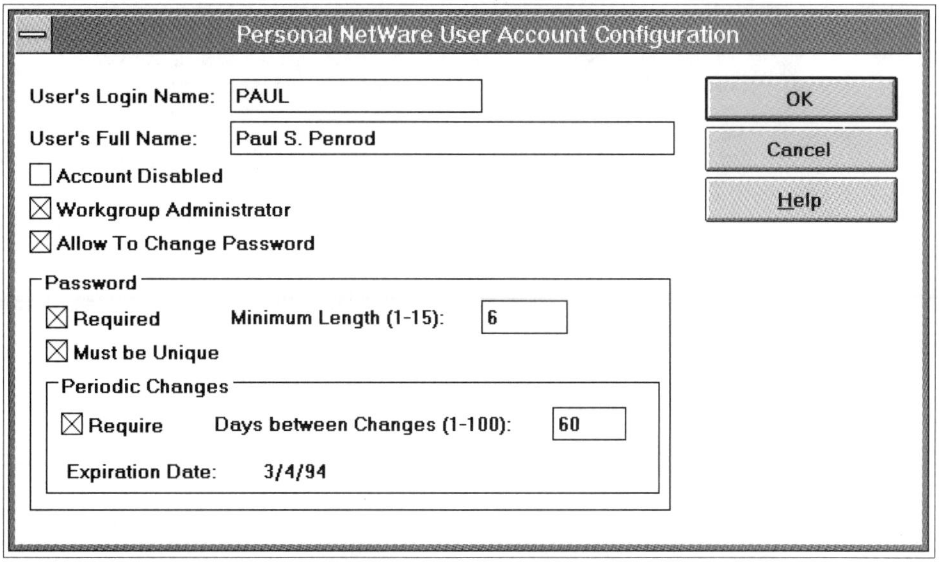

Figure 8.4 The Workgroup Administrator option.

- Separating users into workgroups
- Assigning access rights within workgroups

Separating Users into Workgroups

One of the units that Personal NetWare divides network access into is the workgroup. A workgroup can consist of one or many servers, and it can have one user or many users. Think of it as a logical way to divvy up types of work and resources.

For example, let's examine a company network that has accounting, development, shipping and receiving, and administrative departments using it. These departments each has its own data and functions to manipulate that data specific to its particular needs. One of the logical ways to divide this network into manageable chunks is by establishing workgroups that encapsulate each of the major functions. Then, accounting, development, shipping and receiving, and administration each will have its own workgroup.

This segmentation into workgroups helps protect the data of each workgroup from accidents that could happen when users who don't know what they are doing start trying to manipulate data. Remember, security should be designed

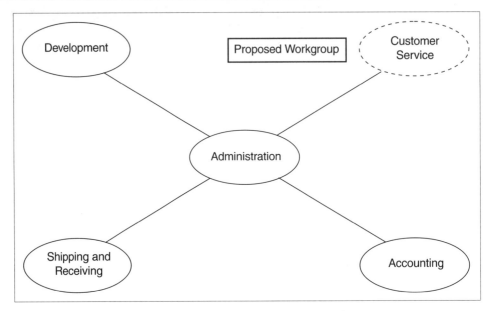

Figure 8.5 Creating a workgroup for customer service.

to allow authorized users to access data. If everyone has access to all data, you are inviting accidents or possibly even sabotage.

Let's illustrate our example further. Customer service for the company is being handled by the administration area of the network. After a period of time, the amount of business done within the realm of customer service has reached a point where it has become a burden to the administrative resources on the network. At this point, the decision is made to create a new workgroup for customer service. Figure 8.5 shows the existing network and the proposed changes.

Figure 8.6 shows how the proposed workgroup will look, and illustrates the current administrative workgroup and what will change. The diagonal dashed line represents the logical split between the physical resources of the administrative workgroup and the newly created customer service workgroup. The small dotted lines represent the former logical connections between the workstations that used to be connected to the Administration server, but now run to the customer service server.

Note that no machines have moved, and no wires have been rerouted or reconnected. The customer service workgroup now encapsulates the workstations and personnel that do that kind of work, while limiting access from the

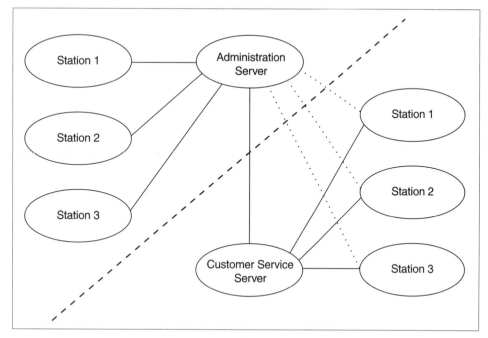

Figure 8.6   Dividing customer service and administrative functions.

outside. That data is safe from unknowing accidents and deliberate attempts at sabotage from those outside of the workgroup. This is done in part by the user database attached to each workgroup. This database keeps track of who is allowed to log in to the workgroup and access the resources attached to it.

Assigning Access Rights within Workgroups

The server functions as a primary device for managing shared resources and delivering data between the logical and physical network components under its control. This means that a server is like a traffic cop. It directs the flow of traffic (data) between workgroup devices based on a user's access rights. How access rights can be used to secure data and access within the workgroup is the focus here.

To begin with, unlike NetWare, Personal NetWare does not provide a volume function that can span several network drives. A Personal NetWare volume only encompasses the designated shared directories on a single logical drive for a server. For example, let's say Joe's PC is a server, and the hard drive is logically divided into C and D drives with each logical drive having shared directories. Both of these logical drives would appear as Personal NetWare volumes. Note that Personal NetWare ties servers directly to a single workgroup as one of its resources. Consequently, any access to a server's volume must be done from within the workgroup itself.

As discussed earlier, sensitive information should be grouped on a single logical drive on multivolume servers, or within a specified directory or directories on a single-volume server. Making a drive public potentially gives access to all data to everyone within the workgroup. In many cases, not everyone within the workgroup needs access to all this information, so how does Personal NetWare control access from within the workgroup?

Personal NetWare controls access from within the workgroup by use of the shared directory function. Once a directory is made public, this function restricts access and usage on a user account to this public directory according to the assigned access rights or privileges for that particular account within the workgroup. A user can be assigned the following access rights: READ, WRITE, NONE, or ALL. These access rights are explained in more detail below.

- **READ:** The user can read data, execute a program from that directory, or scan the directory itself.

- **WRITE:** The user can write data to existing files and create new files. Users can not execute programs, scan the directory, or read data from files.

- **NONE:** The user can see the directory, but cannot read data from files, execute programs, create new files, or scan the directory for information. If there is a subdirectory connected to this directory that the user has permission to read or write to, he or she can go there and perform any read or write functions that are valid for the account.

- **ALL:** When this is set, the user has permission to read, write, create, or execute files from that directory without restriction.

To modify shared directory access for an account in Personal NetWare, do the following. (To do any of the procedures listed here, you must be logged in as SUPERVISOR.)

From DOS (interactive):

1. From the DOS prompt, type **NET ADMIN**, and the main network administration screen will appear.

2. Select the View menu item by pressing **ALT-V**. The View menu selection window will appear.

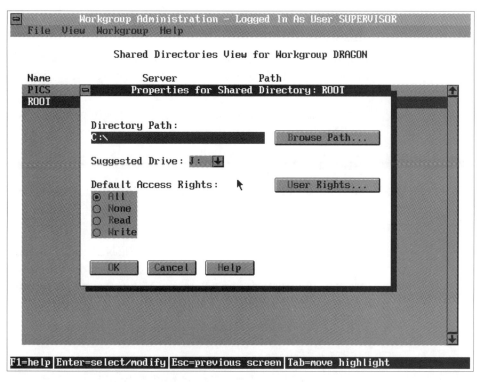

Figure 8.7   The Properties window.

3. Select the Shared Directories option by pressing **ALT-D**. The Shared Directories screen will appear with all public directories and the associated public names for the shared directories displayed.

4. Using the arrow keys, highlight the directory on which you wish to modify the user access rights and press Enter. The Properties window for that directory will appear (Figure 8.7).

Using Default Access Permissions

Most users within a workgroup will require the same permissions for their account. If you set the default access permissions to reflect the majority of users' needs, then only the few accounts that differ need to be changed. In the left-hand corner of the window, there is a selection for default access. Make sure the permission level selected there equates to the bulk of your user accounts.

5. Select the User Rights button by pressing **ALT-U**. This will display the User Rights screen.

6. Using the arrow keys, highlight the user whose permission needs to be different from the default access setting. Press ALT-M to display the Modify screen.

7. Select the access permission for this user. Highlight the OK button and press Enter.

8. Repeat steps 6 and 7 until all user accounts requiring modification are completed.

9. From the User Rights screen, select the Close button and press Enter.

From the DOS command line:

To do this from the DOS command line, use the NET RIGHTS command. This command is used to display and set the rights of shared directories on a Personal Netware server, all directories on a Personal Netware server running Novell DOS 7.0 that has security enabled, and volumes on a Netware server.

To see the access rights of a user to a shared directory, type:

```
NET RIGHTS <directory>
```

For example, to see the rights assigned to the shared directory C:\PAYROLL\JAN, enter:

```
NET RIGHTS C:\PAYROLL\JAN
```

To set the default rights of a shared directory, type:

```
NET RIGHTS <directory> ADD DEFAULT <rights>
```

For example, to allow users to write to the shared directory C:\PAYROLL\JAN, enter:

```
NET RIGHTS C:\PAYROLL\JAN ADD DEFAULT WRITE
```

To remove the default rights of a shared directory, type:

```
NET RIGHTS <directory> DELETE DEFAULT
```

For example, to remove the default rights assigned to directory C:\PAYROLL\JAN, enter:

```
NET RIGHTS C:\PAYROLL\JAN DELETE DEFAULT
```

To set a specific user's rights to a shared directory, type:

```
NET RIGHTS <directory> ADD <user> <right>
```

For example, to add the READ permission to C:\PAYROLL\JAN to user BERT, enter:

```
NET RIGHTS C:\PAYROLL\JAN ADD BERT READ
```

To remove a specific user's rights to a shared directory, type:

```
NET RIGHTS <directory> DELETE <user>
```

For example, to remove user BERT's permissions to C:\PAYROLL\JAN, enter:

```
NET RIGHTS C:\PAYROLL\JAN DELETE BERT
```

To remove all user's nondefault rights to a shared directory, type:

```
NET RIGHTS <directory> DELETE *
```

For example, to remove all the nondefault rights assigned to users with access to C:\PAYROLL\JAN, enter:

```
NET RIGHTS C:\PAYROLL\JAN DELETE *
```

From Windows:

1. From the desktop, double click on the Personal NetWare icon in the Personal NetWare group.
2. Select the Window option from the menu bar. The Window option window is displayed.
3. Select the NetWare option. The NetWare display window will appear, displaying network connections, workgroups, and users.
4. Double click on an existing workgroup icon to display the shared directories, if they are not already displayed.
5. Highlight the shared directory for which you wish to modify user access rights.
6. Select the File menu option from the main menu. This will display the File menu window.
7. Select the Rights option from the File menu. The Personal NetWare Rights window will appear for that shared directory.
8. Select the user account that you wish to modify and select the appropriate rights to assign to it for that shared directory (Figure 8.8).

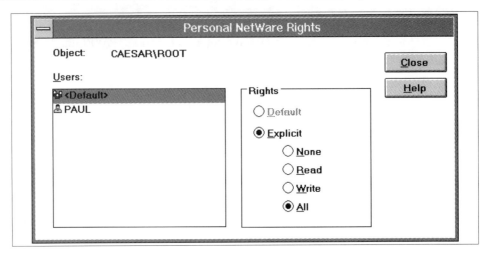

Figure 8.8   Choosing rights for a shared directory.

9. Repeat step 8 until all modification to user accounts is done, and then select the Close button.

10. End the Personal NetWare application.

Who Needs Access to the Network?

Anyone who has work that requires resources on the network should have access to the network. The system administrator and/or the person(s) responsible for the data the potential user needs to access will determine to what extent that person can make use of what is available.

On some networks, there are special accounts called GUEST or ANONYMOUS. These accounts allow anyone restricted access to certain public parts of the network. Usually these accounts are set up to allow people to log in and obtain public information, print documentation, upload and download public domain files and data, run programs, or any other activity that the system administrator has determined will not compromise the security and operation of the network.

When Should They Have Access to the Network?

Restricting user access to the network based on time is another method that the system administrator can use to maintain control over the network. For the most part, networks have open access 24 hours a day. There are, however, circumstances that call for restricting when user accounts can log in to the network.

Think back to GUEST or ANONYMOUS accounts. More often than not, these types of accounts have people outside the organization logging into them. Usually, there are not too many problems associated with this. The system administrator may decide to limit login access to this type of account to the hours during which he is available to monitor the activity. (As a side note, Personal NetWare does not have many direct ways to monitor activity on your network, so you will have to deduce much of what you want to find out if you are trying to be discreet.)

Another reason you might want to limit a user's access to the network for certain time periods is to make backing up the system more efficient. Preferably, there should be no active user accounts while this is taking place. The backup procedure cannot access those files that are in use at the time of the backup, which means there will be missing information, and the backup will not be complete. This can be a problem if the files missed by the backup procedure are damaged or destroyed and cannot be restored.

If the information is sensitive enough, such as classified documents, then management may instruct the system administrator to limit the times a user can be on the system to hours when someone is available to watch the activity on the network directly, thus preventing unauthorized access to this information.

Problem users are another cause for the system administrator to restrict a specific account, enabling him or her to track that user's activities. It's unfortunate that some people make a point of exercising their independence and try to do things they know are questionable. Their actions cause problems for other users and sometimes the network as a whole. Thus, the system administrator may use time access to monitor a problem user.

To restrict times when a user can log in to the network through Personal NetWare, do the following. (To do any of the procedures listed here, you must be logged in as SUPERVISOR.)

From DOS:

1. From the DOS prompt, type **NET ADMIN**, and the main network administration screen will appear.

2. Select the View menu item by pressing **ALT-V**. The View menu selection window will appear.

3. Select the Users option by pressing **ALT-U**. The Users screen will appear with all accounts displayed.

4. Using the arrow keys, select the user account to modify and press Enter. The Properties window for the selected user account will be displayed.

5. Press **ALT-L**, or highlight the LOGIN Times button and press Enter. The Login Time Restrictions window will be displayed (Figure 8.9).

6. Using the arrow keys, cursor over to the day row and hour column you wish to modify, and press the Spacebar. If an asterisk was there before pressing the Spacebar, then it will disappear and the account will not be able to log in during that hour on that day. If there was no asterisk prior to pressing the Spacebar, then one will appear, and the account will be able to log in during that hour on that day.

7. Press **ALT-O**, or highlight the OK button and press Enter to save the changes to the login times for that user account.

8. Press **ALT-O**, or highlight the OK button and press Enter to save the changes to the user account.

From Windows:

This function is not available under the Personal NetWare Windows application.

What about Passwords?

On most networks, user accounts are secured through the use of passwords. Personal NetWare is no different. Passwords are nothing more than unique keys that are used to unlock use of the network for a specific individual. Since all activity on the network is tracked by means of the user account, it is important to make sure that the person assigned to the user account is the one who is actually using it. If more than one person uses a nonpublic account, then access to nonpublic parts of the network can be compromised. Thus, it is important to maintain a one-to-one relationship between account and user.

Password Guidelines

The length of the password determines how hard it is to obtain it by random guessing. As a rule of thumb, it is recommended that passwords be no fewer than six characters long. This makes the number of possible password combi-

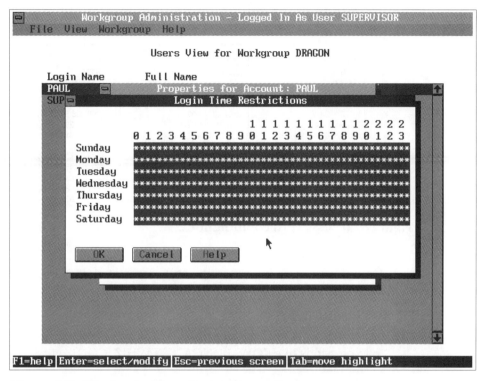

Figure 8.9   The Login Time Restrictions window.

nations large enough (165,765,600 combinations for using just letters of the alphabet) that it tends to discourage all but the most determined. Figure 8.10 shows the possible number of password combinations based on the length and the number of unique characters allowed to create those passwords.

Even though a long password can be difficult to decipher, some people use passwords that make it easy for others to guess what they are. When cracking a password to enter a computer network, professionals take advantage of the fact that most computer network users are unsophisticated and will use common names, numbers, and nouns that are closely associated with them in some manner. Here are some suggestions of things to be aware of when selecting a secure password:

1. Do not use any part of your name as your password. Do not use your first, middle, or last name as your password. This includes initials, partial spellings, abbreviations and nicknames.

Password Length	Possible number of permutations based on length and unique characters available.		
	A-Z 26	A-Z, 0-9 36	ASCII set 127
1	26	36	127
2	650	1,260	16,002
3	15,600	42,840	2,000,250
4	358,800	1,413,720	248,031,000
5	7,893,600	45,239,040	30,507,813,000
6	165,765,600	1,402,410,240	3,721,953,186,000
7	3,315,312,000	42,072,307,200	450,356,335,506,000
8	62,990,928,000	1,220,096,908,800	54,042,760,260,720,000
9	1,133,836,704,000	34,162,713,446,400	6,431,088,471,025,680,000
10	19,275,223,968,000	922,393,263,052,800	758,868,439,581,030,000,000
11	308,403,583,488,000	23,982,224,839,372,800	88,787,607,430,980,500,000,000
12	4,626,053,752,320,000	599,555,620,984,320,000	10,299,362,461,993,700,000,000,000
13	64,764,752,532,480,000	14,389,334,903,623,700,000	1,184,426,683,129,280,000,000,000,000
14	841,941,782,922,240,000	330,954,702,783,345,000,000	135,024,641,876,738,000,000,000,000,000
15	10,103,301,395,066,900,000	7,281,003,461,233,580,000,000	15,257,784,532,071,400,000,000,000,000,000

Figure 8.10   Password combinations.

2. Do not use any words that are closely associated with you. These include such items as:

> Favorite colors
> Acronyms like FUBAR, BOHICA, WYSIWYG, etc.
> Expressions like KOWABUNGA, GEEWHIZ, COOL, etc.
> Hobbies
> Books
> Famous people
> Sports

3. Do not use numbers associated with you, including:

> Social security number
> Student ID number
> Car license plates
> Driver's license number
> Phone number (work or home)
> Birthdays

4. Do not use the names of relatives or close associates.

Once a password is selected for a user account, the tough part commences: having to deal with it. The password is the key to your account, so keep these points in mind:

1. Change the password at regular intervals. This is important for the simple reason that, over time, the chances of someone finding out your password and using it increase. Also, when changing your password, do not recycle old passwords. Recycling makes it easier for someone to get into your account. All they have to do is try passwords you frequently use until they find the one that currently works.

2. If someone knows your password, change it. People who want to cause problems or do questionable things will try to enter the network as someone else to disguise themselves.

3. Do not tell anyone what your password is. This means everyone, even the system administrator. The system administrator does not need to know what your password is, because he or she has the permissions necessary to handle your account directly. If there were a password problem, they would change it and inform you of the change so that you could enter your account and set a new password.

4. Do not write your password down and keep it near your computer. In fact, if the password must be really secure, never write it down. Paper can and will be seen by other people. Unsophisticated users many times will write down their password and keep it handy in case they forget it. Someone seeking access into the network from your computer will search the area around your computer looking for a piece of paper containing your password. If you write down your password and leave it by your computer, chances are, someone will find it.

Setting Passwords in Personal NetWare

Personal NetWare provides the SUPERVISOR with some flexibility in handling passwords to user accounts. Personal NetWare allows for:

- Users to change their own passwords.
- Requiring a password for an account.
- Password attributes that include a minimum length, uniqueness, periodic changes, and the number of days between forced password change.

To modify a user account's password information in Personal NetWare, do the following. (To do any of the procedures listed here, you must be logged in as SUPERVISOR.)

From DOS:

1. From the DOS prompt, type **NET ADMIN**, and the main network administration screen will appear.

2. Select the View menu item by pressing **ALT-V**. The View menu selection window will appear.

3. Select the Users option by pressing **ALT-U**. The Users screen will appear with all accounts displayed.

4. Using the arrow keys, select the user account to modify and press Enter. The Properties window for the selected user account will be displayed (Figure 8.11). The next set of steps will depend upon what you wish to do.

If you want to let the user change his or her own password:

5. If there is not a check mark in the box next to the Allow to change password option, press **ALT-T**, or highlight the box next to it and press Enter or Spacebar. A check mark will appear in the box, and the option will be enabled.

6. Press **ALT-O**, or highlight the OK button and press Enter to save the changes to the user account.

If you want to make a password required for this account:

5. If there is not a check mark in the box next to the Password required option, press **ALT-R**, or highlight the box next to it and press Enter or Spacebar. A check mark will appear in the box, and the option will be enabled. Doing this will activate the options Password minimum length, Must be unique, and Periodic change options for selection.

6. Press **ALT-O**, or highlight the OK button and press Enter to save the changes to the user account.

If you want to change the minimum length for a password (a password must be required for this account in order to use this option):

5. Highlight the field next to the Minimum length option. Enter a number between 1 and 15 to tell Personal NetWare how long the shortest valid password must be to be acceptable. (See the discussion on password length earlier in this chapter).

6. Press **ALT-O**, or highlight the OK button and press Enter to save the changes to the user account.

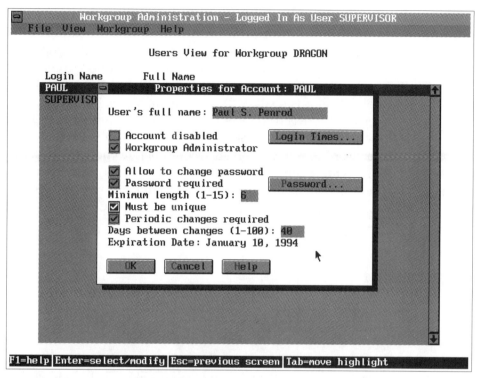

Figure 8.11 The Properties window.

If you want to force a unique password when it needs to change (a password must be required for this account in order to use this option):

5. If there is not a check mark in the box next to the Must be unique option, press **ALT-U**, or highlight the box next to it and press Enter or Spacebar. A check mark will appear in the box and the option will be enabled. When this option is activated, Personal NetWare stores up to the last four passwords used for this account. This is done to encourage the user not to recycle passwords, or at least make the cycle between repeats long enough so it is difficult to penetrate the account with old passwords.

6. Press **ALT-O**, or highlight the OK button and press Enter to save the changes to the user account.

If you want to make periodic changes of the password required (a password must be required for this account in order to use this option):

5. If there is not a check mark in the box next to the Periodic changes required option, press ALT-E, or highlight the box next to it and press Enter or Spacebar. A check mark will appear in the box and the option will be enabled. When this is activated, the option to change the number of days between requiring a new password becomes active as well. The default value is 40 days. To change this value, highlight the field next to the Days between changes option. Enter a value between 1 and 100 days. Generally, 30, 45, 60, or 90 days are common periods of time to allow a password to function on an account before changing it. A rule of thumb is: the more sensitive the information the account has access to, or the more active the account, the more often the password should change.

6. Press **ALT-O**, or highlight the OK button and press Enter to save the changes to the user account.

Conclusion

Security for a network of any kind is not a trivial task. Even for small networks, it is important to plan ahead and understand the needs of the user community at large. A major consideration is balancing those needs with the restrictions necessary to handle sensitive information and orderly operation inside the network. A well thought-out plan needs proper execution in order to function well. The best way to do this is to become very familiar with the tools Personal NetWare provides to implement and maintain security.

Chapter 9

Administrative Chores for the Network

Introduction

With a peer-to-peer networking system like Personal NetWare, everyone should pitch in and help to maintain the network. In a sense, the workgroup as a whole serves as the network administrator; each workgroup member takes responsibility for the data and applications, as well as the shared resources located on the machine under his or her control. It would be best, however, if a user with technical know-how is assigned responsibility for network functions that cannot be managed well through a community effort. This will help to eliminate the "But, I thought you were doing it!" syndrome. And, let's face it. There are some functions, such as backing up the network, that you cannot afford to be done haphazardly.

In this chapter, we will discuss network backup, virus protection strategies, dealing with novice users, and the network printing functions for which a "network administrator" should have responsibility.

Network Backup

Backing up your system prevents you from being held hostage by any number of disasterous events, and should fall under your short list of administrative "must do's." When your system collapses through user errors, equipment failures, or a natural calamity, it is definitely too late to be implementing a backup strategy. It is always a good policy to plan for the worst, so you will never be completely unprepared.

Data Migration

Backing up network data and migrating (archiving) old data is really two sides of the same coin. The difference between regular backups and planned data migration is merely in the intent of the operation. Backing up by making a copy of your Personal NetWare data and placing it on some form of storage media such as tapes or optical disks prevents the loss of data through mechanical failures or human errors. From this copy you can restore any lost or corrupted data to the condition it was in at the time of the last backup. The only data that might be lost are the changes made since the time of the last backup. For this reason, you should strive to keep as current a backup as you possibly can.

Data migration involves data that is archived to save it over time as well as to prevent its unexpected destruction. Once the data being migrated is archived and stored, the space it occupied on the network can be freed for use, a great boon to networks that are short of disk space.

Data migration, however, should be regarded as an addition to backups; it is not intended to take the place of regular backups. For instance, your accounting department will definitely want to save financial records for several years for audit purposes. Files such as these should be migrated off your network and copied onto tapes, floppy disks, or some other form of storage media and saved in a safe place such as a safety deposit box or a fireproof safe. A good rule of thumb for archiving normal everyday data files is three to six months.

Part of your archiving procedure should include recording what data is contained on your storage media and what procedure was used to save it. This will be a tremendous help to whomever is going to restore the data. There is no telling how long this data may be kept, and the system administrator might not always be available. Further, you may also change to a new backup system or procedure in the future.

Backup System Considerations

There are many third-party vendors such as Tecmar, Seagate, and Palindrome that provide complete backup solutions including both the hardware and the accompanying software that you can incorporate into your Personal NetWare network. The differences in hardware capabilities, storage media, and software methodologies used for the vast array of backup devices available today create several issues which need consideration before purchasing a backup system.

Security

With a peer-to-peer network like Personal NetWare, you have one major security problem that you will have to minimize in order to protect against data theft or destruction. To perform a complete backup, you must be logged in as the SUPERVISOR or a user account with rights to all the data, and leaving a workstation logged in with that kind of access to the network while the backup is being performed is not a good idea. Conversely, it is also not very productive for you or somebody else to "babysit" the workstation to make sure no one steals your backups or stops the backup and uses the supervisor privileges for mischief. One way to solve both problems is to limit access to the workstation that is performing the backup by physically locking the room the workstation is in.

An additional way to improve security for your backup system is to set up a specific user account designed for the sole purpose of performing the backup procedure. You could set up the user account BACKUP, for example, with supervisory privileges and mappings to the backup software location. This special account, however, can be restricted so that BACKUP can log in only during the times that you think will be used for regular backup sessions. You can further restrict the BACKUP user account by having a batch file call all the necessary backup programs, perform the backup, and then log the BACKUP account out when the backup is complete. You could also include programs in the procedure that will disable the Ctrl-Break function or enable you to lock the keyboard with a password. Many computers also allow you to physically lock the keyboard with a key.

These precautions should make your workstation reasonably secure from unauthorized access while the backup procedure is running. There is still the problem of the outright theft or destruction of the data once it has been saved to the storage media of choice. If your backup software supports this feature, assign a password to each tape or disk to prevent the unauthorized access to the data contained on it. Always rotate your backups to a safe place off-site such as a safety deposit box or fireproof safe. This not only helps secure your data, but it can prevent destruction of your backup library, archived files, and network drives from a natural catastrophe such as a fire. It would be relatively simple to recover from the loss of one or the other, but not both.

Ideally, your backup system should be set up so that you simply log in as BACKUP, provide any information necessary to start the backup, lock the keyboard through either software or hardware, and leave the workstation inside a secured room.

File Handling Problems

With hardware technology habitually outpacing software capabilities, you should check to see that the software and hardware you eventually choose can handle very large files or an ever-expanding directory structure.

Another important file handling aspect is how your backup software will deal with open files. When files are backed up, there are usually modifications made to that file, such as resetting the *archive needed* attribute. This causes a problem with open files because both the backup software and a user can't be using and therefore modifying the same file at the same time. Requiring that your network be inactive guarantees that all the files will be closed, thereby defusing the issue of what will be done about open files. This is not a very efficient idea, however, since it also guarantees that no work can be done while a backup is being performed. One of the most important principles for planning your backup routine is to make it as easy and convenient as possible for everyone involved so that backups are performed as scheduled.

With this in mind, it is best that backups be performed after hours when the use of the network is lowest. But, what would happen if there was an important project that needed to be finished and users were working late to accomplish this? You would either have to wait until they were finished to perform your backup or skip it entirely. Neither is a very inviting idea.

The programs that allow you to back up while files are open offer several ways to handle the problem of open files. Most back up software packages will halt the backup procedure when they encounter an open file. The person performing the backup then has the option to stop the backup completely, try to back up the file again, or skip that file entirely. The program will usually keep track of all the files that are bypassed in this manner so that they can be backed up later when they are not open.

But, watching a backup being performed can be described as tedious at best. Therefore, it is recommended that you look for software that allows for unattended backups (thus the need for tighter security discussed earlier) so that no one must be available to monitor the backup session. In an unattended backup, you can set the software to skip over and record in an error log any open files found. Or the software can return to an open file several times to try backing it up again. After a predetermined number of unsuccessful tries to backup a file, the software can record the persistently open file and continue on.

Available Types of Media

There are many choices of storage media available such as floppies, optical disks, and magnetic tape. Magnetic tape is probably the most popular because of its relatively large capacity and low cost. There are several common formats in use today, including Quarter-Inch Cartridge (QIC), 8mm Tape, and Digital Audio Tape (DAT). Quarter-Inch Cartridge tape drives record data in serial fashion on long serpentine tracks running the length of the tape. DAT and 8mm tape drives use a method of storing data quite different from QIC. Called helical scan, the method uses rotating read and write heads to magnetize the tapes in short diagonal tracks. DAT cartridges, however, are smaller than 8mm tape cartridges. DAT tape changers are also available that enable you to back up very large amounts of data without having to "babysit" the process in order to change tapes.

Optical drives make use of the same compact disk technology found in your stereo system. In fact, if you looked at a music CD and a CD containing computer files, you would not be able to tell the difference. A laser heats the disk to high temperatures, and a magnetic field is then used to repolarize the affected area with ever-present binary code. There are two types of optical disk technology that are useful to the backup procedure: write-once read-many (WORM) and rewriteable or erasable.

WORM technology lends itself to archiving of very important files because of its ability to write to an optical disk. Once you have written to a WORM disk, it becomes permanent and can't be erased and written over like magnetic media. Obviously, this could be more useful for archiving important files because you would not have to worry about them being over-written by accident. Conversely, this inherent inflexibility makes WORM technology a poor choice of storage media for backups, especially when you also consider how much more expensive optical technology is in relation to magnetic media.

There is a newer optical disk technology that enables you to erase and reuse optical disks just like magnetic disks or tapes. There are even optical disk changers called "jukeboxes" that can hold multiple optical disks. This makes optical disks as convenient as their magnetic counterparts with the added advantage of a shelf life of up to 100 years. However, the cost is still much too prohibitive to warrant replacing magnetic media. This greater cost makes optical media a poor choice for routine backups but is a consideration for use on critical backups of important data.

With the leaps that technology has been taking, hard drives have, in all practicality, become far too large for floppy disks to even be considered as a realistic alternative for regular backup procedures. For instance, if your file server has a 200 MB hard drive, it would take approximately 140 high-density (1.44 MB) floppies to back up your network. Now imagine a 1 gigabyte hard drive. You would be feeding floppies from now until doomsday. There is, however, an alternative.

Recently, optical technology was merged with the concept of a floppy disk to produce a "floptical" disk drive. Instead of the floppy containing a small magnetic disk, it contains a small optical one. Some of the new drives that this merger have produced can now support both media with read/write heads for both types of disk. Nevertheless, floppies are still very slow and best used by individual users to back up important files they do not want lost, erased, or corrupted by accident.

File-by-File vs. Imaging

There are two major flavors of backup software, depending upon the technique used to back up data. The first method is known as *imaging*. With imaging backup software, the operating system is ignored completely. Instead, an exact copy of the hard disk is made by transcribing the sectors, one by one and in order. For this reason, the imaging technique is very fast. All that is happening is that data is copied directly to the storage media with total disregard for the operating system's structures.

Unfortunately, this method is very inflexible. Because the operating system structures are not taken into account when the data is stored on the media, it is difficult to restore a specific directory or even a specific file since a file's bytes are rarely stored on a hard disk in the same place and in order. This is a serious inconvenience when you need to restore a very important file from a backup quickly.

The other and far more popular type of backup software is the *file-by-file* technique. This method copies files instead of sectors. This procedure takes into account the operating system's file and directory structures, which means you can specify which files to back up. Unlike imaging, file-by-file backups are much better at locating and restoring specific files and directories. Most will also allow you to restore files to a directory other than the one they were backed up from. This flexibility usually makes the file-by-file method the best choice.

Error Detection and Correction

There is always the chance that something will go wrong with any operation involving computers. If there wasn't, we would have no need to perform backups. And if that something happens during the transfer of data to the media you have chosen, it is imperative that you have some form of error detection and correction. (Remember, your backup needs to be as accurate as possible since it is your last line of defense against a catastrophic data loss.)

There are two predominant methods of error detection and correction: *read-after-write verification* and *redundant copies* of the data. After a block of data is written to the storage media, the read-after-write method compares the copied block directly to the original block on the hard drive to make sure an exact copy is made. If an error is detected, the block is rewritten to the storage media and the process of reading and comparing to the original is repeated until an exact copy has been made. This method helps eliminate "hard errors," those errors actually recorded on the storage media. The read-after-write method, however, is less effective with "soft errors," which are misreadings of the storage media.

The other popular method of error detection and correction is the redundant copies method. When a block of data is copied to the storage media, a duplicate is copied to a different location on the storage media. If an error is detected during the restore process, the correct information can usually be rebuilt from the two copies of the data. This obvious drawback is in the length of time it takes to back up your network, because you are actually backing it up twice.

Backup Speed and Size

Another thing to keep in mind when you are designing your backup system and procedures is the time it will take to complete a full backup. The less time a backup takes, the less time there is for a power surge or blackout to ruin it. Let's assume that we have 1 gigabyte to back up, and we have a tape drive averaging a relatively fast 10 MB a minute. A complete backup would run about 1 hour and 40 minutes and would probably need only one tape. No problem, right?

Now, consider how long it would take to back up 8 gigabytes of data. We realize that this is a large amount of data, but with hard disks becoming ever larger and cheaper, this much data to back up is becoming more of a reality in even small networks. Back to the example. This much data would take roughly 13 hours and 20 minutes, and would use several tapes depending on the tape size and compression rate. Now time takes on greater importance. If we left this backup at 5:30 P.M. to run overnight, it would still be running the next morning at 6:30 A.M. This also assumes that you have the storage media capable of handling that much data or some sort of media changer, or else you must physically stay on site to insert fresh storage media.

Remember, backups should be as simple and convenient as possible so there is no excuse not to do them. There are many ways that this problem of backup size and the length of time required can be solved. You can have several backup systems, each backing up well-defined portions of the network. More expensive systems with faster drives and larger storage capacities, such as optical jukeboxes and tape changers could be used. There are also simple strategies (described in this chapter) that can help to minimize the inconvenience of large backups. The point here is that the size of a backup and the length of time it will take are issues that should be addressed according to your situation.

Establishing Backup Procedures

Let's take a moment to review what we have covered so far. You should have a backup approach that nullifies security risks. You should also have a software package that has error detection and correction capabilities; it should also be able to adequately handle open files. You will probably have an accompanying tape system because of its large storage capacity and relatively low cost when compared to other media. The tape should be big enough so that the entire network system can be stored on it. If your network is too large for one tape, then a tape changer or a duplicate backup system will do nicely. Next, we will discuss what to do with this setup.

Simple Backup Schemes

Your data is too important to be lost when protecting your network is so easy. Some form of backup, whether full or partial, should be performed *every* day. A simple and effective scheme could include a full backup using a different tape marked for each day. Then, if a file had to be restored from three days earlier, you could go to that tape and restore from it.

Another strategy that would cut down on the time necessary to complete a backup would be to rotate between partial and complete backups. You could do a complete backup once a week and perform a partial backup of only those files that were modified for each of the other four workdays. Between the complete backup and the daily partials, you should be able to restore any file to the condition it was in at the time of the last backup. Make sure in any case that you always have two tapes with complete backups before you begin reusing your tapes. This scheme leaves you with two weeks of history at any one time.

On-Line, Near-Line, Off-Line

As stated, the problem of backup size and speed can be solved through many means, such as redundant systems, tape or disk changers, or mixing complete and partial backup procedures in a planned and intelligent manner. There are other solutions that combine all of these factors with the concept of data migration, which encompases on-line, off-line, and near-line storage.

On-line storage is data that can be immediately accessed, such as data on a hard drive. Near-line storage consists of data that is stored on tapes in a tape changer or optical disks in a jukebox. These files are still accessible from your workstation, but there may be a delay while the tape changer or optical jukebox finds, loads, and reads the correct disk or tape. Off-line storage is data stored on removable media that the user has to physically load and read in order to access.

Combining these storage concepts with your regular backup and archiving methods can improve both. For instance, you could migrate your seldom used data to a near-line storage setting (optical jukebox) where it is still accessible, but leaves room on your network disks for more frequently used files. All of your data should still be saved off-line on removable media.

An elegant way to solve the problem of backup length and size is to use a backup system that keeps a database of files that it backs up, the date each file was backed up, and the location of the file on the storage media. This backup software will, in essence, be doing a complete system backup the first couple of times that a backup is performed. Meanwhile, the database that the software creates and updates is keeping track of the location and age of every file on the storage media. By this, we mean that the database is recording whether each file has been modified since the last backup. When a file has not been modified at all for a certain amount of time, the software tags it as rarely used and will not back it up again until it has been modified. You end up having a complete backup each time you run the procedure, but it gets faster and faster because time is not wasted recopying files where no modifications have been made.

Network Printing

Most users will not have any trouble capturing ports and printing documents and data to them. There are, however, several ways to configure and control the printer ports, print queues, and print jobs that may prove useful from an administrator's point of view.

How Network Printing Works

In order to understand what is different about network printing and how to best use it, we should first take a look at how the print process works with a printer that is directly attached to a desktop computer (local printer). In the application you wish to print from, you normally designate to which printer port (LPT) the printer is attached. This tells the application where to send the print job. You also need to designate that printer driver to use. A printer driver is a program that translates the application commands and formatted text into instructions that the printer will understand. Once the document has been translated into the correct printer's instruction set, the job is sent to the designated printer port to the printer.

Printing to a network printer works in much the same way. There are, however, a few extra steps. The document or data you wish to print is still translated into the printer's instruction set with a printer driver. But instead of traveling to the printer through a printer port, the document or data is intercepted or "captured" before it can reach the printer port. The captured print job is diverted across the network and saved as a file in a special directory or "queue" located on a Personal NetWare server, which is sharing the printer you are trying to use. The print queue is automatically created and named for you when you designate the server's shared resources during the installation process.

The print job waits its turn in the print queue with other print jobs until the printer is ready for it. Generally, the print jobs are processed on a "first come, first served" basis, but you can manually alter the order in which print jobs are processed.

Configuring a Personal NetWare Print Queue

Personal NetWare allows you to set the following configuration options for a Personal NetWare queue:

- Define forms
- Designate a startup form name
- Set the character-per-second transfer rate
- Set the error wait time

- Set the DOS console time-out
- Determine serial port settings
- Designate the spooler directory
- Decide what to do with old print jobs
- Alter the printer status (Windows)
- Enter setup strings (DOS)
- Set access rights

The following further defines these queue configuration terms.

- **Forms:** Forms are used to cause the server controlling the printer to pause so that you can change paper sizes for the printer in question. You can define sizes such as legal or letter. When the server receives a print job in the printer queue that has a form different than what was most recently printed, the server will pause, enabling you to change to the correct stationery or paper size and change the printer status from Halted to Ready.

- **Character Transfer Rate:** The Character Transfer Rate is the number of characters transmitted to the printer each second.

- **Error Wait Time:** The Error Wait Time is the amount of time the server will wait for a response from the printer before it will assume that there is an error condition on the printer.

- **DOS Console Time-out:** The amount of time that a server will wait for its user to respond to a pop-up message before proceeding. The wait can be set for 0 to 300 seconds. The default will cause the server to wait indefinitely.

- **Serial Port Settings:** If you have a serial port, you can use this option to define serial port settings such as baud rate, parity, etc.

- **Spooler Directory:** The spooler directory is the print queue described earlier. It is normaly located at C:\NWCNTL\LPT*n* where *n* is the printer port number. This directory is where all the print jobs are placed until the printer is ready to output them. You can change the default to another directory with this option.

- **Old Print Jobs:** This option tells the server what to do with print jobs that are still in the queue when the server is started. The settings are Hold, Print, or Delete.

- **State (Windows only):** This option tells you the status of the printer. The printer can be either Halted or Ready. This option can be set with the Windows utilities only.

- **Setup Strings (DOS only):** Setup Strings are hexadecimal printer codes or escape sequences that set up the printer for a forthcomming print job. See your printer documentation for a listing of valid escape codes. This option can only be set with the NET ADMIN menu utility.
- **Access Rights:** Just as with other shared resources, you can control the access that users and groups have to the printer.

You must, of course, have Workgroup Administrator privileges on your user account before you can change or set any of the above options. Additionally, you need to have access rights (ALL) to the shared printer (print queue) in question. With shared printers, you can have either ALL or NONE as your designated access privileges.

To set or change any of the above options through DOS, use the NET ADMIN command. From the Administration menu utility, press **Alt-V** to bring the View submeu down, and select the Shared Printers option. As the menu suggests, another way to change the view to the see the shared printers is to press **Alt-P**. This will give you a list of shared printers for the workgroup you are logged in to. Highlight the printer whose queue you wish to modify, and press Enter.

NET ADMIN will show you a screen similar to Figure 9.1. Buttons and fields are available for setting the printer transmission rate, the error wait time period, serial printer information (if you have a serial printer), individual and default user rights, setup strings for the printer, and forms. Pressing Enter while the "Advanced Info..." button is highlighted will bring up the screen shown in Figure 9.2. This screen will allow you to set the startup form name, direct old print jobs, set the DOS console time-out, and set the location of the print queue (Spool Directory).

Configuring the print queue through Windows is just as simple. Open the Personal NetWare user utilities and double click on the NetWare icon. Expand the workgroup tree and highlight the shared printer whose queue you wish to configure. Open the File menu and select Properties. As the menu suggests, you can also press **Alt-Enter**. Whichever way you choose, you will see a screen similar to Figure 9.3.

This screen enables you to set the startup form name, the printer transmission rate, the error wait time, the DOS console time-out, the location of the print queue (Spool Directory); direct old print jobs; and set serial printer information (if you have a serial printer), forms, and the printer's state or status. To set up the individual and default user rights, open the File menu and then select "Rights..." (see Figure 9.4).

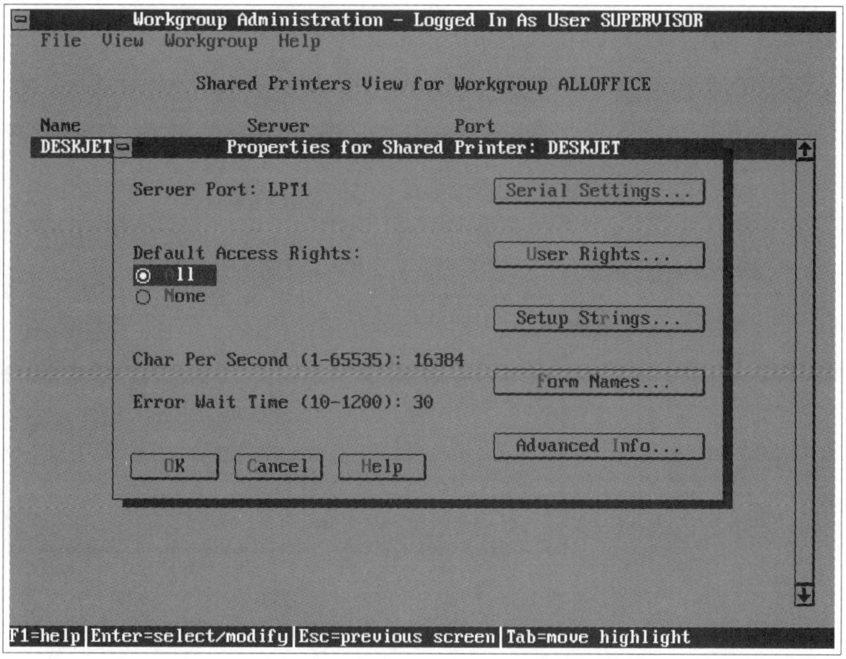

Figure 9.1   Configuring a Personal NetWare print queue through DOS.

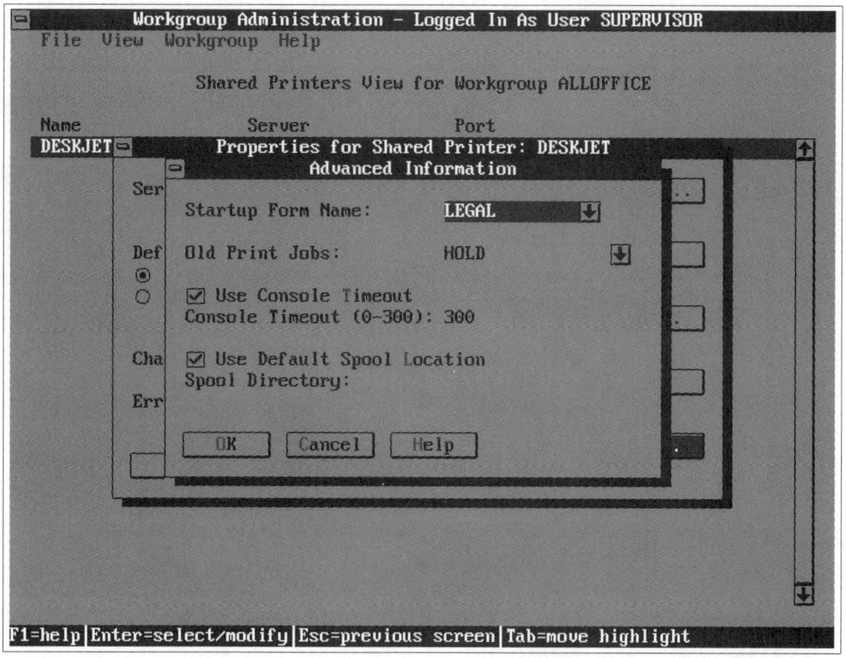

Figure 9.2   Advanced Personal NetWare print queue information.

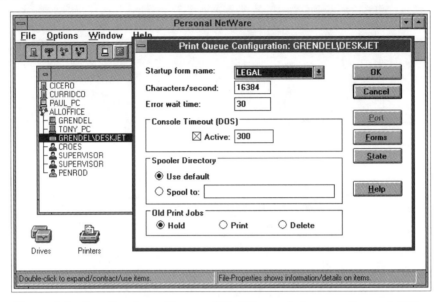

Figure 9.3   Configuring a Personal NetWare print queue through Windows.

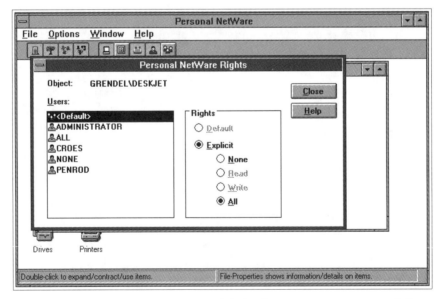

Figure 9.4   Setting individual and default print queue access rights.

Controlling a Personal NetWare Print Queue

Suppose you have just finished a rather large presentation and have sent the associated graphics to the print queue to ouput. Suddenly, an associate runs in and requests a document from you ASAP because he/she must leave to catch a plane. Your presentation graphics will probably take 20 minutes to print completely once they reach the printer. This may sound grim for your associate with poor planning habits, but not to worry, because Personal NetWare gives you a certain amount of control over a print job after it reaches the print queue. It allows you to perform the following actions to print jobs after they have reached the print queue:

- Add print jobs directly to the queue (DOS only)
- Delete print jobs from the queue
- Place print jobs on indefinite hold (restart them as well)
- Change the printing order from "First In, First Out" (DOS only)

To perform the above operations using the Windows user utilities, double click with the left mouse button on the Printers icon. You will see the familiar list of available printers and queues on the right and the currently captured printer ports on the left. Select the appropriate printer port, and double click it with the left mouse button. You will be shown a list of the current jobs in the print queue that is associated with the printer port you chose (see Figure 9.5).

If the print job icon is green (assuming that you are using a color monitor), the print job is currently being processed. Red means the job has been placed on hold, and white signifies any other print job condition. Highlight the job you wish either to place on hold, take off hold, or delete from the queue. Then click your left mouse button on the appropriate button: Pause or Resume to either place the print job on or take it off indefinite hold, or Delete to remove the print job from the print queue.

To perform these operations using the DOS interactive user utilities, type **NET** or **NET USER** at the DOS command line. Press **Alt-P** for the Printing menu, highlight the **Select print queue...** option, and then press Enter. You will be shown a list of print queue names and the server name they are associated with. Select the print queue that contains the print jobs you wish to reorder, add, delete, or place on hold, and then press Enter. You will be shown a screen similar to Figure 9.6, which contains a list of print jobs currently in the print queue.

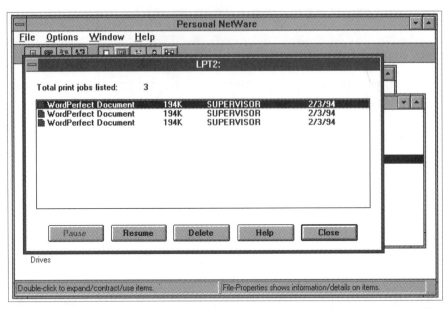

Figure 9.5 Controlling a print queue through the Windows user utilities.

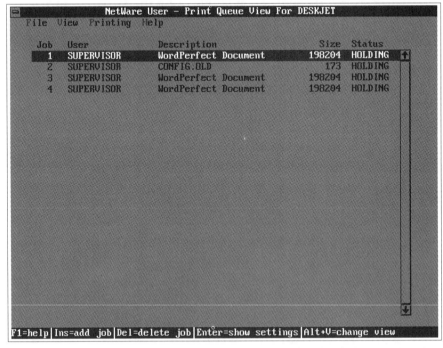

Figure 9.6 Controlling a print queue through the DOS interactive user utilities.

Press **Alt-P** to see the options you can perform on the print jobs in the queue. The available options are Print file... Ins, Delete job... Del, Move job..., and Job settings... Enter. Use the Ins key or the "Print file... Ins" menu option to bring up a screen to capture the name of a print file that you wish to add to the queue. Use the Del key or the "Delete job..." Del menu option to delete the highlighted print job from the queue. To move a print job to a new order in the queue, select the "Move job..." menu option and enter the number for the position you wish the job to be. The other print jobs will be reordered accordingly. To place a print job on or remove it from indefinite hold, use the "Job settings... Enter" menu option or press Enter on the highlighted print job. This option is explained in more detail in the following section.

Changing Port and Print Job Settings

In addition to changing the order of print jobs in the queue, deleting print jobs from the queue, and placing print jobs on indefinite hold, you can affect the following print job settings:

Hold	Places the port on indefinite hold.
Notify	Notifies the user when a print job has completed printing so it can be retrieved.
Form feed	Feeds a blank form following the completion of a print job.
Auto endcap	Closes the print job when the application that created it terminates.
Direct	Begins printing the print job before the print job has been enirely buffered or closed.
Tabs	Specifies the size of a tab character.
Time-out	Specifies the amount of time to wait after the last data was received until assuming the print job is finished.
Form type	Sets a defined form type or paper size.
Banner	Sends a banner to uniquely identify a print job and its owner.
Number of copies	Specifies the number of copies to print.
Setup strings (DOS)	Designates a defined setup string.

All of these printer port settings can be set using the NET CAPTURE DOS command and the appropriate arguments; additionally, all of them, with the exception of setup strings, can be assigned through the Windows user utilities.

To change port and printer job settings—Windows:

1. Open the Personal NetWare user utilities and double click on the Printers icon.
2. Highlight the printer port you wish to change the settings on and select the File pull-down menu and the Properties... Alt-Enter option. As the menu suggests, you can also press **Alt-Enter**. Whichever you choose, you will see a screen similar to Figure 9.7 where you can make the appropriate adjustments.

These printer port settings will be applied to every print job that is sent to the printer in question. You can, however, use the DOS interactive NET or NET USER menu utilities to adjust some of these settings for individual print jobs.

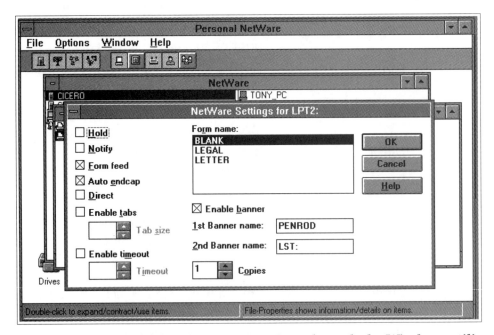

Figure 9.7 Adjusting the printer port settings through the Windows utilities.

To change port and printer job settings—DOS (interactive):

1. Type **NET** or **NET USER** at the DOS command line to start the DOS interactive user utilities.

2. Press **Alt-P** for the Printing menu, highlight the Select print queue... option, and then press Enter. You will be shown a list of print queue names and the server name they are associated with.

3. Select the print queue that contains the print job whose printer port settings you wish to individually modify and press Enter. You will be shown a list of print jobs currently in the print queue.

4. Select the print job you wish to modify and press Enter. A screen containing fields for changing the print job's settings will be shown to you (see Figure 9.8). As you can see, you can change the settings for an individual job for a banner, a form feed, an indefinite hold, user notification upon completion, the current form name, the number of copies, and the size of the tabs.

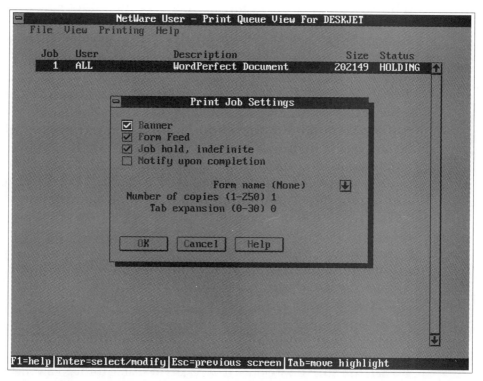

Figure 9.8 Changing individual print job settings.

Virus Protection

A virus is an executable program with one distinct feature: It copies itself using a host process or program to do so. There are many different kinds that perform many different functions (mostly malicious and destructive), but the one thing they all have in common is the ability to replicate.

A good "guesstimate" of the number of different viruses there are would probably be around 2,000, with more introduced every day. And, as anitviral software has become more adept at detecting these critters, the authors of such programs have become more efficient at hiding their creations. The point is, the days of the simple virus are gone. Virus programs are so sophisticated and behave so much like a real biological virus, that the name is justified.

The Enemy Tactics

One way that the new generation of computer viruses have adapted to survive is through a variety of "stealth" techniques designed to mask or camouflage their presence from antivirus measures. Early forms of viruses tricked DOS into thinking the infected file was the same size and unmodified. These viruses went so far as to restore the original file date and turn off the file's archive bit. Newer versions can mimic the file's signature, (a number derived from a mathematical formula used to give a program a unique identifier), thus fooling some antiviral software into thinking the file is not infected. These viruses have a component that intercepts disk I/O requests for DOS and returns false information about file size, and so forth.

Another new-generation virus is the polymorphic variety. Viruses in this category randomly mutate their own code as they replicate. This helps to hide their unique code "signature" from the software designed to scan for it. Other forms encrypt most of their code to mask their presence. When the program is loaded into memory, an unencrypted stub will decode the main portion of the code so that the virus can function.

The scenario is getting worse. The Dark Avenger Mutation Engine (DAME) is a polymorphic encryption engine believed to have originated in Bulgaria (the unofficial virus capital of the world). This virus building tool is widely available and easy to use. The would-be saboteur simply attaches the virus to the engine to build a virus capable of creating hundreds of different strains with each execution.

There are other do-it-yourself virus kits available through a variety of underground bulletin boards such as "The Phalcon/Skism Mass-Produced Code

Generator," the "Virus Construction Set," and the "Virus Construction Laboratory." Some even have GUIs, pull-down menus, and context-sensitive help utilities.

It is estimated that this malevolent atmosphere caused $2 billion in damages to businesses in 1993 alone. This is all compounded by the fact that it is still *not* illegal to write and distribute a virus in this country. Programming is largely thought of as writing, which can run a would-be lawmaker afoul with the First Amendment. Obviously, every network needs vigilant protection.

Antivirus Software

In order to protect your LAN from these electronic disasters, a good antivirus software package must have features able to detect, disinfect, and prevent virus attacks. Some packages address only one of these aspects, while others address all of them. The key is to plan a defense that includes one or more packages to cover all of these points. Some good examples are Fifth Generation's Untouchable, Central Point's Anti-Virus, Cheyenne's InocuLAN, Intel's LANProtect, McAfee Associates's NetShield, and Symantec's Norton AntiVirus.

The methods used to detect virus software have changed since they were first introduced in the mid-1980s. Many antivirus programs still rely mainly on the techniques of scanning for "signatures" or other unusual activity, and "integrity checking" to spot virus contamination. Signature scanning involves searching data for a match to code unique to a particular virus. There is a database of unique code or signatures for each type of virus the program recognizes. Another related form of scanning for viruses is to scan for virus stealth activity, including peculiar system interrupts or virus-like code that cannot be hidden, such as unusual jump instructions.

Integrity checking tries to spot signs of virus activity by comparing files with past information to see if they have been changed. The antivirus program calculates checksums using a variety of methods for a file that it is known to be uncorrupted. These checksums are compared to the new checksums calculated every time a file open request is made. If there is any difference, the antivirus software alerts the user. In this manner, viruses can be detected even if they are new and not yet a part of the signature database that the scanning function uses.

These methods are not foolproof. Some 50 new viruses are created every month. This, of course, creates a problem for the scanning method. If the signature is not in the database of viruses, the antivirus program will not identify this new strain as a virus. Vendor updates to the database are vital. On the other hand, if the database becomes too large, it becomes unwieldy, and performance suffers. To address the issues of performance and updates, some companies, such as Fifth Generation and Central Point, have developed complex mathematical algorithms to detect viruses, even if the signature is not listed in their databases.

The integrity checking method is not without fault, either. Whenever there is a change to a file, the user is alerted, and forced to decide whether the interruption is for a legitimate reason. These "false-positives" can be quite annoying, and may encourage a user to disregard alerts altogether.

Antivirus Hardware

There are also some hardware alternatives to virus protection being bandied about. AMI offers primary-boot protection through Hi-Flex BIOS, which monitors the boot sector, restricts access to it, and alerts the user when an attempt has been made.

Ergo Computing has developed a combination BIOS and software solution called Seat Belt. Seat Belt uses Ergo BIOS which contains Absolute Control of the Environment and Restoration Technology (ACERT) and monitoring software to check for modifications of the PC's master boot record, system files, and partition tables before the system boots up. These files are compared to stored images. If any discrepancies are found, the extraneous code is eliminated, and the A: drive is disabled to prevent booting from an infected floppy.

Western Digital has come up with a system called Immunizer that uses the System Management Interrupt (SMI) found on 386- and 486-based systems. Immunizer is a combination of Western Digital's WD7855 system logic controller and accompanying software, which looks for suspicious activity. Immunizer, basically, write-protects critical areas of the hard disk as well as executable programs. When a write request is directed at a protected area, an alert is sent to the user.

Along the same lines is the Thunderscan PC Immunizer from Electronic Systems and Special Services. This device is an 8-bit card with its own ROM BIOS system that serves as a buffer between the bus and the hard disk controller of a PC and looks for viral activity.

Another 8-bit card is the ViruStop PC Immunizer Card by Multix which monitors activity along the PC bus. Initially, this card scans memory and boot sectors for viral activity, and then screens bus activity, interrupting the user if suspected activity is discovered.

As you can see, there are many different solutions to fit all your needs, both hardware and software. It is important to remember that no solution is fool-proof because of the continual mutation of viral software. A good set of strategies is also needed.

Antiviral Strategies

It is much easier to prevent a virus from entering a computer than to go through the process of excising it from the machine. The following is a list of suggested steps to keep your data from being infected by a virus.

1. **Back up your data frequently:** One strategy that works to foil even early detected viral infections is to back up disks on a regular basis, use different diskettes or tape cartridges each time, and "age" the backups so that after several passes (usually three or four), the oldest one is recycled and becomes the newest backup. This technique works well with early detected infections, since at some point you have a clean backup without the virus. A variation is to back up only the data from the disk using the previous strategy. Since viruses infect program files, it will preserve the data files that you have constructed, while the program files can be restored to the disk from the original distribution media.

2. **Purchase and use an antivirus package:** Any good antivirus software is better than none at all. The keyword here is use. Viruses will infect a system at some point (usually the most inconvenient, according to Murphy), and if the software is not in use, the virus will gain a toehold and create a problem that might have been preventable.

3. **Check all files coming from an outside source:** Many times, viruses will piggy-back on files that are downloaded from public bulletin board systems, Bitnet, and even the Internet. It is good practice to scan any file that comes into your computer from one of these sources. Most system operators and administrators are diligent about checking for such things, but accidents happen. Better to be safe than sorry.

   Floppies are the most frequent carrier of viruses. In fact, it is the preferred medium of distribution. After acquiring antiviral software, check all personal floppies and distribution floppies under your control to give them a clean bill of health. More important, check every floppy that comes to your system from somewhere else. You really don't know where it has been. It could be carrying a virus it picked up as recently as the last system it was inserted into, even if care to prevent infection was taken.

One other suggestion is to write-protect floppies that are going to be read from on other systems. This will prevent a virus from latching on during a read to the disk.

4. **Check all shareware and public domain programs:** Do not purchase and use these programs on unchecked media, especially those from a mail order house. Check them with your antiviral software to guarantee their cleanliness.

5. **Check all commercial packages:** Never assume that because the software is in the original shrink wrap that it is 100 percent safe. There are dealers that have a return policy that allows a purchaser time to try the product and return it for any reason. While they are supposed to return the package to the original manufacturer, some vendors will re-wrap the package and make it available for sale. There have been cases reported where software has been returned with a virus on it. If any part of the shipping package looks like it has been tampered with, such as fingerprints, writing in the manuals, a broken disk pack seal, return it to the vendor for another copy and report it to them.

   ZINC software, in 1992, accidentally shipped first-run copies of its ZINC Interface 3.0 package with the FORM 18 virus on the boot sector of the disks. This created problems for many people. ZINC responded by issuing a letter informing those people who had received the software of the problem and made antiviral software available on a limited basis to clean the disks. Fortunately, the FORM 18 virus is benign and only makes a clicking noise on the speaker when you press a key.

6. **Do not loan original program diskettes to other people:** Loaning out an original puts it at risk of acquiring a virus. Instead, use a copy of the original and either check the disk or format it when it is returned. (This, by the way, presumes that loaning out a copy of the program is legal because of site license agreement or other legal arrangement with the software vendor.)

7. **Do not loan your workstation to other people:** If circumstances require that you share your workstation, make certain that visitors use your diskettes and programs. If they must use their own diskettes, check them prior to use.

8. **Mark all .EXE and .COM files as read-only:** This is a simple way to keep the less sophisticated viruses out of your program files. DOS provides the means to do this with the ATTRIB command. This command changes the

aread-only flag so that normal write operations to a file will fail, thus stopping attempts to modify it. Enter the following commands from the root directory:

```
ATTRIB +R *.EXE /S
```

and

```
ATTRIB +R *.COM /S
```

The commands will make all program files with those extensions read-only, from the root directory down through all the subdirectories.

9. **Mark all DOS executables in shared directories with read-only permission:** This prevents most viruses from latching onto a shared program and traveling from workstation to workstation within the workgroup.

10. **Periodically scan all DOS executable files on workstations:** An ounce of prevention is worth a pound of cure. Even the most diligently managed workstations and servers will, at one time or another, allow a virus to slip in undetected.

11. **Restrict access to the network:** The easiest way to combat virus infections is to restrict access to your network. Provide diskless workstations that will boot remotely (discussed later in this chapter) so that users can't introduce a virus (knowingly or not) through a floppy drive.

12. **Teach users to how to manage their resources:** Education of users is of the utmost importance. Teaching them to use virus scanning software can be important if they do not have diskless workstations.

If you are prepared, a virus attack can turn out to be just a minor nuisance. Taking viruses lightly, however, can lead to some serious trouble with your data's integrity, and imperil your ability to conduct business.

Working with the Novice User

One of the tasks a network administrator will find him/herself performing quite often is working closely with new and novice users. The obvious goal of this task is training. Training to use the network resources, applications, and proper maintenance procedures. The easiest and least frustrating way to do this is to train slowly and in measured steps. Automate and restrict the novice user's network environment as much as possible in the beginning. Personal NetWare provides you with two specific means, in addition to the security functions mentioned in the last chapter, by which you can automate and restrict the user's network environment: user login scripts and diskless workstations.

Login Scripts

One of the simplest and easiest ways to automate a user's network environment is with login scripts. A login script is a set of instructions tailored to a particular user's needs. It sets the user's network environment so that they are ready to work from the beginning of the network training session. These instructions can include drive letter mappings, capturing printer ports, and setting DOS environment variables (see Example 9.1). The point here is to do this automatically so that the novice user does not have to know how to perform these sorts of tasks. You can move on to the more important job of teaching the user how to use the network applications to do his or her job more efficiently. You can even set up different login scripts run by different batch files so the user can have several setups, if necessary.

```
@ECHO OFF

rem ** Login to the net. You may change the user name if you want. **

net login ALLOFFICE\NEW_GUY

rem ** Map Drives **

net map F: GRENDEL_DRVC GRENDEL

rem ** Capture Ports **

net capture LPT2 DESKJET GRENDEL B=Y F=Y H=Y W=0 S=

rem ** DOS Environment Variables **

set PROMPT=$p$g
set TEMP=c:\os\dos\temp
set SHIVA=c:\utils\shiva
set NWLANGUAGE=ENGLISH
set COMSPEC=Y:COMMAND.COM
set PATH=Z:.;Y:.;X:.;W:.;C:\PROGRAMS\WINWORD;C:\NETWARE\PNW\NWCLIENT;
    C:\OS\WIN31;C:\;C:\OS\DOS;C:\UTILS;C:\UTILS\SHIVA;
```

Example 9.1   An example login script.

Creating a login script for a user is a fairly simple procedure. The most important thing to do is set up the workstation exactly as it needs to be. Map the network drives so the user can access the relevant applications and data files. Capture the printers he or she will need to use, and set any other variables that must be in place for the applications and services. Once the workstation has been prepared, use the NET SAVE command line utility or the NET (NET USER) interactive utility to save the network environment to a login script.

Type **NET SAVE /S** to save the current workstation configuration to the Personal NetWare control directory (NWCNTL). Type **NET SAVE /D** to delete the current login script from the control directory. If you want to save the workstation configuration to a batch file, type **NET SAVE** *filename*.**BAT** where *filename* is the name of the file you are saving to. If you type **NET SAVE** with no arguments, the current workstation configuration will be saved as a batch file named NWLOGIN.BAT.

Saving the login script as a bat file will allow you to automate the startup procedure for a novice user even further. Log in as the user, and type **NET SAVE** *filename*.**BAT** to save the workstation configuration. This configuration also will include logging in to the correct user account. Modify the login line of the user's STARTNET.BAT file to read **NET LOGIN @***filename*.**BAT**.

All the user will have to do is turn the workstation on and enter his or her password when prompted to do so. Everything else will be set up automatically.

As mentioned earlier, you can use the NET (NET USER) interactive DOS utility to save a login script. Type **NET** to start the utility, press **Alt-F** to open the File menu, and select the "Save script..." option to save the login script. A note will appear to tell you where the login script has been saved. If you need to edit this script, choose the "Edit script..." option.

Setting Up Diskless Workstations

Setting up a diskless workstation helps out in two areas: improved security and automating the network for novice users. One of the first tasks that you will need to perform in order in implement remote program loading is to prepare the diskless workstation by adding a Remote Boot Programmable Read-Only Memory (PROM) chip to the NIC and creating a Remote Boot Disk Image File (Boot Image).

Preparing the boot image is a little more complicated a procedure. Basically, the procedure involves collecting the necessary files to boot the workstation and log in to the network on a bootable floppy disk. An image of this disk is generated in the LOGIN directory of the Personal NetWare server from which the diskless workstation will boot. When the diskless workstation is turned on, the boot PROM grabs the boot image of the bootable floppy disk and uses it to complete the startup procedure just as if the PC were booting from a floppy or hard drive.

Preparing the Personal NetWare Server

The first step in preparing the Personal NetWare server from which the remote workstation will boot is to create a shared directory called LOGIN. Copy the contents of the RPL directory to the newly created LOGIN directory. The RPL directory is a subdirectory of NWCLIENT. The LOGIN shared directory is where you will generate the diskless workstation's boot image.

Additionally, you will need to copy to the LOGIN shared directory NET.EXE and IBM_RUN.OVL from the NWCLIENT directory, and NETC.MSG from the NWCLIENT\NLS\ENGLISH directory. These are the files necessary to run the NET DOS utilities. Any other program that you call from either STARTNET.BAT or AUTOEXEC.BAT *after* VLM.EXE is loaded, must be copied to the LOGIN shared directory as well.

You must make two additional modifications to the server. The programs RPL.COM and NEARSERV.EXE must be loaded in order for the remote program loading to occur. Probably the best place for these calls to occur is in the STARTNET.BAT file after the call for VLM.EXE. Simply add the lines C:\LOGIN\RPL.COM and C:\LOGIN\NEARSERV.EXE to the STARTNET.BAT file for the server so that they will be loaded automatically when the server is started. This placement does not require that a user account log in to the network from the server before these programs will be run. In other words, do not place the calls following the NET LOGIN command in the STARTNET.BAT.

NEARSERV.EXE Will Not Load If...

If you have a bindery server on the network, NEARSERV.EXE will not load. NEARSERV.EXE can only be used on an exclusively Personal NetWare network. If you have a bindery server, use the remote boot procedures for it.

Preparing the Diskless Workstation

The first step in preparing the diskless workstation, installing the remote boot PROM, is a fairly simple operation, and detailed installation instructions should come with it. You may have to temporarily install a floppy drive in the diskless workstation in order to configure a jumperless NIC or configure the NIC in another similar workstation with a floppy drive and then transfer it.

The second step in preparing the diskless workstation, creating the boot image, is a little more involved. The first order of business is to create a bootable floppy by typing **FORMAT A: /S** at the DOS prompt when the floppy you are going to format as a system disk is in the A: floppy drive. You next need to create or modify an AUTOEXEC.BAT file, a CONFIG.SYS file, and a NET.CFG file designed for the diskless workstation. The AUTOEXEC.BAT should contain the following lines in addition to any others you deem necessary in order to set the environment for the diskless workstation:

@ECHO OFF

LSL

RPLODI.COM   (This line is optional. See "Working with Older Remote Boot PROMs for more information.)

driver.COM   (Where *driver* is the name of the specific NIC ODI driver the diskless workstation will use.)

IPXODI

VLM

NET LOGIN

NET MAP C: LOGIN

SET COMPEC = C:\COMMAND.COM

C:

Place one copy of this file on the bootable floppy that you have created and one in the server's LOGIN directory.

The CONFIG.SYS file should contain the following line, in addition to any others you deem necessary in order to set the environment for the diskless workstation:

LASTDRIVE = Z

You will also need a copy of the Personal NetWare server's NET.CFG file. This file should have the LINK DRIVER section modified to match the settings for the diskless wokstation's NIC. Be sure that both the server you will boot from and the diskless workstation are using the same frame type (for example, Ethernet_802.2).

You should copy to or create on the bootable floppy you have prepared all of the following files:

COMMAND.COM

CONFIG.SYS   (See the previous discussion for modifications.)

AUTOEXEC.BAT   (See the previous discussion for modifications.)

NET.CFG   (See previous discussion for modifications.)

LSL.COM

RPLODI.COM   (This file is optional. See "Working with Older Remote Boot PROMs" for more information.)

driver.COM   (Where *driver* is the name of the specific NIC ODI driver the diskless workstation will use.)

IPXODI.COM

VLM.EXE

CONN.VLM

FIO.VLM

GENERAL.VLM

IPXNCP.VLM

NWP.VLM

PNW.VLM

REDIR.VLM

SECURITY.VLM

TRAN.VLM

The final step in creating the boot image is to generate the image in the server LOGIN directory using DOSGEN.EXE. Move to the server's LOGIN shared directory. Place the bootable floppy with all the appropriate files listed above in drive A: (or drive B:). From the LOGIN shared directory, run DOSGEN.EXE by typing **DOSGEN A:**. DOSGEN.EXE will create the boot image called NET$DOS.SYS and place it in the LOGIN shared directory. On your screen you will see something similar to this:

```
C:\LOGIN>DOSGEN A:
Floppy Type: 3 1/2 inch, 1.44 MB
Total Floppy Space 2880 Sectors
Transferring Data (747 Sectors) to "NET$DOS.SYS"

C:\LOGIN>
```

Reboot the server so that the RPL.COM and NEARSERV.EXE programs will be loaded. You should now be ready for remote login.

Working with Multiple Remote Boot Disk Image Files

What happens if you want to boot multiple workstations from a Personal NetWare server? Because they would all have to be exactly alike so they could use the same files that make up the boot image, down to the settings of the NIC defined in the NET.CFG file, this is not quite so easy to arrange. If the workstations that you wish to boot are not alike, either their AUTOEXEC.BAT, CONFIG.SYS, NET.CFG, or all of these files will be different. You may even wish to use different versions of DOS. Consequently, you will have to make multiple boot disk image files.

The process for dealing with multiple boot images is different in only a few ways. You still will create a boot disk, but you will create one for each workstation setup. If you have five different workstations, you will have five boot disks, each tailored to its workstation. Additionally, you will need to create a subdirectory under the LOGIN shared directory for each version of DOS you will be using, and copy the appropriate system files into each. You will find the process easier if you temporarily install a floppy disk to boot from. This will come in handy later when you need to determine the network address for the diskless workstations.

After you have created all the boot disks, rename the AUTOEXEC.BAT file of each boot disk so that it is unique for each version of workstation. For example, for the first workstation configuration, you might rename the AUTOEXEC.BAT file to STATION1.BAT by typing at the A:> DOS prompt, **REN AUTOEXEC.BAT STATION1.BAT**. In its place on each boot disk, create a new AUTOEXEC.BAT whose only function is to call the renamed AUTOEXEC.BAT (now named STATION1.BAT in our example). Copy all the renamed AUTOEXEC.BAT files (for example, STATION1.BAT) to the LOGIN directory. Finally, using a text editor, create in the LOGIN shared directory a file named AUTOEXEC.BAT, which contains only a single line of 12 blank spaces.

At this point, you will need to create all the boot disk image files. You still will use DOSGEN.EXE to create the boot disk image files, but this time you will provide it with a unique name for the .SYS file that will be generated in the LOGIN shared directory. In the LOGIN shared directory, type **DOSGEN A: STATION1.SYS** (using our previous example) at the DOS prompt. You will see the following (or something similar) on your monitor:

```
C:\LOGIN>DOSGEN A:STATION1.SYS
Floppy Type: 3 1/2 inch, 1.44 MB
Total Floppy Space 2880 Sectors
Transferring Data (747 Sectors) to "STATION1.SYS"

C:\LOGIN>
```

The final step you will need to perform when working with multiple boot image files is to create a boot configuration system file (BOOTCONF.SYS) in the LOGIN directory. The BOOTCONF.SYS file lists each remote workstation and which boot image file it should use. The first order of business is to use the NET INFO command to determine the diskless workstation's network and station address (Figure 9.9). If you have not already done so, install a floppy drive so you can use the boot disk you have made to log in to the network and use the NET INFO command. An alternative would be to set the workstation up using the single boot disk image method, and obtain the two addresses in that way for all the diskless workstations.

The network address and the station address make up the last piece of information that NET INFO shows you, Machine address. The first set of

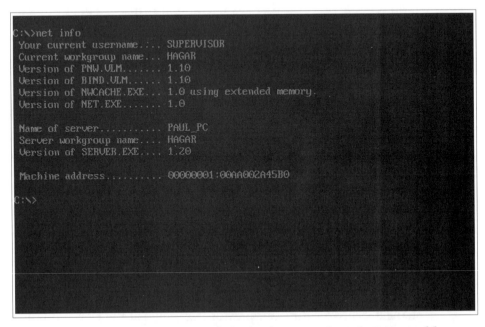

Figure 9.9 Determining the workstation's network and station addresses.

numbers, 00000001 in our example, is the network address. The second set of alphanumeric characters, 00AA002A45B0 in our example, is the station address. Using this information and the name of the boot image file, build the individual lines of the BOOTCONF.SYS using the following elements in this order:

- The number zero and the letter x (0x) to signify a hexadecimal number
- The network address (00000001) in hex
- A comma (,)
- The station address (00AA002A45B0), also in hex
- The equal sign (=)
- The boot image file name (STATION1.SYS)
- A comma (,)
- (Get Near Server) GNS

Our example line of the BOOTCONF.SYS file should resemble:

```
0x00000001,00AA002A45B0=STATION1.SYS,GNS
```

Next, remove the floppy disk installed earlier in the workstation and restart the server so that NEARSERV.EXE and RPL.COM will be loaded.

Working with Older Remote Boot PROMs

There are two basic versions of remote boot PROMs in use with NetWare networks: an older version (old) and a newer enhanced version (enhanced). There are several key differences between them which can affect the boot image generation process. The old version supports only the Ethernet_802.3 and Ethernet_II frame types; the enhanced version does *not* support the Ethernet_802.3 frame type, which makes it very important that you know the frame type you will be using and whether the boot PROM will support it.

The old version of the boot PROM also requires some additional software support. The program RPLODI.COM must be one of the files on the boot floppy from which you are creating the boot image. Additionally, a call to run the program RPLODI.COM must be made in the AUTOEXEC.BAT file immediately following the call to LSL.COM.

Finally, the old version of the boot PROM cannot correctly read a boot image that is created for MS DOS 5.x or better. You must alter the boot image file with RPLFIX.COM so that the boot PROM will be able to read it. Type **RPLFIX NET$DOS.SYS** from the LOGIN shared directory to alter the boot image file.

Conclusion

In this chapter, we discussed the basics of network backup and virus protection. Paying attention to these two issues can prevent a lot of heartache and lost valuable data. We also discussed how to run the network more smoothly through managing the network printing functions and helping novice users get their feet wet. All of these issues are administrative in nature and deserve special attention so that they do not become a problem that causes deterioration in workgroup productivity.

Chapter 10

Working with Other Versions of NetWare

Introduction

S o far, we have been concerned only with Personal NetWare and how to use it to network PCs effectively. But what about using Personal NetWare with other versions of NetWare? After all, they all use the same client software. In this chapter, we will examine some of the strategies for using Personal NetWare workgroups effectively with other versions of NetWare. We will also examine how to take advantage of some of the features provided by the NetWare DOS Requester. In enterprise environments, Personal NetWare is the ideal client. It adds peer-to-peer connectivity and workgroup features to the strong foundation provided in native NetWare.

Understanding Network Routes

In a purely Personal NetWare network, there is no need for network routers. If, you work with other versions of NetWare as part of a larger network, there is a good possibility that the network will have routers running. In NetWare, each server on the network has a unique *internal network number*, and each network segment has a unique *network number*. Whenever data must travel from one network to another, it must cross a router. NetWare uses two types of routers: Internal and External.

Each NIC in a server is connected to an external network with its own network number, while the server's bus is an internal network with a network number. Figure 10.1 shows an internetwork with native NetWare servers and internal routers and Personal NetWare servers and workstations. A *hop* occurs when packets must cross over one network to reach another. With Personal NetWare, there is no integral routing software so Personal NetWare must supply the router with the addresses of other networks it needs to reach. When part of a larger environment, you must use these network routes to reach Personal NetWare servers on other network segments.

A Personal NetWare route consists of two parts: a network number and a node number mask (typically FFFFFFFFFFFF h) in the form *network:node_mask*. For example 00000001:FFFFFFFFFFFF is a valid network route in Personal NetWare. It is also important to remember that a Personal NetWare server uses a different routing table (stored in a binary server configuration file) than the one used by the client software for a workstation (stored in the client software NET.CFG file).

This translates to the fact that a workstation can belong to one workgroup that consists of several nodes on different networks while the server running on the same workstation can be serving a different workgroup consisting of other nodes on other networks. If you find this confusing, you're not alone, but hang on for a minute and we'll straighten this out.

The basic idea behind network routes is to allow workstations on two sides of a network router to be a part of the same workgroup whether they are servers are workstations. It does not matter if your local server (on your station) is supporting a spreadsheet for the workgroup ACCOUNTING while you access services from the workgroup ADMIN on another network, *or* your server is part of the same workgroup as the one you are logged in to, the basic idea is the same. The net result is that you as a user can be logged into a different workgroup than the one your server is a part of. This is convenient if you use the resources of a particular workgroup most of the time (the one your server is a part of) but periodically need services provided by another workgroup.

You can control the routing table for a workstation in two ways. First, you can directly edit the NET.CFG file; and second, you can use the NET WGFIND command. This command locates all of the workgroups it can find from the routers on your internetwork, and places the addresses of those you specify in the NET.CFG file. Once this is done, it is possible for you as a user to access resources from the servers in these workgroups.

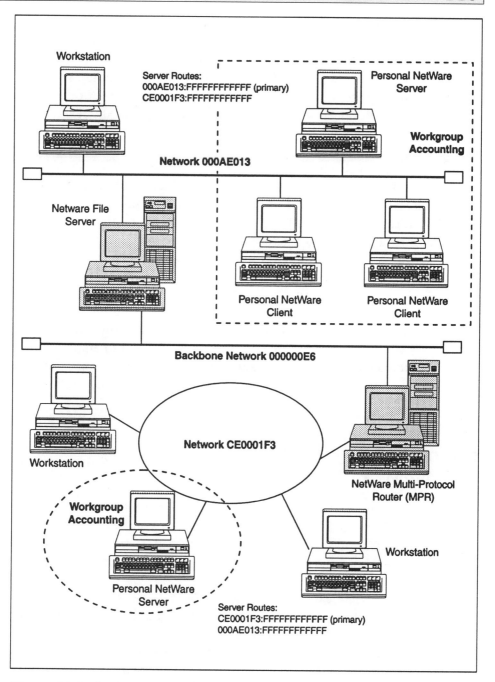

Figure 10.1   An internetwork with internal NetWare routers.

Servers use the routing table for a workgroup to determine which computers are part of the same workgroup, regardless of which network they are on. To access the routing table for a server, you must use NET ADMIN. In NET ADMIN under the Workgroups menu, there is an option for Routes. Selecting this option brings up the current routing table for the workgroup. A workgroup route allows the two Personal NetWare servers on Network 000000AE:FFFFFFFFFFFF and the three servers on network 01BE0020:FFFFFFFFFFFF to be a part of the same workgroup.

You can also have your server play "follow me" when you move from one workgroup to another. From the Servers View in NET ADMIN, there might be a server marked Local in the list, or it might say that the server is Local, in Workgroup SOME_OTHER_WORKGROUP. In the first instance, the server is part of the same workgroup to which you are logged in. In the second, the workgroup you are logged in to (shown at the top of the screen) is different from the one your server is currently part of.

You can change this from within NET ADMIN in one of two ways. The first is to select your server from the list, and then select Properties from the FILE menu. One of the options in this menu is Workgroup, and it enables you to move the server (and its resources if you choose) to another workgroup. The alternative is to use the Create option from under the Workgroups menu. This allows you to create a completely new workgroup and move your server and resources into this workgroup.

Improving Performance and Security on NetWare Networks

The Universal Client allows Personal NetWare networks to integrate seemlessly with NetWare 3.12 and 4.01. This ability to work so closely with other versions of NetWare means you can take advantage of several features that NetWare 3.12 and 4.01 provide natively, which can help you improve security and network performance.

On a small exclusively Personal NetWare network, these issues are not so important. But, when you are integrating your Personal NetWare network into a much larger and varied network with hundreds of clients, multiple NetWare servers, and most likely several router hops between you and your data and applications, these issues of security and network performance can become quite important.

Enabling Packet Burst Mode

To begin with, NetWare Core Protocol (NCP) is a set of procedures that a NetWare server performs in order to accept and respond to a client's request for services. Each request for a service from the server is, of course, divided into the appropriate packet size, and sent one packet at a time to the server (Write Request). In older versions of NetWare, the server responded with an acknowledgment after the receipt of each packet. This process was reversed when responses to the client were sent (Read Request). For every NCP packet, there was an acknowledgment packet returned to the sender (one request/one response).

As you can see, this need to respond to each NCP packet is a very inefficient means of communication. It would save time and cut down on traffic to send all the packets that make up an NCP request or response and not wait for the acknowledgment of the receipt of each individual packet. Then, you could wait until all the packets have been received, and return only one acknowledgment that lets the sender of the request or response know that all the packets were received in good order. This is basically what Packet Burst Mode is all about.

Packet Burst is a protocol that sits on top of IPX and is used to speed the transfer of multipacket NCP requests between a client and a server. For Instance, Packet Burst allows a client to send a read request to the server without the necessity of a reply. Instead, the server simply returns the requested data in a series of packets one right on the heels of another. There is no need for the client to acknowledge the receipt of each packet before the next is sent. In the same vein, when the client sends a write request, all the packets are sent before the server sends a single response acknowledging that all the packets were received. If packets are lost, only the missing packets are retransmitted.

Not all NCP requests can be sent in a single group of packets. Some NCP requests can be very long and require several sets of packets and the associated acknowledgments to be completely transmitted. In order to tune the number of packets for the best network performance, Packet Burst can also adjust itself to the appropriate "burst" lengths through a dual volume-throttling mechanism. This mechanism is made up of an expanding and contracting windows-size algorithm and a packet-transmission metering value. These two parameters are negotiated by each client with the server at the time a connection is established through a complex transmission rate control algorithm.

For any client using the VLM shells, packet burst is automatically an option. In fact, the VLM shells will automatically self-tune the Packet Burst buffers, read and write windows size parameters. Packet Burst is also native to NetWare 3.12, 4.0, and 4.01 operating system code. For older versions of NetWare such as 3.11, you will need to load the PBURST.NLM on the server, and use BNETX.COM instead of NETX.COM with the client software.

It is the older versions of NetWare with which you need be concerned. The next section deals mainly with BNETX, so if you are still dealing with a workstation that does not use the VLM shell, you will have the information you need.

As mentioned, there are three parameters that you can set in the NetWare DOS Requester option section of the NET.CFG file to control Packet Burst with BNETX: buffers, read windows size, and write windows size. The number of buffers is set with the line:

```
PB BUFFERS = number
```

The range for *number* is 0 to 10 buffers with a default of 3. Since there is a default, this line is optional for both BNTEX and VLM. Setting the buffers to 0 turns Packet Burst off for both VLM and BNETX. This is the only line that will affect VLM shells, since VLMs automatically set Packet Burst to on, and negotiate the best settings with the server at the time of connection.

With BNETX, you will need to experiment with the number of buffers to find the best configuration. Each buffer holds one complete frame of the access protocol type your network supports. For example, if you choose 6 buffers and are using Ethernet, the buffers will add 9,000 bytes to the size of your shell. This is not normally a problem unless your shell starts to approach the 64,000 byte segment limit imposed on it.

The Packet Burst read and write windows size is also negotiated automatically for VLM. You can alter the defaults for BNETX with the following lines in the NetWare DOS Requester option section of the NET.CFG file:

```
PBURST READ WINDOWS SIZE = number
PBURST WRITE WINDOWS SIZE = number
```

The range for *number* is 2 to 64 with a default of 16 for read and 10 for write. The default settings have been carefully chosen for greater reliability in a wide variety of installations, and performance increases beyond the default settings is minimal at best. It is recommended that you do not alter the default settings since critical network errors could result if care is not taken.

Utilizing Large Internet Packets

When you are dealing with NetWare networks, chances are good that you will be dealing with routers, either internal or external. One of the benefits of a router is that it segments a network, which reduces traffic. Only packets that need to reach a node on the other side of the router are passed through. This means that, if one segment of the network is experiencing heavy traffic, another segment on the other side of the router will not necessarily be affected since only packets addressed to a destination on the other side will be allowed to pass through.

Normally, when information needs to be passed through a router to a destination on the other side, the packet sizes are automatically set to 576 bytes. This breaks down to 512 bytes of data and 64 bytes of header information. Large Internet Packets (LIP) support permits larger packets to be passed across routers. This will help your network's performance, since fewer data packets and the associated confirmation packets will be required to send a transmission.

LIP support allows packet sizes of up to 4,202 bytes (token ring). Theoretically, packet sizes of up to 16,384 bytes can be supported, but token ring is the largest packet size a normal topology supports. Basically, how large a packet you can send is determined by the largest size packet your particular topology will support.

If both the workstation and the server support LIP, they will negotiate the packet size at the time the connection between the two is made. The router is disregarded when the packet size is set unless the packet size is hard-coded into the router. In this case, the packet size will be forced to remain at the hard-coded value. Additionally, if a station without LIP support connects with the server with LIP support on the other side of a router, the packet size will remain at 576 bytes since both parties do not support LIP.

NetWare 3.12, 4.0, and 4.01 now support LIP natively in the operating system. The support is also built into the VLM shells. If you are dealing with older versions of NetWare 3.x and wish to support LIP, you will need to load PBURST.NLM for the server and the NETX.EXE v3.31 shell for the client.

Turning LIP support on or off is the only parameter you can affect when you are using VLM shells. Typing the line **LARGE INTERNET PACKETS = ON** in the NetWare DOS Requester option section of the NET.CFG file will turn LIP support on. It is, however, unnecessary since LIP support is activated by default. Typing the line **LARGE INTERNET PACKETS = OFF** will prevent LIP support for the workstation.

If you are using NETX.EXE on your client, support for LIP must be turned on by typing the following lines in the NetWare DOS Requester option section of the NET.CFG file:

```
LARGE INTERNET PACKETS=1
```

which turns support on

```
LI FRAME MAX = number
```

where *number* falls in the range of 512 to 16,384 bytes. This line is optional; 512 is set for the default unless otherwise specified.

Enabling NCP Packet Signature

NetWare Core Protocol (NCP) Packet Signature is a feature that improves security by making it next to impossible to forge a valid NCP packet. At the time of connection, the client and the server determine whether packet signature will be used for the session about to be established. There are three outcomes possible: login is unsuccessful, packet signature is used, and packet signature is not used.

If packet signature is used in the session, the client and the server will settle on a unique session key that determines the packet signatures to be used between the server and this particular client for that session only. If a new session is established later, the session key will be different.

For each packet passed between the client to the server, a signature will be generated based on the mutually agreed upon session key, and attached to the packet. If the server determines that the NCP packet has a valid signature attached to it, then the server will accept the packet and process the request. A new signature is attached to the reply request and returned to the client.

If the signature is determined to be invalid by the server for this particular session or missing when one is required, the packet is ignored. An alert is also generated and sent to the server's console and copied into the server's error log file. The client sending counterfeit NCP packets will only be informed that an error occurred during the connection process.

Changing the level of security for Packet Signature is a simple matter. To change the security level from the default value for the server, you simply type the following line at the file server console:

```
SET NCP PACKET SIGNATURE OPTION = number   (default value = 2)
```

The variable *number* can have any of the following values:

0 = The server does not support NCP Packet Signature.

1 = The server signs packets only if requested to do so by the client.

2 = The server signs packets if the client is able to do so.

3 = Packet Signature support is required of the client for a successful login.

This line can also be added to the server's AUTOEXEC.NCF file to make the change last beyond "downing" the server.

The client's level of security is changed in the NET.CFG file. Under the NetWare DOS Requester option section of the NET.CFG file, enter the following line to alter the level of security for the workstation client:

SIGNATURE LEVEL = *number*   (default value = 1)

The variable *number* can have any of the following values:

0 = The client does not support NCP Packet Signature.

1 = The client signs packets only if requested to do so by the server.

2 = The client signs packets if the server is able to do so.

3 = Packet Signature support is required of the server for a successful login.

Setting up Workstations for Automatic Backup with NetWare's SBACKUP.NLM

In a normal Personal NetWare network, backing up the network can be a simple operation. A workstation could have a drive mapping to each of the network hard disks on the various Personal NetWare servers. There are usually 21 drive letters available for this. There probably won't be more than 20 workstation and/or workstation/servers out there anyway, since performance suffers with too many Personal NetWare nodes in the same workgroup. It should be a simple matter to script the backup procedure to access the necessary network drives and back them up.

But what happens when your workgroup is a part of a larger NetWare network, and the policy of the organization is to have a centralized backup scheme for all the network's varied resources? It would not be efficient to have to map a drive letter to each Personal NetWare server and each NetWare volume as well. There may not be enough drive letters to go around. The solution is simple: Use the SBACKUP.NLM utility, and its ability to back up workstations using a Terminate and Stay Ready (TSR) program called a Targeting Service Agent (TSA) (provided with NetWare 3.12, 4.0, or 4.01) to back up your Personal NetWare servers, as well as the other network workstations.

SBACKUP.NLM is a server-based backup package provided by Novell that can back up not only DOS and Macintosh directories and files but also O/S 2 HPFS and NFS files. SBACKUP is executed from the file server console and runs as a file server process, using a backup device attached directly to the file server. The devices, however, only operate with *Device Independent Backup Interface (DIBI-2)* device drivers. If you do not have a DIBI-2 device driver for your backup hardware, you will either need to contact your backup device vendor or check Novell's NetWire service for a current driver.

SBACKUP has two command line options that you can set to control the number of buffers and the buffer size. The number of buffers is controlled with the BUFFER=x option, where x is the number of buffers in the range of 2 to 10 (4 is the default). The size of the buffers is determined by the option SIZE=xxx, where xxx is the buffer size of 16, 32, 64 (default), 128, or 256 KB. The following is an example of loading SBACKUP on the console with six, 128 KB buffers:

```
LOAD SBACKUP BUFFER=6 SIZE=128
```

The feature to SBACKUP that you are probably most interested in, though, is the automated workstation backup. SBACKUP can be used to back up workstations that have the proper TSA loaded. The TSA performs several duties:

- Passes the data request from SBACKUP to the target.
- Receives and processes commands from SBACKUP so that the target's operating system can handle the request for data.
- Receives the requested data from the target and returns it to SBACKUP in standard Storage Management Services (SMS) format.

There are four main steps to take for automatic workstation backup by the NetWare file server:

1. Load the device drivers for controllers or storage devices. (If the SCSI controller and its device driver are ASPI-compatible, you can use TAPEDAI.DSK. Otherwise, consult your vendor, local Novell office, 1-800-NETWARE, or NetWire for a driver for your storage device.)
2. Load TSA_DOS.NLM at the server.
3. Load TSA_SMS.COM at the workstation.
4. Load SBACKUP.NLM at the server console.

Conclusion

This chapter discussed the ins and outs of using Personal NetWare with other versions of NetWare. Because Personal NetWare uses the same ODI technology and VLM Requestor as native NetWare, Personal NetWare is a natural extension that adds workgroup features and peer-to-peer capabilities to the NetWare environment.

Chapter 11

Advanced Topics: Troubleshooting

Novell designed Personal NetWare to be as simple as possible to install and use. Nevertheless, network problems seem to sneak up on all of us eventually. Fortunately, Personal NetWare includes many features and tools that make it easy to locate and correct network-related problems. In this chapter, we introduce a general method for troubleshooting Personal NetWare networks, but the most valuable tools you have for finding network problems are patience, persistence, and the cooperation of your network users. Secondary to these are diagnostic tools like cable testers and the software diagnostics included with Personal NetWare.

We'll give you a few troubleshooting guidelines and describe the diagnostic tools included with Personal NetWare. The explanations and suggestions are by no means comprehensive, but we hope at least to indicate how you might begin to identify a problem, and then give you a set of logical steps that will lead to its resolution.

Sources of Technical Information

As always, your vendor is the final word on technical support. If you encounter problems that you are unable to resolve, or if you suspect compatibility problems with components or other software you are using, don't hesitate to use the technical support services that Novell has in place. Just keep in mind that technical phone support from Novell is not free—Premier Telephone Support costs $2.95 for the first minute and $1.95 a minute thereafter.

In addition to putting you directly in contact with a network engineer, Novell supports an automated voice response system (ASK Novell), a 24-hour bulletin board (408-649-3696, 9600,N,8,1), the Novell Desktop Systems Group FaxBack service (801-429-2700), and the NetWire Forum on CompuServe (GO NETWIRE or GO NOVDESKTOP). The client software for Personal NetWare is identical to all other NetWare versions, so most of the technical information on VLMs applies to Personal NetWare as well.

General Troubleshooting Procedures

The first step toward resolving any problem is determining what the problem is, whether you are troubleshooting a car, a network, or a nuclear power plant. If you already know what the problem is, resolving it is usually a simple or straightforward matter (though it might involve investments in time and money to resolve). The real chore of troubleshooting is isolating the source of the problem in the first place.

Your users will most likely have a black-and-white perspective on the network (and computers in general): It either works or it doesn't. A problem has the potential to lead to a cry of, "The network is down!" Therefore, its a good idea first to translate "The network is down" into "I have a problem here." It is up to you, the person responsible for administering and troubleshooting the network, to educate users about their new responsibilities as network citizens, and to help them understand what causes the problems they experience. Users who are willing to help can be valuable sources of information.

In a networking environment, trouble can come from a variety of sources—many more than you should consider at once. Therefore, it helps to organize possible problems into broad categories before tearing off in the direction of the "fire." Network server problems, workstation problems, and network segment problems can be caused by cabling, component failure, configuration errors, application problems, protocol problems, and user errors, to name a few.

Are Other Workstations Up and Running?

The first step in any network troubleshooting procedure should be to see if other network stations are up and running. If you have a multiple segment/ring network, check to see if other networks are functional.

Check the Other Workstations

If you've had a working network, you can usually isolate a problem very quickly by checking the state of other workstations. If they are not experiencing problems, check the faulty workstation and its client software; if they are not, check the network hubs.

If none of the workstations on a particular segment/ring is communicating, probably the problem does not lie with the workstations, and you have narrowed the problem to either the server(s) or the network components. If other workstations are running, you most likely have a problem with a particular workstation.

Does the Workstation Run as a Stand-Alone Computer?

Although seemingly obvious, more than one eager network troubleshooter has marched off to check network cabling, servers, and network hardware before ensuring that the workstation with the problem is actually running. Make sure that the workstation in question can boot up and function normally as a stand-alone computer before going on what could be a wild goose chase.

If the workstation is functional, and you have verified that other workstations on the network are functioning as well, you have further narrowed the problem to the cabling between the server or hub and the workstation or to workstation configuration. You can probably identify the problem most quickly by checking the NIC and client software configuration at the workstation.

Does the Client Software Load Properly?

In general, software diagnostics messages will give you the quickest and easiest access to troubleshooting information regarding a configuration problem. As explained in Chapter 4, the workstation client software is made up of four main components:

- LSL.COM—the Link Support Layer
- DRIVER.COM—an ODI driver for your network interface card (for example, NE2000.COM or EXP16ODI.COM)
- IPXODI.COM—the NetWare IPX driver
- VLM.EXE—the NetWare DOS requester

Each of these components gives troubleshooting information as it is loaded. When problems occur, you will usually receive an error message that can lead you directly to the source of the problem. Perhaps the fastest way to isolate a problem with the workstation is to remove the call to STARTNET.BAT from your AUTOEXEC.BAT file. (If you use another batch file to load the client software, prevent it from being executed when you reboot your workstation.) Reboot the workstation and manually load each of the elements of the client software, taking note of any error messages that occur along the way.

We have included an example STARTNET.BAT file here to show you the order in which the components are typically loaded.

```
@ECHO OFF
SET NWLANGUAGE=ENGLISH
C:
CD C:\NWCLIENT
REM DPMS should be loaded before NWCACHE
DPMS
NWCACHE 1536 768 /LEND=ON /DELAY=OFF
LH SHARE /F:10240 /L:200
LH LSL
LH EXP16ODI
LH IPXODI
LH SERVER
VLM
CD \
C:\NWCLIENT\NET LOGIN
```

If you have other Personal NetWare servers running on the network, try loading just the client software consisting of this list of software in the following order: LSL, DRIVER, IPXODI, VLM. You should be in the \NWCLIENT directory before running VLM.EXE, as this program depends on the individual (.VLM) files stored in that directory. As each element is loaded, some form of diagnostic or informative message will be displayed. The information displayed by the ODI driver for the network card is not standard; but, for a working NIC, you might expect a sequence such as the following:

```
C:\NWCLIENT>lsl
NetWare Link Support Layer v2.05 (930910)
(C) Copyright 1990-1993 Novell, Inc. All Rights Reserved.

Configuration File "C:\NWCLIENT\NET.CFG" used.
```

```
Max Boards 4, Max Stacks 4


C:\NWCLIENT>exp16odi
Intel EtherExpress(tm) 16 Ethernet MLID v2.30 (930512)
(C) Copyright 1992 Intel Corporation  All Rights Reserved

EtherExpress 16 Adapter configured as follows:

Int 4, Port 360, Node Address 00AA002A3F6A L
Using connector auto-detect
Max Frame 1514 bytes, Line Speed 10 Mbps
Board 1, Frame ETHERNET_802.3, LSB Mode

C:\NWCLIENT>ipxodi

NetWare IPX/SPX Protocol v2.12 (931007)
(C) Copyright 1990-1993 Novell, Inc. All Rights Reserved.


Bound to logical board 1 (EXP16ODI) : Protocol ID 0

C:\NWCLIENT>vlm
VLM.EXE  - NetWare virtual loadable module manager v1.10 (931119)
(C) Copyright 1993 Novell, Inc. All Rights Reserved.
Patent pending.

The VLM.EXE file is pre-initializing the VLMs..............
The VLM.EXE file is using extended memory (XMS).
NMR.VLM  - NetWare management responder v1.10 (931119)
You are attached to server CICERO

C:\NWCLIENT>
```

Notice that the VLM requester informs you that it has successfully attached to server CICERO. If the VLM is not able to attach to a server, it exhibits an error message to that effect.

Different drivers for NICs will respond in different ways. Most, however, will give some indication of a configuration or hardware problem. The next example shows the result of loading an NIC driver with incorrect settings in the NET.CFG file:

```
Intel EtherExpress(tm) 16 Ethernet MLID v2.28 (930115)
(C) Copyright 1992 Intel Corporation  All Rights Reserved

EtherExpress 16 Adapter configured as follows:

Int 3, Port 320
Using BNC connector
Max Frame 1514 bytes, Line Speed 10 Mbps
Board 2, Frame ETHERNET_802.3, LSB Mode


EtherExpress(tm) 16 board not found.
The following is a list of probable causes:

1) I/O conflict with another adapter
2) EtherExpress 16 not installed
3) NET.CFG I/O address differs from the EtherExpress 16
   board's I/O address.
EXP160DH-DOS-6: The adapter did not initialize. EXP160DH did
not load.
```

This particular vendor even suggests a few areas to check. Most newer cards are completely software configured, but older cards might require that you set dip-switches, jumpers, or both. Most NICs use an I/O port somewhere in the range of 200-3FFh, an IRQ (PC interrupt) between 2 and 11, and shared memory in the PC somewhere between A0000 h and DFFFF h.

No other devices in the PC may conflict with the settings specified for the NIC. In order to load the NIC driver, the settings specified in the NET.CFG file must match the settings on the card. The information the driver needs varies depending on the NIC manufacturer, but an I/O port and an interrupt value are common.

If the Client Software Loads, Can You See Other Servers?

Often, the client software for the workstation will appear to load normally, but the workstation will not be able to "see" some of the network servers (or any servers). This type of problem is often related to the settings in the NET.CFG file which control many aspects of the individual client software components. We have included a sample NET.CFG file here to explain the effect that individual components might have on a "missing server" problem:

```
Link driver EXP16ODI
  PORT 360
  FRAME Ethernet_802.3

NetWare DOS Requester
  FIRST NETWORK DRIVE = F
  NETWARE PROTOCOL = PNW,BIND,NDS
  PREFERRED SERVER = CICERO
  PREFERRED WORKGROUP = ALLOFFICE
  WORKGROUP NET = 00000001:FFFFFFFFFFFF
  Network Printers = 4
  VLM = AUTO.VLM
```

There are two areas to check immediately if you are having trouble locating network servers, even though the client software appears to have loaded correctly. The first is the frame type specified in the NIC driver section (EXP16ODI in this case). Personal NetWare, NetWare 3.12, and NetWare 4.x have all moved to a default frame type of Ethernet_802.2 for Ethernet networks. If you are on an internetwork that has NetWare 2.x or NetWare 3.11 servers running, you won't be able to see these servers unless both your workstation and the server are configured to the same frame type. You can add additional frame statements to support multiple frame types.

The second area to check is the NETWARE PROTOCOL heading under the requester section. This item specifies which client support the VLM requester on the station will include. The PNW option specifies that the workstation will be able to use resources from Personal NetWare servers; similarly, the BIND and NDS options allow the workstation to use resources from bindery-based (Net-Ware 2.x, 3.x) servers and NetWare Directory Services (NetWare 4.x) servers respectively. If the proper client support is not loaded at the workstation, it will not be able to see the other servers on the network.

Troubleshooting Network Equipment

If more than one user on a particular network segment is down, check your network hubs. A power failure, spike, or brownout (temporary reduction in power) will often lock up hubs and other networking devices like bridges, routers, and repeaters.

If your's is a local isolated network based on simple workgroup hubs, check the hubs for any diagnostic indicators. If all else fails, try resetting the hub, but not if there are some workstations on the network that are able to communicate. Doing so will probably interrupt their network sessions.

If you are part of a larger internetwork that encompasses bridges, repeaters, and/or routers, seek the help of the internetwork designers or support personnel before attempting to solve a local network problem. On an internetwork, anything you do (including resetting or modifying the operation of network equipment) can have drastic effects elsewhere on the network. If you are in doubt, don't mess with it!

Cabling Problems

Cabling problems can account for a variety of unexpected results on your network.

Thinwire Ethernet

If you have a bus topology Ethernet network running on RG-58U (commonly called *thinnet*, *thinwire*, or *cheapernet*) and none of the workstations is communicating, there are a few ways to quickly check if the cabling is the problem:

1. Make sure that both ends of the network segment have been properly terminated. A properly terminated network has a connector containing a 50 ohm resistor connected to each end, and one end (and one only) is connected to earth ground.

2. Make sure that a user has not improperly disconnected his/her workstation from the network. With thinwire Ethernet, if a cable is removed from one end of the T connector, rather than removing the entire T from the network card, the network will be disrupted.

3. Use a terminator to shorten the network to a single cable segment between two network nodes. If these two nodes work, continue to add additional network segments, one at a time, until you encounter a problem.

Good quality RG-58 has a nominal resistance of about 2 ohms/100 feet. Since the network is terminated on both ends with a 50 ohm resistor, it is also possible to troubleshoot thinnet with a simple Digital Volt Meter (DVM). With all workstations on a particular segment powered down or disconnected from the segment, you can use the DVM to measure the resistance found across the outer and inner conductors of any T connector—it should be around 25 ohms plus a nominal resistance added by the length of the cable.

If your meter reads a very high resistance value or off-scale, you probably have an "open" (broken wire or connection) somewhere on the segment. Conversely, if you read a very low value, you most likely have a "short" (grounding between the inner and outer conductors). If you find either of these problems, you can determine the direction of the problem by separating the cable ends from the T connector and performing the same measurement on each cable end. You can usually use this method to follow the problem along the cable to its origin. This is not the most elegant method of troubleshooting, but it is effective.

Twisted Pair

Twisted pair wiring is often more difficult to troubleshoot. Twisted pair is often used for Ethernet and Token Ring networks. Fortunately, if you have a cable problem with a star topology network, the network hubs are often capable of dealing with the problem so that a minimal number of users are affected. Again, if more than one user is down, the problem might be in the hub. If only a single user is down, the link to the workstation or the workstation itself is suspect.

Change is the nemesis of twisted pair networks. There is a tendency for network connections to be fragile, especially if the network uses telco-style punch blocks or poor-quality connectors. Often, the cure to twisted pair cabling problems is ensuring that the connections at the punch block are good, or replacing the connector on the end of the cable. However, other problems might require more significant measures.

Some of the trouble spots include stolen pairs on a wire trunk (the installers of the intercom system might have borrowed a pair of wires), crosstalk and other forms of interference (the ballast in a florescent light for example), frayed cables, and cable breaks. If you have it in your budget, a network cable tester makes troubleshooting a much more pleasant task. Most of these diagnostic tools respond with messages such as "short found at 15 feet" or "12 dB loss detected" and other human-understandable diagnoses.

Whether you use coaxial, shielded, or unshielded twisted pair cable, there are numerous testers available on the market for rating and troubleshooting cable plants. If, however, you are having significant trouble with a twisted pair network, we recommend that you enlist the assistance of network trouble-shooter or the company that performed the network cable installation.

Using Personal NetWare Diagnostic Tools

Personal NetWare includes a comprehensive set of tools to assist you with network diagnostics and troubleshooting. It includes both a set of DOS-based diagnostics and a Windows diagnostic utility for gaining access to information about the clients and servers in your Personal NetWare workgroup. These utilities provide access to information about the configuration of servers and clients, statistics from the protocol layers, and packet information. The DOS-based utilities are accessible through the standard NET utility. The Windows-based version of the diagnostics is added as an icon to the Personal NetWare group during installation.

In order to get the greatest benefit from these tools, there is an additional VLM that you should load at the workstation or server. The NetWare Management Responder (NMR.VLM) adds capabilities for reporting the CPU type, the amount of disk space available, the amount of disk space used, and the display type for every workstation on which it is loaded. You can make sure that this VLM is automatically loaded with the requester by specifying it as an option during installation or by running setup and accessing management options. In either case, a new line will be added to the requester section of the NET.CFG file for the workstation:

```
Link driver EXP16ODI
        PORT 300
        FRAME Ethernet_802.3

NetWare DOS Requester
        PREFERRED WORKGROUP = HEOROT
        FIRST NETWORK DRIVE = F
        NETWARE PROTOCOL = PNW,BIND
        SHOW DOTS = ON
        USE DEFAULTS = ON
        VLM = AUTO.VLM
        VLM = NMR.VLM
```

You can add this line manually to the NET.CFG file of any workstation that you want to monitor. Once this VLM has been loaded, all the capabilities of the diagnostics software are available for that workstation.

DOS Diagnostics

The DOS diagnostics are accessible in two ways: Either type **PNWDIAGS** at the command prompt, or access them as a command line option of the NET utility with NET DIAGS. In either case, you will be presented with the Main Menu of PNW Diagnostics, as shown in Figure 11.1.

Select Data

This DOS version has some capabilities that go beyond what is available in the Windows diagnostics. While the Windows diagnostics can monitor only connection information and statistics for Personal NetWare workgroups and the servers and clients in a particular workgroup, the DOS diagnostics can monitor either workgroups or entire network segments.

In Chapter 10, we explained the concept of internal and external routers and NetWare network numbering. As we determined there, each network segment on an internetwork of servers has a unique network number. Any network device on a particular segment has its own address composed of two parts, its device address and its network address. By selecting to monitor a particular network, data on all of the devices residing on that network become available to diagnostics.

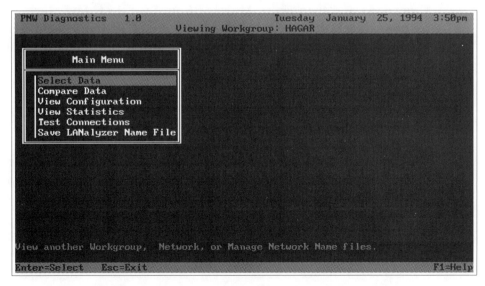

Figure 11.1 The main menu of Personal NetWare diagnostics.

The first menu item in the DOS diagnostics, Select Data, allows you to select either a Personal NetWare workgroup or a specific network number. There are four options in the Select Data Menu:

- **Workgroup:** This option brings up a list of known Personal NetWare workgroups available through the routing table on your station.

- **Network:** This option enables you to see all the networks known to the routers on your internetwork and select a particular one for monitoring. The two remaining menu items are related to this one.

- **Refresh:** This option scans the network to refresh the list of network nodes available depending on whether you have selected a network or a workgroup. It will add nodes that have just been turned on or added to the network, and remove those that are no longer there.

- **Associate:** This option only applies when you elect to monitor a network rather than a workgroup. It queries the devices on the network to associate names with the devices it finds. If the node is a Personal NetWare server with NMR loaded, the name will be the server name. Otherwise, diagnostics will attempt to locate the user name used to connect the device to the network.

In the following example, we selected a network from the list of available networks and then chose Associate from the Select Data Menu. Figure 11.2 shows this list of available networks. Figure 11.3 shows the diagnostic utility querying the network to associate names with the nodes on that network.

Compare Data

After selecting a workgroup or a network to view, the next step might be to choose Compare Data from the main menu. Compare Data allows you to select a group of network nodes to measure, and four options for the type of data you want to compare. The possible groupings are Servers, Workstations, or All Nodes; network statistics options are:

- Traffic
- Resource Distribution
- Resource Efficiency
- Local/Remote

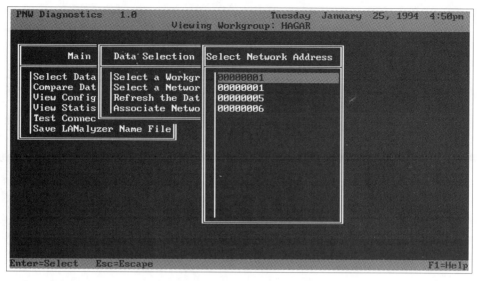

Figure 11.2   List of available network addresses.

The Traffic option enables you to measure the number of packets sent and received by individual network nodes. As Figure 11.4 shows, the nodes are listed by name, network address, and type. The node types include C for client, S for

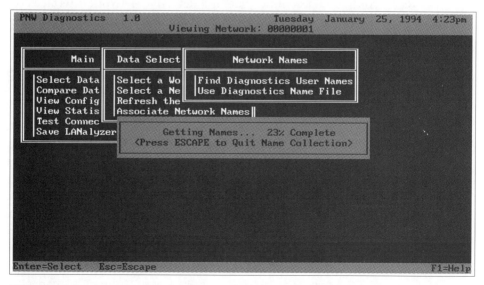

Figure 11.3   Associating names with network nodes.

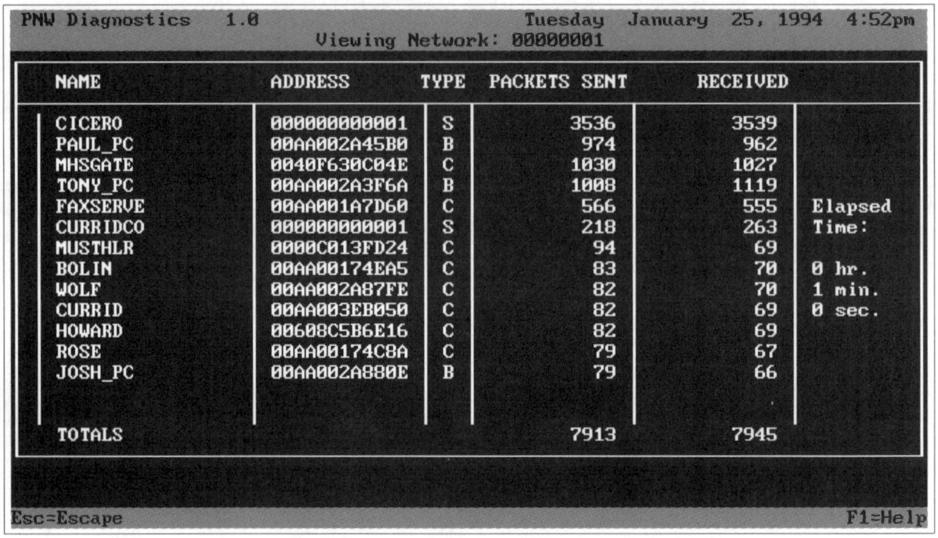

```
PNW Diagnostics   1.0                   Tuesday   January   25, 1994   4:52pm
                         Viewing Network: 00000001

   NAME              ADDRESS       TYPE  PACKETS SENT      RECEIVED

   CICERO            000000000001   S        3536           3539
   PAUL_PC           00AA002A45B0   B         974            962
   MHSGATE           0040F630C04E   C        1030           1027
   TONY_PC           00AA002A3F6A   B        1008           1119
   FAXSERVE          00AA001A7D60   C         566            555       Elapsed
   CURRIDCO          000000000001   S         218            263       Time:
   MUSTHLR           0000C013FD24   C          94             69
   BOLIN             00AA00174EA5   C          83             70       0 hr.
   WOLF              00AA002A87FE   C          82             70       1 min.
   CURRID            00AA003EB050   C          82             69       0 sec.
   HOWARD            00608C5B6E16   C          82             69
   ROSE              00AA00174C8A   C          79             67
   JOSH_PC           00AA002A880E   B          79             66

   TOTALS                                    7913           7945

Esc=Escape                                                            F1=Help
```

Figure 11.4   Measuring network traffic with PNW diagnostics.

server, B for both client and server (such as a personal NetWare server), and N for a node that has an IPX driver loaded but is neither a server nor a workstation. Using these measurements, it is possible to determine which nodes on the network are generating the most traffic. This might help to identify an incorrectly configured network node or a defective network interface controller.

The Resource Distribution option displays all the nodes on the network segment. For each node, PNW Diagnostics will attempt to determine the CPU type, Display type, available disk space, and total disk space. As you can see in Figure 11.5, different information is displayed for different types of network nodes. For example, CICERO and CURRIDCO are NetWare 3.1x file servers. Only the available and total disk space figures are available for these servers. JOSH_PC, TONY_PC, and PAUL_PC are Personal NetWare servers. For both JOSH_PC and TONY_PC, the NMR.VLM has been loaded. As the figure shows, these two nodes display all information. PAUL_PC, on the other hand, looks just like the rest of the network nodes because NMR is not loaded.

The Resource Efficiency option works very much like the Resource Distribution option with one main distinction. As Figure 11.6 shows, the display type has been replaced with a number denoting ACTIVITY which is a measure of how busy a particular network node is. This number is useful in helping to determine which servers on the network are supporting the greatest load, which gives you the opportunity to make adjustments in network capacity planning.

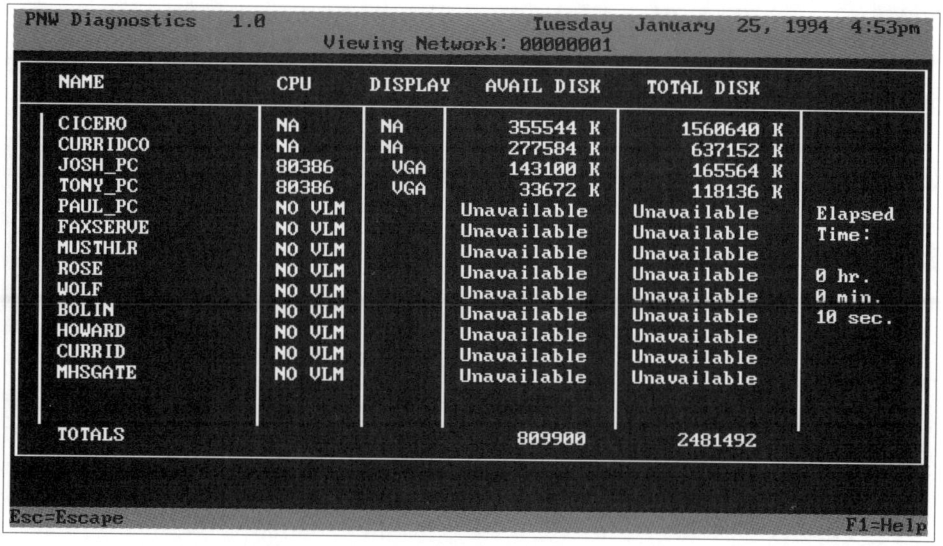

Figure 11.5 Measuring network resource distribution with PNW diagnostics.

The last option under Compare Data, Local/Remote, is a measurement of the division of labor on Personal NetWare workstations that are serving as both servers and clients. As Figure 11.7 shows, all nodes on the network segment are

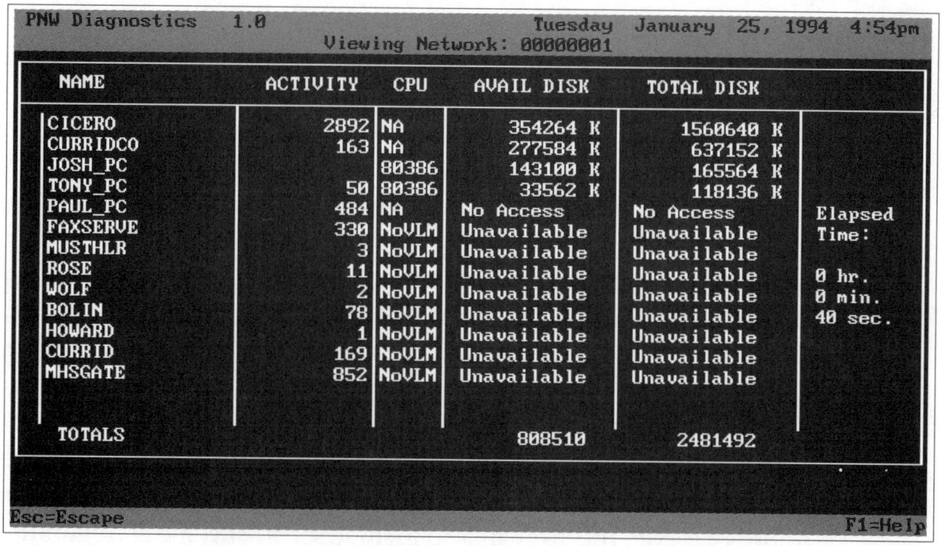

Figure 11.6 Measuring network resource efficiency with PNW diagnostics.

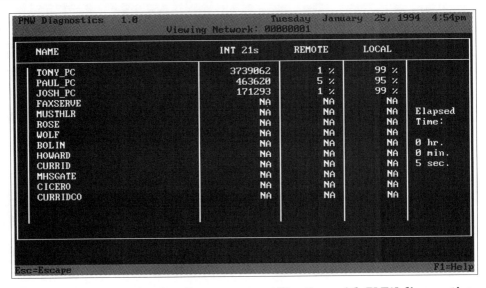

Figure 11.7   Measuring local vs. remote utilization with PNW diagnostics.

listed by name, but only those that are Personal NetWare servers display any statistics. The three columns display figures for INT 21 calls (a call to a network resource), CPU utilization for remote processes, and CPU utilization for local processes.

View Configuration and View Statistics

To this point, all the options we have discussed measure statistics in real time. While these data are useful, there are two additional options that provide a great amount of detail about the configuration of a network node and IPX/SPX protocol statistics. When you select either View Configuration or View Statistics, PNW Diagnostics gives you an opportunity to group network nodes, just as Compare Data did: servers, workstations, and all network nodes. Once you have selected a grouping, a list of network nodes appears by name and network address.

View Configuration displays information about nodes and clients that includes the type of network card installed in the node and its settings, the versions of IPX and SPX protocol stacks, and their current configuration. If the node is a server, this list will also include server specific configuration information. These reports can be saved to disk in ASCII text format, and are an excellent resource for network documentation. The following example is for one of the Personal NetWare servers in our test workgroup.

```
CONFIGURATION  TONY_PC 00AA002A3F6A

Configuration Information:

    OS Type                           DOS
    OS Version                        5.0
    CPU                               80386
    CoProcessor                       80387
    Video                             VGA
    System Memory                     640
    Total Extended Memory (XMS)       12,831 Kb (Approx.)
    Available Extended Memory         10,783 Kb (Approx.)
    Total Expanded Memory (EMS)       0 Kb
    Available Expanded Memory         0 Kb
    Floppy Drives                     2
    Hard Drives                       1
    C:                                120,971,264 Bytes
    Serial Ports                      1
    Parallel Ports                    3
    Mouse Driver                      Present

  Server Specific Information:

    Server Name                       TONY_PC
    Server Description                Tony's Server
    Work Group Name                   ALLOFFICE
    Workgroup ID                      1414085863
    OEM Name                          NOVELL
    Server Version                    1.20
    Size in Memory                    34,912 Bytes
    Workgroup Auditing                On
    Share Loaded                      Yes
    Local Security                    Off
    Print Buffer Size                 512
    Receive Buffers                   3
    Receive Buffer Size               1024
    I/O Buffers                       0
    I/O Buffer Size                   2048
```

```
                        Current        Configured
Connections             0              4
Tasks                   0              8
Open Files              0              50
Workgroup Directories   1              2
Workgroup Printers      0              1
```

Cache Specific Information:

```
Cache Version                         1.0
Type of Memory Used                   EMS
Maximum Size                          4096 Kb
Minimum Size                          2048 Kb
```

Network Information:

```
LSL Version                           2.5
Maximum Network Boards                4
Maximum Protocol Stacks               4

Network Card Name                     Intel EtherExpress 16
Node Address                          00AA002A3F6A
Frame Type                            ETHERNET_802.3
Driver Version                        2.30
Line Speed                            10
Bus Types Supported                   Unknown
Interrupt Used                        4
I/O Address                           360 h
I/O Range                             10 h
Memory Address                        0 h
Memory Size                           0 h
DMA Channel                           Not Used

Protocol Stack Name                   IPX
Module Version                        2.12
API Version                           3.30
Maximum Open Sockets                  20
Maximum Sockets Used                  20
Maximum SPX Connections               15
Maximum SPX Connections Used          3

NET.CFG Path                          C:\NWCLIENT\NET.CFG
```

As you can see, PNW Diagnostics provide a tremendous amount of configuration information about the node. It even tells you from which NET.CFG file the workstation is currently configured.

Like View Configuration, View Statistics provides a good deal of historical and version information about the network protocols in operation on a particular node. As with View Configuration the reports from View Statistics can be captured as ASCII text files by pressing the **F-10** key. The example below comes from one of the Personal NetWare servers on our test network that was running NMR.VLM. Stations with the responder VLM running provide far more information than those without it.

```
STATISTICS   JOSH_PC 00AA002A45B0


   Client Name:   PENROD
   Server Name:   JOSH_PC
   Network Address: 00000001:00AA002A45B0

   LSL Statistics

     Total Transmit Requests        89400
     Get ECB Requests               0
     Get ECB Failures               0
     AES Events Count               881465
     Postponed Events               86385
     Cancel AES Failures            0
     Total Received Packets         120925
     Unclaimed Packets              12034

   MLID Statistics

     Network Card Name              Intel EtherExpress 16
     Node Address                   00AA002A3F6A
     Frame Type                     ETHERNET_802.3
     Total Transmit Requests        89400
     Total Packets Received         108891
     No ECB Available Count         13643
     Too Big Transmit Request       0
     Too Small Transmit Request     0
     Receive Overflow Count         0
     Receive Too Big Count          116
```

```
Receive Too Small Count              0
Miscellaneous Transmit Error Count   0
Miscellaneous Receive Error Count    0
Transmit Retry Count                 0
Receive Checksum Error Count         0
Receive Mismatch Count               0
```

Protocol Statistics

```
Protocol Stack Name                  IPX
Total Packets Transmitted            90460
Total Packets Received               84874
Ignored Received Packets             12047
Malformed Packet Count               0
Open Socket Failure Count            0
Listen ECB Count                     81552
ECB Cancel Failure Count             1005
Find Route Failure Count             0
```

SPX Statistics

```
Establish Connection Requests        113
Establish Connection Failures        0
Listen Connection Request Count      35
Listen Connection Failure Count      0
Send Packet Count                    1957
Target No Receive Buffer Count       223
Bad Send Packet Count                0
Send Failure Count                   0
Abort Connection Count               0
Listen Packet Count                  5377
Bad Listen Packet Count              0
Incoming Packet Count                7420
Bad Incoming Packet Count            0
Suppressed Packet Count              10
No Session Listen ECB Count          0
Watchdog Destroyed Sessions          23
```

Personal NetWare Server Statistics

```
Server Name                          JOSH_PC
Work Group Name                      ALLOFFICE
```

Total Packets Received	152
Number Of Bad Packets	0
Packets Not Processed Immediately	0
Number Of Lost Responses	0
Peak Connections Used	1
Peak Open Files	0
Peak Client Tasks	0
Watchdog Packets Sent	0
Clients Watchdogged	0
ECB Reposts With No Buffers	73
Send Packet With ECB Active	0
Total Slist Requests	755
Server Busy Packets	2
Server Busy Packets No Buffers	0
Unknown Requests	16
Write Behind Misses	0
Read Cache Hits	0
Read Cache Misses	0
Reads Too Large	0
Critical Errors	0
Saved Large DOS Area	4
Saved Small DOS Area	937
Starvation Counter	0
Write Behind Hits	0
Cache Blocks In Use	0
Packet Queue Runs	150
Idle Loop Wait Hits	0
Client Int 21 Calls	1,842,401
Total Int 21 Calls	1,843,179
Password Failures	5
Current Number Of Free Buffers	0
Current Number Of Semaphores	0

Personal NetWare Cache Statistics

Current Size	2048 Kb
Read Requests	382094
Actual Reads	3754
Write Requests	2758
Actual Writes	864
Disk Errors	0
Memory Errors	0

Test Connections

The final option in Personal NetWare diagnostics, Test Connections, provides a means of exercising the network by sending packets to other workstations and measuring the number that are received correctly. There are two options in Test Connections: a point-to-point test and an all points test. The point-to-point test is a focused test of 10,000 512-byte packets sent between two network nodes that you specify.

The all points test uses each network node in turn as the sending station to send a specific number of packets to every other node. The data on the packets are kept for all nodes. Figure 11.8 shows the results of an all points test.

After the test has been run, two additional options, Send Detail and Receive Detail, are available at the bottom of the screen. By highlighting a particular node and pressing either **F-6** or **F-8**, you can see either the number of packets sent by the station that were correctly received by every other station or the number of packets that this station correctly received from every other workstation. Using these tools, it is possible to identify problem network cards and communications problems between network nodes.

Windows Diagnostics

The Personal NetWare Windows diagnostic utility is launched from the Personal NetWare folder added to Windows during the installation of Personal NetWare. Most of the information available in the DOS PNW Diagnostics is available in the Windows version, but only for the workgroup in which you are currently authenticated.

The main menu of Personal NetWare Diagnostics appears in Figure 11.9. The button bar across the top is a quick way to reach most of the functions. The doorway on the far left exits the utility; the three buttons immediately to the right of the exit button allow you to select groups of either servers, workstations, or both. The five buttons on the right allow you to select which graph to display for the current group. Graph possibilities are: network traffic, network disk space, network utilization, workgroup traffic, or all four graphs at once in a tiled windows display.

As you can see in the figure, we are currently viewing the servers for the workgroup ACCOUNTING. The workgroup name and other status information appear in the status bar at the bottom of the window. When an individual node is selected, its address also appears in the status line.

```
PNW Diagnostics   1.0                   Tuesday  January  25, 1994  5:04pm
                        Viewing Network: 00000001

                     ALL POINTS TEST - 702 Packets
      Node Name        Address       Sent by Node        Sent by Network
                                     Received by Network Received by Node

      CROES           00AA002A3F6A        701    99 %       701    99 %
      PENROD          00AA002A45B0        702   100 %       699    99 %
      FAXSERVE        00AA001A7D60        702   100 %       690    98 %
      MUSTHLR         0000C013FD24        701    99 %       694    98 %
      ROSE            00AA00174C8A        700    99 %       702   100 %
      WOLF            00AA002A87FE        686    97 %       702   100 %
      BOLIN           00AA00174EA5        702   100 %       702   100 %
      HOWARD          00608C5B6E16        691    98 %       700    99 %
      CURRID          00AA003EB050        690    98 %       702   100 %
      CROES           00AA002A880E        687    97 %       702   100 %
      MHSGATE         0040F630C04E        702   100 %       662    94 %
      CICERO          000000000001        698    99 %       702   100 %
      CURRIDCO        000000000001        698    99 %       702   100 %

 Esc=Escape    F6=Send Detail    F8=Receive Detail              F1=Help
```

Figure 11.8   Results of an all points test on Network 00000001.

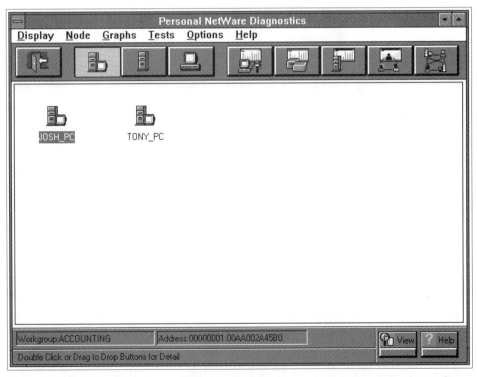

Figure 11.9   The opening window of the Personal NetWare Windows diagnostic tools.

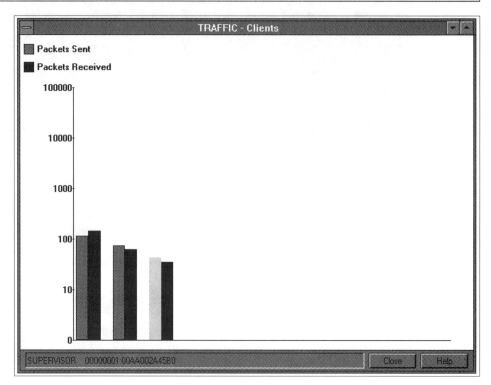

Figure 11.10   The Traffic graph in the Windows diagnostic tools.

To access the statistical and configuration information for a particular node, select the node from the opening window and double click or press the View button in the lower right-hand portion of the window. The first window to appear will be the station configuration details, with a new button at the bottom to display node protocol statistics. As in the DOS version of the diagnostics, this information can be saved to an ASCII file.

Selecting the Traffic graph will produce a result similar to the one in Figure 11.10. The number of packets sent and received by each node in the workgroup will be drawn. As you can see, when a particular bar graph is selected, the network user name and node address appear in the status line. Selecting either the Disk or Utilization graphs will yield similar results. In the Utilization graph, you can elect to display utilization as either the number of client requests versus server requests or as the percentage of server-to-client requests.

Selecting the Workgroup Traffic graph produces a result similar to the one in Figure 11.11. This graph changes over time as the traffic in the workgroup does.

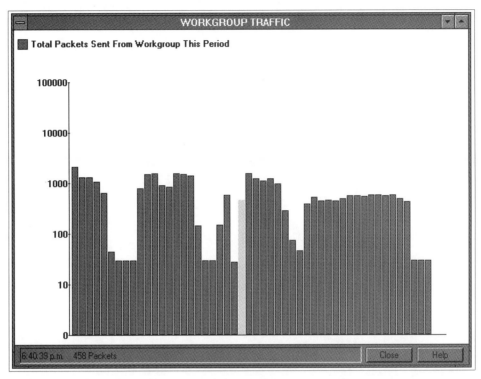

Figure 11.11   The Workgroup Traffic graph in the Windows diagnostic tools.

At any time, you can identify the number of packets sent during a particular period by selecting that bar in the graph and reading the status line.

We covered a lot of ground in this chapter. We discussed a set of general guidelines for network troubleshooting, including a few questions that help to quickly narrow the scope of network problems. We talked about troubleshooting the network cable plant and diagnosing problems with the configuration of the workstation client software. And finally, we covered some of the uses of the Personal NetWare Diagnostics tools.

Upgrading NetWare Lite Resources

Many NetWare Lite users will be happy to know that the introduction of Personal NetWare does not mean that they will have to rebuild their networking environments from scratch. Personal NetWare provides a utility for transferring NetWare Lite server settings, user accounts, shared resources, and current rights to the appropriate Personal NetWare locations and format.

The upgrade path is very simple. Your first task is to use the procedures outlined in Chapter 4 to install the Personal NetWare software on the old NetWare Lite server. The new Personal NetWare workstation will, of course, need to also perform as a server as it did under NetWare Lite.

Ideally, you want the server you are upgrading to be the first server on the network. Then create a workgroup using the SETUP /FIRST or NET ADMIN commands. The workgroup you create will be the location to which you transfer all the pertinent NetWare Lite information.

If you have more than one server to upgrade, then only one can be the first one. You can simulate this "first server" situation either by unloading SERVER.EXE on the already upgraded Personal NetWare servers, or by isolating the NetWare Lite server whose network information you are about to migrate. You can then create a unique workgroup to receive the old NetWare Lite information. When this server rejoins the network, you can join the work-group(s) you intend to keep with the NET JOIN command.

After you have installed the Personal NetWare server software and used the SETUP /FIRST command to create a workgroup, it will have two active accounts (both without passwords): the owner of the workstation and the SUPERVISOR account. In fact, the SETUP /FIRST command should end with you logged in to the owner of the workstation account. You will, however, need to log in as the workgroup SUPERVISOR so you will have all the rights necessary to access the appropriate information.

You are now ready to begin the NetWare Lite resource transfer. Simply type **NLMIGRAT** at the DOS command line prompt to begin the transfer. That's it. You're done. You will not even need to supply any information to the program. NLMIGRAT knows to look in the NWLITE directory off the ROOT directory for the NetWare Lite resource information that it needs. This information will then be transferred to the Personal NetWare NWCNTL directory off the ROOT directory.

Restart your computer and join your workgroup to the workgroup(s) you intend to keep if you had to simulate the "first server" condition. The only housekeeping task you will need to perform is reassigning passwords to the transferred user accounts. The passwords will not transfer with the rest of the user account information because they are encrypted.

Appendix B

NetWars

Introduction

Welcome to NetWars. Who says software can't be fun, much less addictive. NetWars is your basic killing-time-space-shoot'em-up-while-the-boss-is-not-looking kind of program. You wander through space looking for bad guys that come at you from all directions. A quick trigger finger and nerves of steel will make you the toughest law west of cyberspace. It may be a little difficult at first, but after a few games you will get the hang of it. The addicting part comes later.

The most obvious benefit of NetWars is that it improves your eye-hand coordination with the keyboard and mouse. This is important, as many programs require intensive use of a mouse and keyboard to get any work done. This rationalization often works well when you are caught red-handed.

How to Play

You can play NetWars with just a keyboard, or with a mouse and keyboard. If you do decide to use a mouse, a mouse driver must be loaded ahead of time. To start the game, simply enter the command **NETWARS** from the DOS command line. The title screen will be displayed. You can elect to play in single-player mode or multiplayer mode.

Once you have selected the mode you want to play in, the next screen is displayed. This screen contains graphics on all the ships you will see during

253

your voyage. This screen flips back and forth with the High Score table (where you can put your moniker if you're good enough). A menu bar is displayed at all times at the top of the screen. The menu bar has the following options on it:

- Game
- Controls
- Sound
- Graphics
- Press F1 for help

You can access the menu options in two ways. If your mouse is active, then place the pointer over the option and click the left mouse button. From the keyboard, hold down the Alt key and press the key of the letter that is underlined in the option you want to use. After you set the sound, graphics, and keyboard/mouse control just the way you like it, press the Enter key.

The next screen asks you to select the difficulty level you want to start with; 1 is the easiest, 8 the most challenging. With the mouse or arrow keys, move the selection box over the difficulty level you want, and press the Enter key.

The third screen shows the active ships you will encounter. Included with the display is information on how many there are at that level, their speed, their turning ability, and shield strength. Now that you know what you're facing out there in the great silicon beyond, press the Enter key and you're there.

As you drift in the starlit void, you will notice your screen is not quite empty. On the bottom right is your radar. This 3D grid shows your relative position to objects of interest—mainly pods and bad guys. At the upper left is the velocity grid, which indicates your direction of acceleration as a vector applied across six axes. It is much easier to look at than describe.

Below that are two bars, one showing velocity and the other shield strength. When you press the Ctrl key, the velocity bar moves down, indicating reverse thrust. Pressing the Shift key moves the bar upward, indicating forward thrust. The shield indicator doesn't move unless you are struck by a missile or other object.

In the center of the screen are two pairs of crosshairs, one stationary, the other attached to your guidance system and artillery. The secondary pair responds to your mouse and/or keyboard direction commands, and adjusts the ship's course and gunnery accordingly. By pressing the left mouse button or the Enter key in single player mode, shots are fired from the stationary pair of crosshairs. The trajectory of the shots is exactly opposite the movable set of crosshairs, except when both sets of crosshairs are dead center. This may take some getting used to.

Now the fun begins. Enemies appear on your radar and start taking pot shots at you while trying to steal your pods. Annoyed by their audacious behavior and stunning accuracy, you pursue them and sustain damage. Not to worry, those satellites will protect you. By collecting them, you find that your shields are restored, and you may even get a Christmas present or two, such as extra fire power or extra thrust.

Back in hot pursuit, you dodge left and fire. You dodge right and fire. Quickly, you climb out of the way of a pirate into the waiting arms of a missile. BOOM! ARRRRGH!!! Now you know you're dead. But wait, there is still one trick left. Line up the enemy in your sites and press the Ctrl-Enter key combination to launch "fire and forget missiles." These self-tracking missiles will find their target. You may go down in flames, but the enemies will pay dearly for their temerity.

Multiplayer Mode

Multiplayer mode is slightly different. In single-player mode you get beat up by the computer. In multi-player mode, other people do the honors. Multiplayer mode allows you to choose from up to eight universes with four people maximum for each universe.

Before starting, you select your spaceship with the mouse or keyboard. You then type in your name, and press the Enter key to start the game. If the universe you've selected is already full, you can select the Spectate Current Game option to observe the action. If you want to change universes, select a different universe from the menu bar.

One other goody available in multiplayer mode is a cloaking device. This nifty feature lets you sneak up on people unannounced. One problem though: The cloaking device can be destroyed if you are hit while using it.

Well, that's about it. The rest you have to discover on your own. A little tactical hint, though: Set your "hot keys" before playing at the office.

Appendix C

Glossary

100BaseVG (voice grade)—Hewlett Packard's version of "Fast Ethernet" which can be implemented over normal UTP phone line. 100BaseVG is a more radical departure from the normal Ethernet mold. 100BaseVG abandons the CSMA/CD access method and replaces it with a quartet signaling system in order to reach the 100 Mbps transfer rates.

100BaseX—One of two "Fast Etherent" solutions currently gaining industry support. 100BaseX is backed by a consortium of vendors lead by Grand Junction, and operates under the basic principle of speeding up the transmissions to reach 100Mbps while maintaining the access method of CSMA/CD.

10BaseT—Ethernet run over unshielded twisted pair at 10 Mbps.

8mm—A type of magnetic tape cartridge for storing data electronically.

Access Rights—Access rights refer to the restrictions placed on a user account to such shared resources as shared directories. Default rights are granted to the workgroup as a whole, but the SUPERVISOR can restrict rights such as reading, writing, or access to the resource for a specific account.

Archiving—The process of saving important or little-used data to storage media so it will be available when needed again, while removing it from the network drives to free up space.

Attached Resource Computer Network (ARCNet)—A network access protocol commonly used because of its extreme reliability and versatility. ARCNet uses a token passing scheme to access the network and pass data at roughly 2.5 Mbps.

American Standard Code for Information Interchange (ASCII)—A code for assigning a unique number to each letter and numeral as well as many other characters such as @, $, % ,#, ?, !, :, (,), etc.

AUTOEXEC.BAT—A batch file that carries out any DOS commands that you wish during the boot process such as starting a menu program or logging into Personal NetWare.

Backing Up—Process by which an electronic copy is made of the network data and stored on a removable media such as magnetic tapes or optical disks to protect the network from unforeseen and destructive circumstances such as mechanical failure, human error, or sabotage.

Backplane—A special bus in enterprise hubs into which the hub's modules plug. The backplane can be divided into separate network segments or channels through microsegmentation to support the traffic of various protocol modules. These channels are dedicated to supporting the particular protocol's maximum bandwidth (i.e. 10Mbps for an Ethernet channel).

Bandwidth—The amount of network traffic that can be supported at any one time; the rate of information flow. For example, an Ethernet network segment can support 10 Mbps. As the number of nodes on the segment increases, so does the amount of traffic that is contending for the use of the network; consequently, collisions will increase and traffic throughput will decrease.

Basic Input/Output System (BIOS)—Instructions stored in read-only-memory (ROM) that tell a computer how to use devices like floppy drives, disk drives, input/output ports, and keyboards.

Boot Configuration System File (BOOTCONF.SYS)—A file located in the LOGIN directory of the Personal NetWare Server from which workstations remotely boot. This file is necessary when multiple boot images need to be used. It lists each remote workstation and the boot image file it should use.

Boot Image—A file located in the LOGIN directory of the Personal NetWare server from which a diskless workstation will boot. This file is an image of the files necessary to boot the workstation and log in to the network. It is as if the workstation were booting from a bootable floppy disk. When the diskless workstation is turned on, a boot PROM located on the workstation's NIC will use the boot image of the bootable floppy disk to complete the startup and network access procedures.

Bridge—A device that links two or more LANs. A bridge looks at the address of each packet that it sees on all of the LANs attached to it and decides if the packet is intended for a node on the LAN it originated from or is intended for a node on a different LAN. If the packet's destination is on the same network it originated from, the packet will not be retransmitted across the bridge to any of the other networks. If the packet is intended for a node located on a network different from the network it originated on, the packet is buffered and then retransmitted to the correct network. The packet is not altered in any way. This means the bridge must connect networks using the same protocol. This selective retransmission of packets helps to keep heavy traffic on one network from congesting the other networks attached through the bridge, while allowing communication between the networks. Whenever a node comes on-line, it transmits an "I'm here" signal that is used by the bridge to update its tables of addresses so it will know which nodes can be reached through which ports. This can become cumbersome when the number of nodes rises and requires larger address tables.

Bus (Linear) Topology—A topology where the cabling begins with a node on one end of the network and connects the next node and the next after that until all the nodes have been connected. Unlike a ring, however, a bus or linear topology has two distinct ends to the cabling, both of which usually need to be terminated or grounded

Cache Buffer—A specially defined area in a computer's memory used to store repetitively called data.

Capture—The act of yielding control of a DOS logical port to Personal NetWare. Capturing is done to allow for printer access from the network and for print spooling.

Carrier Sense Multiple Access with Collision Detection (CSMA/CD)—A contention-based network access scheme that allows a node to listen for a collision rather than waiting for an acknowledgment or lack of one to detect a collision. This can be described as "listening while talking," and helps to minimize the propagation delay or the time it takes for a network message to be sent and acknowledged. Ethernet uses CSMA/CD.

Checksums—The antivirus software calculations made using a variety of methods for a file when it is known to be uncorrupted. These calculations are compared to the new calculations made every time a file open request is implemented.

Client/Server Applications—With a client/server application, the application's processing tasks have been divided between the client computer and a server. The server is dedicated to performing part of the work instead of just providing access to information. Both computers dedicate resources (like CPU power and RAM) to running the application.

Client/Server Networks—Client/server networks are those in which client workstations access data and resources from servers. Application processing (using word processors and spreadsheets, for example) occurs on the client workstation using its processor and RAM. The server merely provides access to file and print services.

Clone—Originally, clone referred to any desktop computer that copied the original architecture of the IBM Personal Computer. Now, the term normally applies to PCs that are built from parts not produced by the builder.

Coaxial (Coax)—Coax cable consists of a core of either one large solid wire or many smaller wire strands twisted together. The core is surrounded by a layer of insulation, which is itself surrounded by a braided wire mesh to ground out electromagnetic interference before it can affect the signal-carrying inner core. Coax cable is called coaxial because the inner core and the surrounding outer conductor share the same axis.

Collision—When two nodes try to transmit at the same time using a contention-based access protocol, the signals they send will corrupt each other or "collide."

Compact Disk-Read Only Memory (CD-ROM)—An optical disk from which information may only be read. A CD-ROM drive has only read heads; there are no write heads to transfer data to the optical disk.

CompuServe—A worldwide public e-mail and data network service.

CONFIG.SYS—A file that DOS uses during the boot process to configure the PC's hardware components so they can be used by applications.

Connection Commands—These commands deal with aspects of the network that involve connecting things such as workgroups, servers, user accounts, directories, printers, and server extensions.

Console—Monitor and keyboard from which activity for a service is controlled (file server console, network management console, etc.).

Contention—One of the two major methods that a network access protocol can use when determining if a node can transmit accross the network. The contention-based form of accessing the network allows a node to transmit whenever it has a packet of information ready to go. The node will then listen for confirmation from the node the packet was intended for, verifying the packet was received in good order. If a confirmation message is not received, the node that sent the original packet will resend it.

Copper Distributed Data Interface (CDDI)—A high-speed protocol that uses a special bidirectional token passing scheme to obtain speeds of up to 100 Mbps over unshielded twisted pair cable.

Digital Audio Tape (DAT)—A type of magnetic tape cartridge used to store data. DAT drives use helical scan recording.

Data Grade—A more expensive rating of unshielded twisted pair.

Data Migration—The process by which files are moved off the network drives based on a prerequisite level of inactivity. These files can be moved to near-line or off-line storage.

Desktop—Another name for a PC.

Device Independent Backup Interface (DIBI-2)—A device driver that allows you to attach a backup storage device directly to a NetWare file server so that you can use SBACKUP as a file server process to back up your network.

Digital Volt Meter (DVM)—A device for measuring the resistance found across the outer and inner conductors of any thinnet T connector to determine if there is a short or open (broken) connection along a particular thinnet run.

Disk Caching—Disk caching is a feature designed to improve performance of disk-intensive applications by designating a cache buffer in memory to store often-called data. Performance improves because data can be read more quickly from memory than from a hard drive or floppy diskette.

Disk/Tape Changers—Devices that allow access to multiple magnetic tapes or optical disks without the need for human intervention to load the requested media.

Diskless Workstation—A workstation without either floppy or hard drives. These workstations use a process called Remote Program Loading to boot from a nearby server using a boot image and a boot PROM.

DOS Protected Mode Services (DPMS)—A feature for Personal NetWare that allows you to conserve conventional memory by giving you the ability to load programs outside of conventional memory while still running in protected mode.

Driver—A program that serves as an interface between the operating system or application and the device it is intended to control.

Extended Industry Standard Architecture (EISA)—An industry standard developed by a consortium of computer manufacturers based on a 32-bit bus, and meant to provide a more powerful architecture than ISA. Sixteen-bit and 8-bit ISA boards will still work in EISA machines, but 32-bit EISA boards will not work in ISA machines.

ENIAC—An early computer that used vacuum tubes and was programmed by physically rewiring it.

Ethernet—Ethernet is a contention-based protocol that was originally developed by Xerox but was wisely allowed to become an industry standard (IEEE 802.3). Ethernet uses a contention scheme called Carrier Sense Multiple Access with Collision Detection (CSMA/CD) to access the network, and normally operates at 10 Mbps.

Fast Ethernet—A protocol for running Ethernet over unshielded twisted pair at 100 Mbps. There are two solutions currently being considered as possible standards and marketed under the name Fast Ethernet: 100BaseVG and 100BaseX. Both solutions have subcommittees of the IEEE 802 committee setting a standard for them.

Fatigue—A condition where network cabling is bent sharply enough or repeatedly so that the wire conducting network signals breaks and interrupts network traffic.

Function Commands—These commands direct the network to conduct such processes as write entries in the audit log, share directories and printers, synchronize clocks and batch files, print, send messages, save network connection information, and take the server down.

Fiber Distributed Data Interface (FDDI)—A high-speed protocol that uses a special bidirectional token passing scheme to obtain speeds of up to 100 Mbps over fiber optic cable.

Fiber Optic—Fiber optic cable uses light signals to transmit messages through a hollow cable instead of passing electrons along copper wire. Light photons are not normally affected by electromagnetic background noise like electrons are, so fiber optic cable can carry a perfectly clear signal through the electronically noisiest of environments.

File-by-File Backup—This method of backing up networks concentrates on copying files instead of sectors. Since this procedure pays attention to the operating system's file and directory structures, it permits you to specify which files to back up as well as to restore.

Floptical—Merger of optical technology with the concept of a floppy disk. Instead of the floppy cartridge containing a small magnetic disk, it contains a small optical one. Some of the new drives that this merger has produced can now support both media with read/write heads for both types of disk.

Frame—A packet of information used by nodes on a network to communicate. The frame's attributes are defined by the protocol the nodes are using.

Gateway—A gateway is used to give PC networks access to devices that have a different architecture and method of communicating such as mainframes and minicomputers. Fax gateways, e-mail gateways, and connections to CompuServe are some common uses of gateways other than connecting to legacy hardware.

Glass House—Refers to the special, controlled environments that large mainframe computers require.

Helical Scan—Method for saving data electronically to tape by using rotating read and write heads to magnetize the tape cartridges in short diagonal tracks.

Hop—When frames are passed from one network to another across a router.

High Performance File System (HPFS)—OS/2's native file system.

Hub—A device that repeats a signal it receives from one port to all of the remaining ports; thus the origin of another name, the repeater. It is used to connect the different nodes on a star topology network. The hub is often known as a concentrator, since all of the network cabling connects or concentrates at the hub. More advanced hubs have special features such as backplanes and bridging/routing functions.

International Business Machines (IBM)—Computer hardware and software giant that helped to spawn the PC revolution with the introduction of the IBM PC.

IEEE 802 Committee—The Institute for Electrical and Electronic Engineers committee for standardizing LAN communication.

Impedence—Electrical resistance of copper wire that helps to compensate for "noise" produced by the electromagnetic fields of any nearby electricle devices such as fluorescent lights, telephone lines, and/or power cables.

Integrity Checking—A method of spotting signs of virus activity by comparing a file's current checksums with past checksums to see if they have been changed. The antivirus program calculates checksums using a variety of methods for a file when it is known to be uncorrupted. These checksums are compared to the new checksums calculated every time a file-open request is made.

Internal Network Number—In NetWare each file server has its own unique network number assigned to its bus. This is known as the internal network number for the server.

Interrupt ReQuest (IRQ)—A signal or call for a service or calculation to be performed by the microprocessor. The microporcessor suspends its current activities, performs the service or calculation, and then continues with the interrupted operations.

Imaging Backup—Imaging backup software ignores the operating system completely. Instead, an exact copy of the hard disk is made by transcribing the sectors one by one and in order. The imaging technique is very fast, because data is copied directly to the storage media with total disregard for the operating system's structures. Because the operating system structures are not taken into account when the data is stored on the media, it is very difficult to restore a specific directory or even a specific file since a file's bytes are rarely stored on a hard disk in the same place and in order.

Industry Standard Architecture (ISA)—The basic design for the IBM PC was copied so widely that it became the industry standard for desktop computers based on the Intel chipset. One of the features is a 16-bit bus.

Jabbering—A node that is malfunctioning—constantly sending messages—is said to be "jabbering." This can cause enough collisions so that little or no effective network traffic is possible.

Jukebox—An optical disk changer is often referred to as a "jukebox" because of many similarities to both the old record and now the new CD jukeboxes. In the same way that you select the song you want to hear and the jukebox loads the correct CD, so it is with old files on optical disks set up to be in near-line storage.

Jumper Settings—Boards that are added to a PC often have banks of pins that can be "jumpered" with small pieces of metal, usually surrounded by plastic, to allow currents of electricity to flow in a specific pattern across the banks of pins. The specific patterns tell the board such information as which IRQ, memory address, I/O port to use, and other information that the board will need in order to work properly in the PC. If these settings can be set with software and stored in special memory chips on the add-in board, the board is call "jumper-less."

Kinked—A condition common to coax cabling where it is bent very sharply. The core pushes through the insulating layer to ground to the outside shielding, which causes transmission errors.

Large Internet Protocol (LIP)—LIP is a feature of NetWare that helps to improve performance by allowing larger packets to be passed across routers. If both the workstation and the server support LIP, they will negotiate the packet size at the time the connection between the two is made. The router is disregarded when the packet size is set, unless the packet size is hard-coded into the router.

Local Area Network (LAN)—A collection of computers linked by cabling in order to communicate and share peripheral resources, data, and applications.

Login—The process of establishing a connection to the network through a user account.

Login Script—A file containing commands to set up a user's environment that is run after a connection and valid login has been completed. A login script does for a network environment what the AUTOEXEC.BAT file does for the DOS environment.

Logout—The process of breaking the connection to the network for a user account.

Mainframe—A large-scale computer that is meant to serve hundreds of users through terminals. All the processing is performed on the mainframe's CPU instead of allowing some of the processing to be done at the workstation, as with a PC network. Mainframes are very expensive, need a controlled environment, and require specialized staff to program it as well as perform other care and feeding chores.

Mapping—The act of publishing a DOS logical directory for use on the network. Mapping a directory makes it and all of its contents available for public use, with any access right restrictions attached.

Multiple Access Unit (MAU)—A token ring hub.

Micro Channels Architecture (MCA)—A proprietary architecture produced by IBM.

Microsegmentation—Process by which an enterprise hub's backplane is segmented into separate channels dedicated to a single network segment's traffic.

Minicomputer—A scaled-down version of the mainframe. The concept of centralized processing and data storage is the same.

Mobile Workers—Workers who have to conduct business away from the normal base of operations or corporate structure.

Murphy—American sage and philosopher.

NetWare Core Protocol (NCP)—Procedures that the operating system of a NetWare file server performs to accept and process requests for information or services from a client workstation.

NetWare Core Protocol (NCP) Packet Signature—A security feature of NetWare that (depending on the level of security specified) requires a workstation to attach a "signature" to any NCP packets sent to a particular file server. If this if not done, the packets will be discarded and an alert generated. The signature is unique to the workstation and is established at the time a connection to the file server in question is made.

NetWare DOS Requestor—The program VLM.EXE and accompanying VLMs (.VLM) files that form a modular replacement for the older NETX software.

Near-line—Refers to files and data that are stored on removable media but are accessable (with a slight delay) through the use of devices such as optical jukeboxes and tape changers that require no human intervention to load the requested tape or platter.

NET Command Summary:

NET ADMIN	Starts the NET command's interactive network administration utility program.
NET AUDIT	Displays network auditing status and makes entries in the network audit log.
NET CAPTURE	Creates/deletes a shared printer resource.
NET CONNECT	Lists all workgroups and servers to which you are connected. Connects to a server or NetWare 4.x tree.
NET CONSOLE	Lists all clients connected to a Personal NetWare server.

NET CONTEXT	Views or changes current NetWare 4.x context. The command is valid only if you are connected to NetWare 4.x.
NET DIAGS	Starts the Net command's interactive network diagnostic utility program.
NET DOWN	Shuts down a Personal NetWare server and disconnects all clients.
NET HELP	Displays a list of help topics, or help on a listed topic.
NET INFO	Displays information about network software, workgroup, server, and the user account invoking the command.
NET JOIN	Allows a user to join a different Personal NetWare workgroup.
NET LINK	Views, saves, or changes the number of link setting retries, the time-out, and send delay for all messages sent from your computer.
NET LOGIN	Command to log in to a Personal NetWare workgroup.
NET LOGOUT	Command to log out of a Personal NetWare workgroup.
NET MAP	Lists, publishes, or unpublishes a shared directory or NetWare volume.
NET NTIME	Synchronizes all server clocks in your workgroup to the computer from which the command is invoked.
NET PLIST	Lists available or specific printers.
NET PRINT	Prints a file to a Personal NetWare shared printer.
NET RECEIVE	Sees, blocks, and sets time-out of network messages sent to your account.
NET RIGHTS	Adjusts access rights (READ, WRITE, ALL, or NONE) of shared directories.
NET SAVE	Saves current Personal NetWare network environment. This includes drive letter mappings, shared printers, and DOS environment variables.
NET SEND	Sends a network message.
NET SETDOG	Sets the watch dog timer for a server. This program checks intermittently to see if the clients on that server are still active.

NET SETPASS	Changes the password for your workgroup, on a Personal NetWare server, or for a directory tree.
NET SHARE	Shares a directory or printer.
NET SLIST	Lists available workgroup servers, bindery-based servers, and Netware 4.x trees.
NET SYNC	Synchronizes batch files for operations with multiple clients and/or servers.
NET TIME	Sets your computer's clock from a server's clock.
NET ULIST	Displays a current list of active users within a workgroup or on a NetWare server.
NET VLIST	Lists all shared directories and NetWare volumes.
NET WAIT	Pauses for a specified number of seconds.
NET WGFIND	Lists workgroups on the network.
NET WGLIST	Lists workgroups on LAN segments listed in your workgroup's routes.
NET XLIST	Lists service extensions.

NET.CFG—A file that provides the information necessary to define the correct abilities your connection to the network is supposed to have other than the default settings.

Network—A group of computers that can communicate with each other in order to share peripherals, applications, and data.

Network Access Method—A method that a protocol uses to determine whether the node can transmit accross the network. Currently, there are two main schools of thought: contention and token passing.

Network Access Protocol—A network access protocol is a standardized way for nodes to access the network to send packets of information to each other. It determines how those packets of information are structured and how fast they can get to the node for which they were intended.

Network-Centric—This term means the emphasis is on the network as a resource and not on the individual servers providing services. For example, a user on a network-centric network requires only a single login point for the services and resources necessary to perform his/her work become available. On a server-centric environment, the user must log in to each server from which he/she requires services or information.

Network Number—An eight-digit, hexadecimal number that uniquely identifies a network segment. In NetWare, a NetWare server's bus and each protocol bound to an NIC, as well as each frame type the protocol uses, require a unique network number.

Network File System (NFS)—File format type used by UNIX.

Network Interface Controller (NIC)—A piece of hardware that allows a network node (workstation or server) to access the network media. It is generally an add-in board or card that is placed in a computer's expansion slot.

NWCACHE—Program that provides disk caching for Personal NetWare workstations and workstation/servers.

Off-line—Refers to files and data that are stored on removable media and are not accessible unless someone loads the requested media.

One Request/One Response—A process during which an NCP packet is sent and an acknowledgment is generated that the packet was received in good order before the next NCP packet is sent.

On-line—Refers to files and data that are stored on network hard drives and are immediately accessible.

Open Data-Link Interface (ODI)—Technology upon which the NetWare client software is based. It allows for support of multiple protocols on a single NIC as well as multiple NICs in a single workstation.

Packet—A unit of information used in network communication. A packet is basically divided into addressing information and data sections. The addressing information contains directions that help route the packet to the proper destination and navigate the many communication layers. The data portion contains the part of a message that will be reassembled and acted upon once all the packets containing all the portions of the message reach the destination.

Packet Burst—A feature of NetWare that allows a client and a server to dispense with the need for the one request/one response method of ensuring that NCP packets arrive in good order. Packet burst allows all of the packets that make up an NCP read request to be sent without the normal required acknowledgment of the packet's receipt. The acknowledgment comes in the form of the requested data. For write requests, all the packets are sent and only a single acknowledgment is generated to let the sender know that the packets were received in good order.

Password—A keyword, phrase, or collection of alphanumerics that allow a user account access to the network and its resources. This usually is supplied only at login time.

Permissions—Permissions determine a user account's capabilities with respect to network administrative functions. Only a SUPERVISOR account, or an account with supervisor permissions, can modify another user account's permissions.

Personal Computer (PC)—Originally, the PC was IBM's revolutionary desktop computer. This computer was so successful and so widely copied that its architecture became an industry standard, and the term PC has become a generic term referring to all desktop computers based on the Intel chipset.

Peer-to-Peer (Desktop)—A method of networking where there is no need for dedicated servers. Instead, some workstations on the network publish their own hard drives, printers, and other resources to other nodes on the network. These workstations are, in effect, both servers and clients. If your computer is configured as a server, the resources on your network workstation become available to your peers, and the resources of other servers become available to you.

Polymorphic Virus—A virus that randomly mutates its own code as it replicates. This helps to hide its unique code "signature" from the antiviral software designed to scan for it.

Print Job—Information or data and printer commands telling the printer how to handle the information and data sent to it.

Print Queue—A special directory where print jobs are placed until the printer that services the queue is ready to print them.

Printer Driver—A program that translates the application commands and formatted text into instructions that the printer will understand.

Printer Port—Printer ports under MS-DOS are logical devices that communicate directly with hardware. There are three parallel and four serial ports that are supported directly by MS-DOS and Personal NetWare. They are LPT1, LPT2, LPT3, COM1, COM2, COM3, and COM4. Personal NetWare uses these logical devices when capturing a printer port.

Propagation Delay—The time it takes for a packet of information to be sent accross the network and acknowledged.

Quarter Inch Cartridge (QIC)—A type of magnetic tape cartridge for storing electronic data.

Random Access Memory (RAM)—A computer's electronic storage area used by the operating system to hold information temporarily. Information stored in RAM is lost when the PC is shut off.

Read-After-Write Verification—During a backup procedure, one method of error detection and correction compares the original data on the network drive to the data written to the storage media. If they do not match, the data is rewritten and rechecked until an exact copy of the data is made on the storage media.

Read Request (NCP)—A request by a client for information that a server possesses.

Redundant Copy Method—A method for error detection and correction during a backup procedure. When data is copied to the storage media during a backup, a duplicate copy is also copied to a different location on the storage media. If an error is detected during the restore procedure, the data can usually be reconstructed from both copies.

Remote Boot PROM—A chip that you can add to your NIC that has just enough knowledge of IPX to establish a connection to a nearby server and load a boot image to complete the login procedure.

Resources (shared/non-)—Resources include peripherals such as modems, printers, and scanners, as well as drives such as CD-ROM, tape, hard, and diskette. Even the microprocessor and memory can be considered part of a computer's resources. In Personal NetWare, the peripherals, and the disk drives can be shared or made available for workgroup users to access. A computer's microprocessor and memory cannot be shared.

Read-Only Memory (ROM)—Information that can only be read but cannot be altered.

Ring Topology—A topology where the cabling connects all the nodes to form a large ring so there is no real beginning or end to the network cabling. Each node, however, is only connected to the two neighboring nodes located on either side of it in the cabling structure. Ring topology, as described here, is not currently in use in PC networking today.

Root—The highest directory in a directory structure. All other directories are subdirectories of the root.

Route—Personal NetWare does not have routing software to form an internal router as with NetWare, but it does understand routing. When a Personal NetWare server is located on a different network segment from the rest of the workgroup, packets are addressed with the network address of the network segment the workgroup is on, and identical packets are also produced with the network address of the network segment with the stray Personal NetWare server. Two different "routes" or network addresses are associated with the workgroup, so identical packets will be produced to go to the nodes needing them on both of these routes.

Router—A router serves much the same purpose as a bridge: to join networks and keep traffic from crossing it unless necessary. A router can do a few things that a bridge can't, however, such as alter the information package by encapsulating it when necessary to cross a network with a different protocol. A router also uses network addresses to cut down the size of the address tables that it must keep in order to route packets correctly. A bridge keeps track of all active nodes, but a router keeps track only of the nodes directly attached to it and all the networks that are available. A router will look at the packet's destination network to decide which port to send the packet through to reach that network. When the packet reaches the router with that network address, then that router will know that the destination is one of the nodes directly attached to it and will send the packet through the correct port to reach it.

Routing Table—A list of network addresses associated with the workgroup. When packets are broadcast to the workgroup, identical packets will be created, addressed, and routed to each network that has nodes associated with the workgroup.

Remote Program Loading (RPL)—Establishing a connection and loading the proper programs to log in to the network from a boot image stored on a server, and not from a bootable resource at the workstation.

Security—The act of restricting access to network resources to a "need to access" basis so as to maintain confidentiality and orderly information flow.

Server—A network device that provides a service to the network such as print, fax, e-mail, database access, file, etc.

Setting Commands—These commands modify information that controls network behavior of such things as network messaging, packet time-outs, packet retransmits, user account behavior, etc.

Shared Resources—These are resources such as logical drives, directories, and printers that are published to the network for general access by user accounts within a workgroup. Publishing or sharing resources to a workgroup is done by the NET MAP (mapping a drive), NET CAPTURE (capturing), or NET SHARE (sharing a directory) commands.

Shielded Twisted Pair (STP)—Shielded twisted pair (STP) has one or more pairs of conductors twisted together so that they provide the proper impedance. STP goes a step farther than unshielded twisted pair by providing a layer of insulating material around the twisted pairs of conductors and often has a braided shielding conductor around all of that. This layer of insulation and the outer conductor provide better protection or "shielding" against electromagnetic noise.

Signature Scanning—A method of detecting virus activity by searching data for a match to code unique to a particular virus.

Simple Network Management Protocol (SNMP)—An industry standard protocol for communication between a network management console and the network devices that the console monitors, like routers, hubs, and now Personal NetWare workstations.

Sneaker Networks—Sharing resources by physically going to a workstation that has the resources you need and using them at that workstation. Your shoes or "sneakers" are literally the means of accessing these resources.

Stand-Alone—When a PC is not networked, it is considered to be a stand-alone environment, since it is isolated and must rely on only its own resources, data, and applications.

Star (Collapsed Ring) Topology—A topology where each node has its own length of cable connecting it to a piece of equipment called a network hub located in a central location. When the hub receives a signal from one node connected to it, the hub will repeat the signal to all the other nodes that are connected to it simultaneously.

STARTNET.BAT—A file created by Personal NetWare and called by the AUTO-EXEC.BAT file. This file loads the the universal client and the Personal NetWare software specified by the user during setup, as well as initiates the login procedure.

Supervisor—A NetWare and Personal NetWare account with special status. This type of account gives a user access to all areas, user accounts, and resources of the network. The supervisor account has the ability to manipulate them directly. A supervisor account can grant supervisor privileges in whole or in part to any other user account. When full privileges are granted, then that account becomes a supervisor account as well.

System Administrator—This is the person responsible for the care and feeding of the network. Generally, this person has the SUPERVISOR account and handles chores such as adding and deleting users, sharing of network resources, and security.

Termination—Grounding the ends of a bus network so that network nodes will have a point of reference from which to interpret the electronic signals transmitted by the cabling.

Thinnet—Ethernet run over RG-58U coax cabling at 10 Mbps; also known as thinwire, 10Base2, or cheapernet.

Token—A special packet that is passed from node to node which allows a node to transmit packets onto the network in a token passing access scheme.

Token Passing—One of the two major methods that a network access protocol can use when determining whether a node can transmit across the network. Token passing requires that a node be in possession of the token before packets can be sent. When a node is finished transmitting or has run out of time, it will retransmit the token for the next node that needs to transmit to grab.

Token Ring—Token Ring uses the token passing scheme and operates on a star (collapsed ring) topology. IBM was one of the major backers of this protocol when it first gained popularity in the early seventies. Token Ring is presently the only protocol that has the blessing of the Institute of Electrical and Electronic Engineers' 802 Committee, and has been codified into the IEEE 802.5 standard.

Topology—A network's topology describes how the workstations of that network are connected with cabling. There are three types: ring, bus or linear, and star.

Trap Target Addresses—Trap target addresses serve as the places where notification can be sent if a specific situation for which the management system has been configured to look for, such as the use of invalid passwords, occurs.

Targeting Service Agent (TSA)—A TSR that allows NetWare's SBACKUP.NLM to access a workstation's local hard drives in order to back them up.

Terminate and Stay Ready (TSR)—A program that remains in memory in order to continue performing a function; or, after it has completed its function, it will wait until it is needed to perform its function again.

Universal Client—The NetWare client software that can access any version of NetWare. The universal client software consists of the following programs: LSL.COM, the ODI driver for the NIC, IPXODI.COM, and the NetWare DOS Requester (VLM.EXE and the accompanying VLMs).

Unshielded Twisted Pair (UTP)—UTP is most commonly used when cabling telephone systems. UTP cabling usually consists of at least two conductors twisted together to form a cable with at least six twists per inch to provide impedance or electrical resistance that helps to compensate for noise produced by the electromagnetic fields of nearby electrical devices.

User Account—An account, like a credit card or checking account, that identifies a user on the network, and determines what on the network they can or cannot do. User accounts are used by Personal NetWare to validate a person as a legitimate member of a workgroup.

User-name—A user-name identifies a user account to the network.

Virtual Corporation—A company where the people performing the services are not necessarily employees and are not likely to be found in the same geographic location. The talent necessary to perform a service does not always have to come from regular employees but is often contracted to team members on a project-by-project basis.

Virus—An executable program with one distinct feature: It copies itself using a host process or program to do so. There are many different forms that perform many different functions (mostly malicious and destructive), but the one thing they all have in common is the ability and intent to self-replicate.

VLM (Virtual Loadable Module) Shells—Another name for the NetWare DOS Requester. Replaces the older NETX shells.

Voice Grade—One of the cheaper ratings for unshielded twisted pair cable.

Workgroup—Is a group of people brought together to perform a function or task. In Personal NetWare, a workgroup is a unit of user accounts that need to share resources and information in order to complete their specific tasks.

Workgroup Administrator—Generally, a person assigned the task of supervising the use of the workgroup server. This person does not necessarily have a supervisor account or supervisor privileges. If they do not have supervisory privileges, they must be the owner of the server.

Workstation—A computer on the network where work is performed by users. In Personal NetWare, these workstations can also act as servers if they have been designated to share resources. These servers are still considered workstations, since users can perform work on them.

Write-Once-Read-Many (WORM)—These CD-like disks are used for archiving purposes since any information written to them remains there permanently.

Write Request (NCP)—A request by a client to send information to the server.

Index